RENEWING ISLAM BY SERVICE

PIM VALKENBERG

RENEWING ISLAM BY SERVICE

A CHRISTIAN VIEW OF FETHULLAH GÜLEN AND THE HIZMET MOVEMENT

THE CATHOLIC UNIVERSITY OF AMERICA PRESS
WASHINGTON, D.C.

The paper used in this publication meets the minimum requirements of American National Standards for Information Science — Permanence of Paper for Printed Library Materials, ANSI Z39.48-1984.

∞

Library of Congress Cataloging-in-Publication Data
Valkenberg, Pim, 1954–
Renewing Islam by service : a Christian view of Fethullah Gülen and the Hizmet Movement / Pim Valkenberg.
pages cm
Includes bibliographical references and index.
ISBN 978-0-8132-2755-9 (cloth : alk. paper) 1. Gülen, Fethullah. 2. Gülen Hizmet Movement. 3. Service (Theology) 4. Islam — Relations — Christianity. 5. Christianity and other religions — Islam. I. Title.
BP80.G8V35 2015
297.092 — dc23
2015001835

Ignoto Christo inter Turcos

CONTENTS

ACKNOWLEDGMENTS

Everyone who has been engaged in interfaith dialogue knows how much we learn from others, not only about them but also about ourselves. That is why mentioning the names of the persons who have travelled with me along the paths of dialogue is more than a formality. My journey started in the Netherlands, where I was fortunate to meet people like Emrullah Erdem, Alper Alasağ, Ümit Taş, Alaattin Erdal, Marianne Vorthoren, Iris Creemers, and Gürkan Çelik. They are engaged in different foundations and organizations like Islam & Dialoog, Cosmicus, and Dialoog Academie, and they allowed me to gain some knowledge of their faith inspired by Fethullah Gülen.

Since I moved to the United States in 2006, I have met many Turkish friends who volunteer in several organizations such as Rumi Forum (Washington, D.C.), Niagara Foundation (Chicago), Institute of Interfaith Dialog (Texas), Pacifica Institute (California), and Rumi Forum (Maryland). Among them, I mention Ali Yurtsever, Erkan Tuncer, Emre Çelik, Jena Luedtke, Zeki Saritoprak, Yetkin Yildirim, Dogan Koç, Muhammed Çetin, Jeff Yavuz, Mustafa Kurtoglu, Huseyin Saribasak, Serdar Bozdag, Mehmet Saracoglu, Rasit Telbisoglu, and Mehmet Cicek.

When I visited Turkey in August 2009 in order to do research for this book, I was able – thanks to the never-ending engagement of Alper – to meet some very hospitable supporters of Fethullah Gülen in Izmir and in Istanbul. I would like to thank Mahmut Genç, Hüseyin Bingül, Hasan Bozaslan, Arzu Çingay, Mohamed Bakari, Cemal Karaata, Bülent Taş, Şerif Ali Tekalan, Mustafa Duğral, Akif Topal, Bişar Esen, Cemal Yavuzer, Mehmet Eldem,

Gürbüz Dönmez, Yusuf Pekmezci, Ahmet and Müleyke Gürkan, Senai Özyasar, Ömer Özkan, İhsan Taşpinar, Mehmet Portakal, Mehmet Küçük, Mehmet Yildiz, Necdet İçel, Mehmet Bafali, Sinan Koyun, İhsan Yilmaz, Zeki Sakman, Bahadır Tantay, Mustafa Akçay, who represent again many organizations that put into practice the central idea of Hizmet or "service" in order to please God.

Next, I would like to thank a group of people who do not belong to the Hizmet Movement but who can be considered very knowledgeable friends of the movement. They were the ones who reminded me of the fundamental trustworthiness of this movement in ways that were often related to their own faith: Thomas Michel, SJ, Sidney Griffith, John Borelli, Ian Williams, Simon Robinson, and Greg Barton. Also, I would like to thank the members of the group from Rumi Forum, Maryland chapter, with whom I traveled in Turkey and shared so many stories: Charles Meyers, Sister Eileen Eppig, Maryland state senator Delores Kelley, Marie-France and Jean-Pierre Le Boudeur, Indrani Mitra, Ömer Yuce, and again, Hüseyin Saribasak.

Finally, I would like to thank Salih Sayilgan who assisted me in the final editing of this book as my research assistant at the Catholic University of America, as well as James Kruggel and Trevor Lipscombe who enabled me to publish a book in a field that is new to CUA Press.

This is a long list of names. It shows some awareness that we cannot do much by ourselves. As the great theologian Abu Hamid Muhammad al-Ghazālī reminds us in his book on divine providence, God often comes to our help using the arms of our friends. Some of these friends showed such engagement with a stranger that I could not help but recognize in them the face of Christ.

Teşekkürler

INTRODUCTION

Writing a book about Fethullah Gülen and the faith-based service movement that is inspired by him is part of my mission as a Catholic theologian. Being involved in dialogue with Muslims for some time, I have often noticed that Turkish Muslims who belong to this movement are bridge builders between cultures and religions. They represent an important development in the Muslim world that is usually overlooked in the public media. Therefore, even though I have never met *Hocaefendi* Fethullah Gülen himself, I am convinced that the movement that is associated with his name forms a very important contribution to the improvement of Christian-Muslim relations.[1]

Yet the subject matter of this book has been somewhat elusive. Even though the so-called Gülen Movement has been the topic of a sharply increasing number of publications in the last ten years, most of these publications have their origins in a number of international conferences on the Gülen Movement organized by local branches of this movement in Turkey, Europe, and the United States. Most of these publications are historical and sociological in nature, which means that they can be used to understand the nature and the scope of the movement and the basic ideas of the man who is generally described as its source of inspiration. Yet most of these publications clearly represent perspectives of insiders, and therefore scholars who wish to endorse "objective" points of view

1. *Hocaefendi* is a Turkish word meaning "esteemed teacher" or "venerable teacher." This is the honorary title that persons who are inspired by Fethullah Gülen use as a token of their indebtedness to his teaching. It is sometimes used by outsiders as well as a sign of their respect – in this manner I will use the title throughout this book.

in the social sciences often disregard them. Still others, mainly active on the Internet, write to defame Gülen and the movement by concocting sometimes wildly speculative tales. Even though I am not primarily interested in these positive or negative approaches to the Gülen Movement, I need to take them into consideration since they are part of the ambiguous public persona of the movement, and the person at the center of the movement, that are the central focus of attention in this book.

The most important reason, though, why it is difficult to keep the subject matter of this book in focus is of a theological nature: what I describe in this book is ultimately not about Fethullah Gülen or a movement named after him at all, but about the divine source of his work. In some of my interviews with companions and students of Hocaefendi in Izmir, I have discussed this matter, and they agreed with me that Gülen is not happy at all with any attention directed to his person. It is this awareness that the center of attention should be the divine inspiration rather than the human person that distinguishes a theological approach as given in this book from a sociological or a historical approach as given in most articles and books about Gülen.

This, obviously, creates a problem. How to write a biography in which attention is drawn not primarily to the life of the person who is being described, but to the source of inspiration that cannot adequately be described? The Christian tradition has created a separate genre to solve this problem: the literary genre of hagiography, or "lives of the saints." Yet it would be difficult for me to describe Fethullah Gülen as a saint, since such a characterization would be problematic for a religion in which many puritans decry the veneration of saints as one of the excesses of Sufism. Although I would not hesitate to say that I have discerned in the life and works of Hocaefendi some of the characteristics that I appreciate in some of the Christian saints – God-centeredness, simplicity, asceticism, and a style of living for others – it would ill behoove me to use words that might create misunderstandings when they cross religious borders. Therefore I have chosen to use the Islamic tradition of speaking about a "renewer" (*mujaddid*) of an important aspect of Islam, namely faith-based service (*hizmet*).[2] The importance of this notion of "service" in the movement explains why it self-identifies as Hizmet in Turkish. In this book I will describe Gülen as a "renewer of Islam by service," by drawing attention to the idea of "pleasing God" (*rıza-i İlahi*) that underlies Gülen's theocentric spirituality and his engagement to renew the religion of Islam through the service of humankind. Because the service to humankind is more important than the person of Fethullah Gülen, I prefer to talk about the Hizmet Movement rather than the Gülen Movement even though this introduces a little-known Turkish word.

Since I started working as a Christian theologian in the field of Christian-Muslim relations, people have often asked me what they could do to enhance the quality of relationships between the adherents of these two religions. My answer to Christians asking this question has always been: try to find Muslims who are solidly rooted in their own Islamic tradition while they are at the same time open to dialogue with us, and work with them to promote better understanding and cooperation.[3] I have found these Muslims – it would be more accurate to say that they found me – in the Turkish Hizmet community, first in the Netherlands, and later in the United States and in Turkey. That is why I will concentrate on these three areas in this book.

Many non-Turkish, non-Muslim authors who write about Fethullah Gülen and the faith-based service communities inspired by him have come to know the person and the movement through local volunteers who invited them to collaborate and to participate in their activities to promote interfaith dialogue and mutual un-

2. In this book I will use Turkish and Arabic terms within parentheses whenever this is useful to indicate specific religious connotations of these terms. Since most of the words with religious connotations in Turkish are derived from the Arabic, I do not usually indicate whether the word is Turkish or Arabic.

3. A similar argument for involving conservative Muslims as dialogue partners can be found in Ian Markham, *Engaging with Bediuzzaman Said Nursi: A Model for Interfaith Dialogue* (Burlington, Vt.: Ashgate, 2009).

derstanding between nations and religions. I think it is important to preserve this "local flavor" of my first experiences with supporters of Fethullah Gülen's ideas, and therefore I begin this book not with a biography but with the story of these local experiences with volunteers of the Hizmet Movement in the Netherlands, followed by a somewhat broader overview of their place in present-day Dutch society. This chapter will also discuss the change in the political situation in Northwestern Europe and the growing suspicion that persons and organizations belonging to the Hizmet encountered as a consequence of this. The contested nature of the Hizmet Movement and its activities in both Turkey and the West necessitates an explanation of the specific nature of my approach as a Catholic theologian to this Islamic form of renewing faith by service. I will give this explanation at the end of the first chapter in a section on comparative theology and its contribution to the academic study of interreligious dialogue.

The second chapter will introduce the readers to the context within which the life and work of Fethullah Gülen need to be placed in order to be properly understood: the development of Turkey in the twentieth century from the Ottoman Empire through the secular state toward an experiment in cohabitation between the AKP government and secular powers in the military and judiciary state elite.[4] I will also address the recent tensions between the government and the Hizmet Movement.

This will give the basic background against which readers may appreciate an introduction to the life and the main works of Fethullah Gülen in the third chapter. In the last couple of years, some important studies about the person of Fethullah Gülen and about the movement inspired by him have been published in English. Moreover, the movement itself has organized a sizeable number of conferences and published the contributions to these symposia both in print and on a number of websites. This means that scholars now have access to a wealth of information and a good

4. AKP is the Justice and Development Party (Adalet ve Kalkınma Partisi in Turkish).

number of interpretations published in English in the last couple of years. Since most of these interpretations are of a historical or sociological nature, the theological approach offered in this book may add a fresh point of view that, moreover, claims to resonate with some of the core values in the life and works of Fethullah Gülen. Being an outsider to the Turkish language and culture, and to the Islamic faith, I am nevertheless convinced that the Christian theological approach in this book may help not only to understand the renewal of faith by service that is characteristic of the Hizmet Movement, but also to contribute to better relationships between Christians and Muslims. In order to show how Fethullah Gülen can speak to different audiences in different ways, the third chapter gives an analysis of his intellectual heritage in which the different types of religious and educational activities of Hocaefendi are distinguished as strands in his discourse. This chapter also elaborates on some of the most important events in Gülen's life that have been crucial for the origin and further development of the movement that is associated with his name. For this purpose I visited a number of places and interviewed some of the sponsors of the Hizmet in Izmir in August 2009.

The fourth chapter broadens the horizon for an appropriate evaluation of Gülen's life and works by looking at three of the main sources of his theology. While many authors have explored the connections between Fethullah Gülen and Mawlānā Jalāl ad-Dīn Rūmī (1207–1273), as well as Bediuzzaman Said Nursi (1877–1960), only a few authors have addressed the role of the Qur'ān in Gülen's work. Many Muslims may think that it is not necessary to explore the relation between the Qur'ān and Gülen, since it goes without saying that Gülen's work is based on the Scripture revealed to Prophet Muhammad, yet for non-Muslims it may be important to highlight this relationship and its role in forms of religious communication between Muslims such as sermons (*vaaz*) and religious conversations (*sohbetler*). In this chapter I will also show how the relation with the Qur'ān shapes a specific strand in Gülen's discourse that is directed to fellow members of the Muslim community and therefore different in scope and extent from the more general discourse that Gülen communicates to the wider world. The remainder of the fourth chapter introduces the two authors who have shaped Gülen's thinking and writing profoundly, that is, Jalāl ad-Dīn Rūmī and Said Nursi. I will present Rūmī, Nursi and Gülen as three Anatolian renewers of Islam in a tradition coined by Abu Hamid Muhammad al-Ghazali (1058–1111) and his *Ihyā' 'Ulūm ad-Dīn*.[5]

From the fifth chapter onwards, the focus is not so much on Gülen himself but on the faith-based service movement that he inspired. In these chapters I will give an analysis of the structure of this movement, and of the main fields in which it performs its service: education, dialogue, and charity. First, I will give an overview of the structure of the movement, its financial resources, and its public communication media, mainly following the analyses by a number of social scientists.[6] I will also pay attention to the relation between the network structure of the Gülen Movement and the forms of discourse that are transmitted through this network.

In chapter six I will discuss the three most important service activities of the network: education, dialogue, and charity. I will show how the activities of the Hizmet Movement are connected with Gülen's analysis of the root causes of the diseases of modern society. In this respect, Gülen follows Said Nursi who made a similar analysis of the diseases that caused the backwardness of the Islamic world

5. See Oliver Leaman, "Nursi's Place in the *Ihya'* Tradition," *The Muslim World* 89 (1999): 314–24; Ihsan Yilmaz, "*Ijtihad* and *Tajdid* by Conduct: The Gülen Movement," in *Turkish Islam and the Secular State: The Gülen Movement*, ed. M. Hakan Yavuz and John L. Esposito, 208–37 (Syracuse, N.Y.: Syracuse University Press, 2003).

6. See Bekim Agai, *Zwischen Netzwerk und Diskurs: Das Bildungsnetzwerk um Fethullah Gülen (geb. 1938): Die flexible Umsetzung modernen islamischen Gedankenguts*, Bonner Islamstudien 2 (Schenefeld: EB-Verlag, 2004); Mehmet Ergene, *Tradition Witnessing the Modern Age: An Analysis of the Gülen Movement* (Somerset, N.J.: Tughra Books, 2008); Muhammad Çetin, *The Gülen Movement: Civic Service without Borders* (New York: Blue Dome Press, 2009); Gürkan Çelik, *The Gülen Movement: Building Social Cohesion through Dialogue and Education* (Delft: Eburon, 2010); Helen Rose Ebaugh, *The Gülen Movement: A Sociological Analysis of a Civic Movement Rooted in Moderate Islam* (Dordrecht: Springer, 2010).

in his famous Damascus Sermon in 1911.[7] In the footsteps of Nursi's analysis, Gülen often indicates poverty, ignorance, and disunity as the three basic enemies that Muslims have to fight in order to do justice to their faith. Jesuit father Thomas Michel, one of the first Christian theologians to recognize the importance of both Nursi and Gülen for present-day dialogues between Muslims and Christians, has convincingly shown how Gülen decided to combat these evils through three sorts of activities.[8] First, in the 1980s, the battle against ignorance was central in building a great number of schools and other educational institutions; next, in the 1990s, in order to combat disunity between believers and human beings, a number of dialogue activities were deployed both in Turkey and around the world. Finally, the beginning of the twenty-first century saw the beginning of the fight against poverty through organizations such as Kimse Yok Mu, which can be translated as "Isn't there anybody who cares?" In this way, the followers of Gülen follow his analysis in developing activities that can be summarized as the *hizmet*, the Turkish word for service, which is also the name for the Gülen Movement in Turkey. They open schools to overcome ignorance, they open dialogue institutions to overcome disunity, and they organize charity to overcome poverty.

I will also pay attention to the way in which the network functions internally and externally. The internal function of the network is mainly to create a meeting place where like-minded people can discuss the values they share and the ways in which they can pursue these values in present-day society. Often, the network functions as a meeting place for businessmen and social entrepreneurs. Many charitable activities find their origin in this business network. The last part of this chapter focuses on these acts of charity as a way

7. Said Nursi, *The Damascus Sermon*, trans. Şükran Vahide, 2nd ed. (Istanbul: Sözler Neşriyat, 1996). See also Thomas Michel, *Insights from the Risale-i Nur: Said Nursi's Advice for Modern Believers* (Clifton, N.J.: Tughra Books, 2013).

8. Thomas Michel, SJ, "Fighting Poverty with Kimse Yok Mu," in *Islam in the Age of Global Challenges: Alternative Perspectives of the Gülen Movement*, Conference Proceedings, Georgetown University, Washington, D.C., November 14–15, 2008, 523–33 (Washington, D.C.: Rumi Forum, 2008).

to be a faith-based service community. The external function of the network is to create a platform for discussing contemporary questions with all social and religious strata of society. In Turkey, the most important organizations that represent the Hizmet Movement are the Journalists and Writers Foundation (Gazeteci ve Yazarlar Vakfi), the Abant Platform (Abant Platformu) and the Intercultural Dialogue Platform (Kültürlerarasi Diyalog Platformu). In Europe and the United States, a number of organizations focus on intercultural and inter-religious dialogues, among other activities, by organizing lectures and group travels to Turkey. My analysis will focus on the way in which Gülen's discourse on these forms of dialogue inspires the faith-based service community. The schools and other educational opportunities created by the Hizmet Movement are first of all a service to the wider community, offering opportunities to participate in excellent education without any overt pressure to embrace a specific religious point of view. At the same time, the teachers clearly function as models in the movement, and they are considered as key figures in building up a "golden generation" (*altın nesil*) of service-minded intellectuals. In this way, education is the most visible way in which Gülen's thoughts and actions contribute to the betterment of society.

The seventh and last chapter will compare the faith-based service movement inspired by Gülen with similar faith-based service communities in the Christian tradition. I do not want to suggest that Gülen or the people inspired by him are dependent on these Christian traditions, but I am convinced that similar notions of piety, worship, service, and community can be distinguished across the boundaries of religious traditions. For me as a Christian theologian working at different Catholic universities, it has been fascinating to see how several aspects of the God-centered service embodied in the life and the works of Fethullah Gülen, and in the persons who try to follow his example in committing themselves to a life of faith-based service, find resonances in similar notions, examples, and movements in several forms of Christian religious life. While most of the Christian religious orders choose a particular life-form characterized by monastic contemplative life (*vita contemplativa*, for instance the Benedictines), or active renewal of church and society in education, mission, and charity (*vita activa*, for instance the Jesuits), or again in a mixed life centered on preaching and a life of poverty (*vita mixta*, for instance the Dominicans and Franciscans), some contemporary religious movements such as the Sant'Egidio community and the Focolare Movement combine elements of these traditional forms of life. This final chapter cannot do justice to a description of all these forms of religious life in Christianity nor of the many parallels with the religious life inspired by Fethullah Gülen. But it is my hope that glimpses of the analogies in religious life may at least lead Muslims and Christians to the awareness that it is the same God we worship and the same world we aim to serve. With his characteristic humility, Gülen refrains from speaking about himself as a renewer, although in a recent interview he said: "I have tried to revive Islamic tradition that celebrates modernization and economic progress."[9] From this perspective it is possible to see Fethullah Gülen and the faith-based service movement he inspired as an important sign of renewal in the world of Islam. As Mehmet Ergene has shown in his book about Gülen, the term "renewal" (*tajdīd*), or "revival" (*iḥyā'*) aptly describes how Islam can renew itself, and how Muslims can make a difference.[10] Even though I come from a different faith background, I can discern how the life of Fethullah Gülen and the faith-based service movement he inspired are a truly unique way to answer God's call to make a difference in this world.

It is my hope that those who are acquainted with the person and the thought of Hocaefendi M. Fethullah Gülen will recognize in this approach at least some of the basic religious convictions that drive them in their work, and that outsiders will find some

9. Interview in Nevval Sevindi, *Contemporary Islamic Conversations: M. Fethullah Gülen on Turkey, Islam, and the West,* edited with an introduction by Ibrahim M. Abu-Rabi', trans. Abdullah T. Antepli (Albany, N.Y.: State University of New York Press, 2008), 74.

10. Ergene, *Tradition Witnessing the Modern Age*, 106–13.

support to let go of their suspicion of everything that is said and done in the name of Islam. Some of these outsiders might think that Catholic theologians who want to dialogue with Muslims in the years after 9/11 are naïve and may even betray their own faith. I can only say that I try to follow in the footsteps of a few great Catholic theologians who sensed the presence of God in the life of some Muslims, and therefore devoted quite some energy in supporting the relatively unknown faith-based service community inspired by Fethullah Gülen. Faced with a situation in which Islam and Turkey are presented in various media outlets, mainly in Europe, as a threat and a danger, we can only avoid the self-fulfilling prophecy of a "clash of civilizations" if we turn toward those who offer an alternative of hope and collaboration for the future. In its declaration *Nostra Aetate,* the Second Vatican Council fifty years ago embraced such an alternative, and both Fethullah Gülen and Pope John Paul II have agreed that Muslims and Christians should learn their lessons from the past and engage in shaping a better future together, trusting that this is why God created them after all.

RENEWING ISLAM BY SERVICE

1

DIALOGUE-MINDED TURKISH MUSLIMS IN THE NETHERLANDS

IT MAY BE somewhat strange to start this book by focusing on Muslims in the Netherlands since the movement inspired by Fethullah Gülen obviously started in Turkey. Yet it makes sense to tell first about the encounters that motivated me, a Catholic theologian at that time working at a university in the Netherlands, to research the spiritual background of my partners in dialogue. Later in this book I will tell how my study of Fethullah Gülen and the movement he inspired was deepened by a number of contexts and encounters in the United States of America and in Turkey, but it was the first encounter with this faith-based service community in the Netherlands that determined the way in which I began to understand this Muslim community from a Christian theological perspective. According to this perspective, rooted in the encounter with the risen Lord, a religious other should be seen not as just a random passerby but as a possible sign from God, and therefore also as possible guidance toward God. This may sound quite strange to some, but Christians live with stories from the New Testament in which the stranger can become a sign and a light leading us to a better understanding of God.[1]

1. Pim Valkenberg, *Sharing Lights on the Way to God: Muslim-Christian Dialogue and Theology in the Context of Abrahamic Partnership* (New York: Editions Rodopi, 2006), 9.

Of course, the Christian tradition has not often looked at Islam to improve its understanding of God, since it has mainly conceived this new religion as a heresy that might be tolerated if necessary, but should be opposed and challenged whenever possible. Half a century ago, though, the Second Vatican Council, in its declaration *Nostra Aetate,* gave a fresh approach to the relation between the Roman Catholic Church and other religions. In this document, the council expressed its high regard for the Muslims who "worship God, who is one, living and subsistent, merciful and almighty, the Creator of heaven and earth, who has also spoken to men. They strive to submit themselves without reserve to the hidden decrees of God, just as Abraham submitted himself to God's plan, to whose faith Muslims eagerly link their own."[2] A bit earlier, in November 1964, the same council declared in its document *Lumen Gentium,* on the church, that "the plan of salvation also includes those who acknowledge the Creator, in the first place among whom are the Muslims: these profess to hold the faith of Abraham, and together with us they adore the one, merciful God, mankind's judge on the last day."[3] These texts indicate that the Roman Catholic Church wanted to discontinue the history of mutual quarrels and dissensions, in order to promote better understanding between two religions that adore the one God of the Abrahamic faiths.[4] Dialogue is the word that is now used to indicate how both religions try to come to this better understanding of one another in hopes of thereby understanding God better.

INVITED BY THE ISLAM AND DIALOGUE FOUNDATION

In my personal history, the notion and the practice of interreligious dialogue have become very important since I started to work

2. Francesco Gioia, ed., *Interreligious Dialogue: The Official Teaching of the Catholic Church from the Second Vatican Council to John Paul II (1963–2005)* (Boston: Pauline Books and Media, 2006), 44.

3. Gioia, *Interreligious Dialogue*, 48.

4. Michael L. Fitzgerald and John Borelli, *Interfaith Dialogue: A Catholic View* (Maryknoll, N.Y.: Orbis, 2006), 109–21.

as a theologian at the Catholic University of Nijmegen (now renamed as Radboud University) in the Netherlands. My M.A. and Ph.D. studies at the Catholic Theological University at Utrecht had prepared me by giving me some expertise both in the field of Catholic theology — I wrote my thesis about Thomas Aquinas and his use of Scripture — and in the field of comparative religion — I studied with Jacques Waardenburg at Utrecht State University — but it did not prepare me for serious theological dialogue with Islam. Therefore, I decided to study Arabic in the Humanities Department of my own university, so that I would be able to read at least the Qur'ān and *hadith* literature, and to study classical Islamic theology with some assistance.

Shortly after I arrived in Nijmegen, the Department of Theology decided to start a new program in religious studies in which the relationship between religions in contemporary Western Europe would be the main focus. Because of my double background in Christian theology and the comparative study of religions, I was asked to coordinate this new program. It soon began to attract more students than the classical study of Christian theology and later developed into a separate Department of Religious Studies. In this new program of religious studies, I lectured in systematic theology and world religions, but in my research I began to concentrate on the theology of religions in which Christian theologians reflect on the relation between Christianity and other religions. Now such reflection can be done in a quite abstract, philosophical way — as it has certainly been done in the history of Catholic theology, in which thinking about other religions was subsumed under thinking about Christianity as the true religion and the Roman Catholic Church as the true church. But encounters with other religions led more and more theologians to think that an authentic theology of religions cannot be done without encountering religious others.

At that time I lived in the city of Utrecht, which has a sizable Muslim population. In the footsteps of my wife, who worked as a pastoral life director in one of the Roman Catholic parishes, I tried to engage in dialogue with Muslims at the local level in hopes of generating experiences that could help me in teaching about interreligious dialogue. While the project in which she participated succeeded in bringing together Dutch women and women of guest-worker families in order to teach the Dutch language in a homely setting, I was able to reach out to some of the Moroccan Muslims in the neighborhood. We even tried to form a small group but failed because of a lack of continuity in Muslim participants: they were manual workers who were not really used to telling stories about their religion, let alone to sharing these stories with religious others.

I met a new group of Muslims at the beginning of the new millennium when the journal *Begrip Moslims-Christenen* ("Understanding between Muslims and Christians") celebrated its twenty-fifth anniversary with a symposium that attracted a good number of Muslims. I was excited when I found out that these Muslims were not only young and bright but that they actually wanted to talk about their own faith with religious others. They were members of a new group that called itself "Islam and Dialogue." Unfortunately, this group was mainly active in the western part of the country (Rotterdam and Amsterdam) and it did not have a local branch in Utrecht or Nijmegen, the cities where I lived and worked. Yet such local branches would soon be developed so that I received, shortly after the dreadful events of September 11, 2001, an invitation for an *iftar* dinner. This dinner has a specific social function in the tradition of Islam, since in many Muslim countries it is customary to break the fasting (*saum*) during the month of Ramadan with a communal dinner. Modern Muslim groups like to include Christians and other believers especially during the month of Ramadan. The SEMA Foundation in Nijmegen, an institution that runs a boarding school where children of Turkish provenance can do their homework and live together under supervision, extended an invitation for an *iftar* dinner to my wife, who worked in one of the Roman Catholic churches, and I was happy to be able to accompany her. During the *iftar* meal, one of the Turkish hosts introduced himself to me as Emrullah Erdem, a freelance interpreter who also acted as coordinator of the Nijmegen branch of the Islam and Dialogue foundation. Having studied Arabic and Islam at the university where I worked, he proposed to collaborate in the future in organizing interreligious dialogue events. I was glad to accept this invitation, since it seemed that finally I had met my Muslim dialogue partners.[5]

The first project in which we collaborated was a short course on Islam and Christian-Muslim relations for one of the Roman Catholic parishes in Nijmegen. Since I consider myself to be a specialist in the field of Christian-Muslim relations, but not in the field of Islam proper, I was happy to be able to share my teaching with a Muslim, and so we lectured together about the history and the future of Islam and Christian-Muslim relations. I also invited Emrullah to participate in a number of dialogue sessions for my freshmen students in the religious studies program since, in teaching them about interreligious dialogue, I wanted to add some hands-on experience of dialogue with Muslims and Jews.

After the events of September 11, 2001, the Department of Theology and Religious Studies of my university decided to discuss the possible relationship between concepts of God and religious violence during one of its public events for all students and alumni. Since I had been asked to introduce the lectures at that conference, and to edit the conference proceedings, I did some research on the immediate reactions to September 11, and I noticed that the large majority of these reactions either struck an accusatory note in attributing violence to religion in general and to Islam in particular, or a defensive tone in appealing to a nonviolent religious core. Such a defense can of course be expected if a specific religion is time and again connected with violence in the mass media, but from an academic point of view it does not sound entirely convincing. Along these lines I noticed an interesting contradiction in

5. I am aware of the fact that the notion of "invitation" (*da'wa*) has a strong missionary connotation in Islam. Tittensor remarks that "despite its protestations to the contrary, the Movement is very much a *da'wa* (missionary) organization." See David Tittensor, *The House of Service: The Gülen Movement and Islam's Third Way* (New York: Oxford University Press, 2014), 9.

the self-representation of the Islam and Dialogue Foundation. In its mission statement, it says that "the essence of Islam is peace, mercy, grace and tolerance; that strife, violence and terror are out of place in Islam; and furthermore, that all religions have these principles in common so that we should refrain from all quarrels in order to lead our tormented earth to a peaceful and blissful future."[6] In its printed public relations brochure, however, the foundation includes the following English quotation: "Loving affection and detesting hate are the most distinguishing qualities of a heart exuberant with faith."[7] I liked this quotation because it expressed beautifully how a religion that is aimed at promoting peace and love can in certain circumstances lead to violence. So I asked my friends of the Islam and Dialogue Foundation where they found the quotation, but they said they did not know. Since the quotation kept puzzling me, I did some research and after some time found out that it should probably be attributed to Fethullah Gülen, the source of inspiration of a widespread movement to which the Islam and Dialogue Foundation clearly belonged.[8] In one of his speeches on dialogue I found the following quotation: "The most distinctive feature of a soul overflowing with faith is to love all types of love that are expressed in deeds, and to feel enmity for all deeds in which enmity is expressed."[9] Similar quotations can be found at other places in Gülen's books, although he sometimes also says that the faithful soul should love its enemies as well. Although I found it somewhat strange that the members of the Islam and Dialogue Foundation were not able to identify the quotation, its obvious religious power triggered me to engage more in reading the works of Fethullah Gülen as they became available to me.

6. www.islamendialoog.nl (accessed June 11, 2008); my translation of the Dutch mission statement.

7. Quotation from a pamphlet spread by Stichting Islam & Dialoog in 2001.

8. Later, I found similar quotations in the works of Said Nursi. On the relationship between Nursi and Gülen, see chapter four.

9. Quotation from the compilation *Fethullah Gülen: Advocate of Dialogue* by Ali Ünal and Alphonse Williams, trans. Ali Ünal (Fairfax, Va.: Fountain Publications, 2000), 198.

At the same time, actual dialogues organized with the Islam and Dialogue Foundation were more important, since the form of comparative theology in which I am engaged sees this form of theology as a secondary reflection on the actual practice of dialogue.[10]

At the practical level, I began to collaborate with the Islam and Dialogue Foundation when Emrullah Erdem asked me to become involved in a public event celebrating Abraham (*Ibrāhīm*) as the forefather of Jews, Christians, and Muslims. I invited a group of students and faculty of the religious studies program at our university to join this collaboration, and after some time we extended the invitation to one of my Jewish colleagues, Tzvi Marx, who brought along the great resources of his Folkertsma Foundation for Talmudic Studies. The venue of the event was Museum Park Orientalis in the city of Groesbeek near Nijmegen. This museum was originally founded to enable visitors who could not afford to travel to the Middle East an impression of the life of Jesus in its original setting. Later, the board of directors of the museum tried to develop a new policy that would give more attention to the multicultural character of the Middle East, but the Roman Catholic bishop of 's-Hertogenbosch who had the authority to steer the course of the museum as a canonical institution, was opposed to highlighting other cultures and religions since—as he argued—the museum was originally meant to underscore the uniqueness of Jesus Christ. Whereas the bishop used an exclusivist theological argumentation to defend his canonical rights, the board of directors argued in favor of the policy of multiculturalism that was sponsored by the Dutch government in the 1990s. The Islam and Dialogue Foundation had its own reasons to organize an event focusing on Abraham, and these were neither exclusivist nor multicultural. They wanted to engage in interfaith dialogue and collaboration on the basis of texts from the Qur'ān such as:

O humankind! Surely We have created you from a single (pair of) male and female, and made you into tribes and families so that you may know

10. Valkenberg, *Sharing Lights on the Way to God*, 206–9.

one another (and so build mutuality and co-operative relationships, not so that you may take pride in your differences of race or social rank, and breed enmities). Surely the noblest, most honorable of you in God's sight is the one best in piety, righteousness, and reverence for God. Surely God is All- Knowing, All-Aware.[11]

So the Catholic bishop and the Muslim foundation have in common that they base their points of view on religious sources, but they diverge in the way in which they apply these sources. While the bishop wants to preserve the museum's Catholic identity in a way that does not leave room for religious plurality, the foundation aims at appreciating this plurality.

I was quite surprised when Emrullah told me that an important spokesperson from the Vatican had agreed to come and give a speech on the occasion of our public event on Abraham. To my knowledge, any Vatican authority would have contacted the local bishop first, and I would have been surprised if the bishop had consented to his coming to an event at the venue of this museum, especially one that would promote interfaith collaboration. Yet it turned out that the visitor from the Vatican was a Jesuit priest: Father Thomas Michel, the secretary for interreligious dialogue for the Jesuit Curia in Rome, and so I understood how a Jesuit was able to come and stimulate interreligious dialogue without consulting the local bishop. I will come back to this special position of the Jesuits and the similarities between them and Gülen's faith-based service communities at the end of this book.

The public event in June 2003 brought together several hundred participants with Muslim, Christian, Jewish, and secular backgrounds. If we look at the event with a view to its contents, the three lectures on Abraham from Jewish, Christian, and Muslim points of view were the most important; but if we look at it as a ritual event, several other elements proved to be important. Representatives of

11. Qur'ān 49:13. Quotations from the Qur'ān are usually taken from Ali Ünal's English interpretation (*The Qur'ān: With Annotated Interpretation in Modern English* [Somerset, N.J.: Light, 2006]), since it is clearly connatural with the thoughts of Said Nursi and Fethullah Gülen, who are often quoted in the annotations.

the three Abrahamic religions referred to the basic rituals of their religions by blowing the *shofar* (a reference to the Jewish festival of *Shavuot*), by reading from the Acts of the Apostles (commemorating the Christian festival of Pentecost), and by reciting from the Qur'ān (*sūrat Ibrāhīm*). Politicians affirmed the importance of collaboration between the Abrahamic religions for the progress of good relationships at the local and the European level. And, most importantly, a group of dancers and musicians performed a part of the *sema*ʿ ritual that is associated with Jalāl ad-Dīn Rūmī and the whirling dervishes of his Mevleviyya Sufi order. When I was asked to introduce the concluding panel discussion, I pointed out that an effective dialogical event needs to connect the intellectual, practical, and spiritual levels. As the Pontifical Council for Interreligious Dialogue has stated on several occasions, since we are human persons living together, dialogue should be a matter not only of expert opinions but of life, action, and finally religious experience as well.[12] Or, to put it differently: in order to bear fruit, an interreligious dialogue should have an intellectual, a ritual, and a spiritual dimension. This was the case as well in another symposium on "Religions and Peace in the Light of Forefather Abraham," organized in 2004 by another organization inspired by Fethullah Gülen, the Intercultural Dialogue Platform in Istanbul. The second part of this symposium was an academic gathering in Istanbul where we listened to a substantial number of speeches in plenary sessions, but for the first part of the symposium the participants traveled by plane to Mardin in southeast Turkey where an impressive number of religious dignitaries gathered to express their support for Abrahamic peace. The ritual dimension of this symposium was expressed most strongly when the dignitaries individually crossed a bridge on the podium to join one another with their religious symbols, forming the background for schoolchildren with olive branches and doves, and a Turkish singer performed, expressing the intention to work together for world peace.[13]

12. Fitzgerald and Borelli, *Interfaith Dialogue: a Catholic View*, 28.

13. An impression of this event was published in *Today's Zaman*, written by Abdulhamit Bilici, May 18, 2004 (www.todayszaman.com, accessed June 24, 2009).

In June 2004 we organized a second symposium "In the Footsteps of Abraham" in the Netherlands. Again, the public event, with important speakers and ritual contributions from the three religions, was held at the open air museum, but it was preceded by a smaller gathering at the Radboud University in Nijmegen for which a number of students and professors from the university's religious studies program had taken the initiative. Because Ertürk ("Alper") Alasağ, the coordinator of the Islam and Dialogue Foundation in the Netherlands, decided to enroll in our religious studies program and to participate in our dialogue group as well, it was quite easy to coordinate the organization of this event with the Islam and Dialogue Foundation. Moreover, we invited the Folkertsma Foundation for Talmudic Studies to become our Jewish partner once more. Organizing the symposium of 2004 by three different groups with different religious and cultural backgrounds was itself an exercise in intercultural and interreligious collaboration at the practical level.

The main speaker at this symposium was Karl Josef Kuschel from the University of Tübingen in Germany, author of a book on Abraham in the Jewish, Christian, and Muslim traditions.[14] His book formed the occasion for some debate between theologians who favored Kuschel's proposal for collaboration between the Abrahamic religions, and others who disliked this idea because it might water down the differences between Christianity and Islam. This was a way to engage some Evangelicals into the world of the "Abrahamic ecumenism" as well.

The organizers of the 2004 symposium decided to publish the results of this symposium and its predecessor in a volume edited by its board members in Dutch.[15] Furthermore, the group institutionalized itself into a foundation so that it could attract private

14. Karl-Josef Kuschel, *Streit um Abraham: was Juden, Christen und Muslime trennt—und was sie eint* (Munich: Piper, 1994).

15. Pim Valkenberg, Ertürk Alasag, Greco Idema, Janneke Teunissen, and Carla Robertson, eds., *In de voetsporen van Abraham* [In the footsteps of Abraham], (Budel: Damon, 2004).

and public grants. One of its newer activities is maintaining a website and an e-mail newsletter.[16] For a number of years, the group collaborated with the Islam and Dialogue Foundation and the Folkertsma Foundation in organizing interreligious weekends for young Christians, Jews, and Muslims, in hopes that such "Abrahamic learning communities" might develop into a new and youthful "Abrahamic network."[17]

COLLABORATION IN A CONTEXT OF GROWING SUSPICION

My contacts with a representative of a second foundation associated with the Gülen network in the Netherlands began at an *iftar* dinner in the city of Boxmeer, three (lunar) years after I met Emrullah Erdem at a previous *iftar* in Nijmegen. This time it was Gürkan Çelik, who introduced himself to me as the national president of the Cosmicus Foundation, an organization that, according to its website, "aims to advance the education, development and careers of students and alumni through educational, cultural, social and scientific activities and projects."[18] He invited me to participate in organizing a number of symposia at Dutch universities in which people who can be seen as forerunners in peace from diverse cultures would be introduced in a comparative perspective. We organized a first conference in Nijmegen in 2004, and three more conferences in 2005. Some of the contributions to these symposia were collected in a booklet and presented by the Cosmicus Foundation to its members and sponsors.[19] The basic idea behind this

16. The website (in Dutch) has been continued for a few years as www.interreligieuze-werkplaats.nl (accessed June 16, 2009).

17. For further information, see Pim Valkenberg, "Towards 'Abrahamic Learning Communities': How to Learn from Violence and Prejudices in Interreligious Polemics on Abraham and his Family," in *Your Heritage and Mine: Teaching in a Multi-Religious Classroom*, Studies on Inter-Religious Relations 43, ed. Lena Roos and Jenny Berglund, 154–62 (Uppsala: Swedish Science Press, 2009).

18. English text on www.cosmicus.nl (accessed June 19, 2009).

19. Gürkan Çelik, Paul Cobben, Joannemie van Dijk, and Pim Valkenberg, eds., *Voorlopers in de vrede* [Forerunners in Peace] (Budel: Damon, 2005).

conference was that it would be fruitful to counter the prevailing idea of a "clash of civilizations" between "Islam and the West" by showing how influential personalities from different religions and cultures have shown us a way to peace rather than conflict. Fethullah Gülen was among these personalities, together with Pope John Paul II, Mawlānā Jalāl ad-Dīn Rūmī, the Dalai Lama, Mother Teresa of Calcutta, Rabbi Nachman of Breslov, Saint Francis of Assisi and Desiderius Erasmus. Gürkan Çelik and I pursued the same idea in an article on Fethullah Gülen and Pope John Paul II that has been published in several versions, most recently as part of Gürkan's Ph.D. thesis.[20]

A few years later, we again organized a symposium in which we compared Gülen and Erasmus as bridge builders between cultures and religions, but in the meantime the atmosphere had changed. The apparent success of some of the schools that are part of the Cosmicus Foundation had drawn attention from some journalists and politicians. These journalists remarked that the Dutch government had subsidized schools that contributed in their eyes not to integration but to isolation and segmentation of Turkish Muslims in the Netherlands. Moreover, they suggested that the Gülen Movement might have a hidden agenda in promoting the introduction of the *sharīʿah* in the Netherlands.[21] This led to quite some publicity about the followers of the Gülen Movement in the Netherlands, occasioned by a news item on Dutch public televi-

20. See Gürkan Çelik and Pim Valkenberg, "Gülen's Approach to Dialogue and Peace: Its Theoretical Background and Some Practical Perspectives," *International Journal of Diversity in Organisations, Communities and Nations* 7, no.1 (2007): 29–37; Gürkan Çelik, *The Gülen Movement. Building Social Cohesion through Dialogue and Education* (Delft: Eburon, 2010), 147–61.

21. Even though I prefer to use the words "Hizmet Movement" rather than "Gülen Movement" as I explained in the introduction to this book, I will refer to Gülen Movement whenever this is the term used in the public media by outsiders, since this term suggests that Gülen somehow is the mastermind behind this movement. As I wrote before, insiders now begin more and more to speak about the Hizmet Movement (or service movement, or volunteers movement) since this emphasizes the role of the people who do the actual work of the movement. Yet, for me as a theologian, it also refers to the divine origin of the service accomplished by members of the movement, inspired by Fethullah Gülen.

sion in the summer of 2008. Questions were raised in Parliament, and several political parties asked that the government withdraw its subsidies to Gülen-oriented organizations. As a consequence, one of the Dutch organizations that was to cohost the conference on Gülen and Erasmus withdrew its contribution, but fortunately another organization that carried the name of Erasmus decided to stay on board. The conference was successful and its results were published in a small book a few months later.[22] Because of all negative publicity, Gürkan Çelik withdrew from the Cosmicus Foundation and founded the Dialoog Academie (Dialogue Academy), a network and dialogue institute based in Rotterdam, the Netherlands. One of its most recent activities was a conference, "Mapping the Gülen Movement" in Amsterdam on October 7, 2010.[23]

My collaboration with Muslim organizations inspired by Fethullah Gülen has thus far clearly followed the pattern of multiculturalism, a point of view that is even better known and more debated in Europe than in the U.S. Yet new initiatives were met with growing suspicion because the political climate had begun to change in the new millennium. In order to understand this change in the perception of multiculturalism in the Netherlands and in many other countries in Northwest Europe, we need to look at the situation of Muslim immigrants in these countries in order to understand the consequences of the change in the political climate for the supporters of Fethullah Gülen.[24] Even though the terrorist attacks culminating on September 11, 2001, caused a heightened, largely negative publicity about Islam and its supposedly radical

22. Iris Creemers et al., eds., *Erasmus en Gülen. Inspiratoren voor vrede en dialoog* [Erasmus and Gülen: Inspiring peace and dialogue] (Budel: Damon, 2009).

23. The conference papers have been distributed to the participants as a booklet: *Mapping the Gülen Movement: A Multidimensional Approach*. Publication of these papers together with some other contributions about the situation of the Gülen Movement in Europe is under consideration with a well-known academic publisher in the Netherlands for 2015.

24. The following paragraphs were written by Alper Alasağ and Pim Valkenberg for presentation at a conference on the Hizmet Movement and Peacebuilding organized by Rumi Forum in Washington, D.C., in October 2013.

nature, the change in the political climate – reflected in the public media – had local causes as well. Right-wing politicians began to perceive the presence of foreign workers and their growing families in the Netherlands no longer as a positive contribution to the economy, but as a threat to the employment of Dutch citizens. Scholars of sociology and economics started to say that the idea of a multicultural society had turned out to be a complete failure. Instead of integrating into Dutch society, the foreign workers and their families appeared to isolate themselves in linguistic and cultural ghettoes. Some politicians started to indicate Islam as the root cause of the problems because of its resistance against some of the basic values of Western society, such as equality, freedom, and the separation between church and state. In 1997 and again in 2001, the famous right-wing politician Pim Fortuyn summarized these ideas in a book-length pamphlet.[25] When he was murdered in 2002 during a very successful political campaign, many people saw this as a sign that Fortuyn was right in his ideas about the incompatibility between Islam and Western culture, even though the person who murdered him was an animal-rights activist. But the murder – this time by a radical Muslim – of Theo van Gogh in 2004, shortly after he had made a critical film on the position of women in Islam together with the politician Ayaan Hirsi Ali, signaled the reality of Huntington's (and Fortuyn's) thesis about the "clash of civilizations" for many Dutch citizens. A few years later, another right-wing Dutch politician, Geert Wilders, would create one of the biggest one-issue parties with his resistance against Islam as the source of all problems in the Netherlands. In 2008 Wilders made another film about Islam in which he threatened to burn the Qur'ān. Even though he has been persecuted for hatred against Islam, he has never been sentenced in court since the judges found that he only provoked hatred against Islam, but not against specific Muslims.

Even though most politicians were not as vociferous against

25. Pim Fortuyn, *De islamisering van onze cultuur. Nederlandse identiteit als fundament* [The Islamization of Our Culture: Dutch Identity as Foundation] (Rotterdam: Speakers Academy, 2001).

Islam as Fortuyn or Wilders, many of them shared their conviction that the integration of foreigners in Dutch society had failed and that the government needed to be stricter in the admission and treatment of foreigners. Since Turkish and Moroccan Muslims were the most visible groups of foreigners, they were looked at with some suspicion, particularly when they received financial support from the government.

In the summer of 2008, the Hizmet Movement became the focus of widespread negative attention when *Nova*, a news program about present-day events and issues broadcast on one of the Dutch public television channels, presented a long news item on some of the Cosmicus schools. The program suggested that the schools, while receiving large subsidies from the Dutch government, created an atmosphere that went against the purposes for which government money had been granted. While the schools carried a very favorable public image, with splendid academic results and successful examples of integration into Dutch society, *Nova* made the suggestion that they simultaneously fostered a secret agenda of segregation and "Islamization." Journalists interviewed an anonymous student who left one of the "houses of light" because of what was described as indoctrination and promotion of strict Islamic values and behavior. The journalists found out that the schools were part of the Gülen Movement, which they described as a very hierarchical organization with strict rules. Some Turkish journalists gave their negative opinion about Gülen as an authoritarian ruler and an Islamist who secretly wants to introduce the *shari'ah*. They also quoted a famous Dutch scholar of Turkish Islam who said that it could very well be that schools inspired by Gülen, while publicly promoting multicultural openness and integration, might in fact favor a climate of isolation and withdrawal from Dutch society. The journalists also suggested that members of the different organizations of the Hizmet were not straightforward about their membership of the Gülen Movement. They interviewed some influential Turkish Muslims in the Netherlands who denied having any connection with Gülen. In doing so, the Turkish

Muslims were driven by a long history of the persecution of religious groups in Turkey and by the ongoing defamation campaign against Gülen since the military "soft coup" in 1997. This conflict came to a climax in 1999 with a video that was broadcast in which Gülen seems to instruct his followers to engage in a secret infiltration of state institutions. Supporters of the Hizmet, however, claim that this video was fabricated. The video has been exported to the many countries where members of the Hizmet are active. We will discuss the specific Turkish context in the next chapter, but a reticence that might have been necessary in the context of Turkish state-promoted secularism can easily be seen as hypocrisy, and even as outright lying, in Dutch society with its ideals of open communication. So when the journalists were able to show that the Turkish professionals who denied their relationship with Gülen used his name all the time in their offices and on their websites, it confirmed the innuendo that they were members of an organization with a secret agenda. While members of the Hizmet Movement stress that there is no central organization and that they do not receive any direct orders from Gülen or anyone else, opponents suggest that there are secret channels of communication.

This aspect of the publicity around the Hizmet Movement is not typically Dutch; closer inspection shows that many allegations go back to journalists in Turkey who work for periodicals that defend the strictly secular heritage of Mustafa Kemal Atatürk and accuse the Hizmet Movement of secretly trying to impose Muslim *shari'ah* on a secular nation. So, on the one hand, those who are critical of the Hizmet talk about its strategic ambiguity, while those who support the movement talk about a strategic defamation of the Hizmet.[26] Behind all of this is the question: is there a secret "master plan" behind the movement? Turkish-American scholar Hakan Yavuz offers the following observation:

26. Joshua Hendrick, *Gülen: The Ambiguous Politics of Market Islam in Turkey and the World* (New York: New York University Press, 2013); Dogan Koç, *Strategic Defamation of Fethullah Gülen: English vs. Turkish* (Lanham, Md.: University Press of America, 2012).

People who have been persuaded by Gülen's message help with, and invest in, such activities, especially those related to education. Although these activities are decentralized and the movement itself is loosely knit, because the activities are conducted by like-minded people in different places, it looks like a single organizational structure is directing them from above. This is why critics of the Gülen movement tend to portray it as a single hierarchical "organization" controlled by an *eminence grise* who operates behind the scenes.[27]

The news item about the Cosmicus schools in the *Nova* program occasioned a number of questions in Dutch parliament, not only by notorious "anti-Islam" politicians but also by members of mainstream political parties who wanted to make sure that no government money would be given to organizations favoring withdrawal from Dutch society instead of integration into it. Consequently, representatives of four different political parties in the Dutch parliament wanted to know from the national government whether organizations in the Gülen Movement had received subsidies from the government, and whether it agreed with the *Nova* journalists that these organizations in fact obstructed the integration of Turkish Muslims into Dutch society instead of promoting it. They also wanted the government to start an official inquiry about the identity and the activities of the Gülen Movement in the Netherlands. On behalf of the government, the minister responsible for immigration issues responded that government money was given in 2002 to a number of the schools and other educational institutions mentioned in the *Nova* news item; however, there was no indication that any of them were instrumental in radicalizing Muslims. Concerning the identity of the Gülen movement, the minister wrote that there was no evidence that this is a strictly guided "monolithic" movement, rather it is a network of local organizations with similar ideals. These ideals can be characterized as religiously conservative but in no way danger-

27. M. Hakan Yavuz, *Towards an Islamic Enlightenment: The Gülen Movement* (New York: Oxford University Press, 2013), 76.

ous to the state. Consequently, there is no reason for a thorough investigation.[28]

Meanwhile, questions remained in the national Parliament about the practices in the boarding schools and the "houses of light," and about Gülen's ideas that still seemed to be very ambiguous in the eyes of many politicians. Therefore, the government decided to start an official investigation in February 2009. The result of this investigation was published in September 2010 in a report written by Islamicist Martin van Bruinessen of Utrecht University. In the summary of his report, van Bruinessen comes to the conclusion that the Gülen Movement has a socially and morally conservative character and that it lacks transparency in its organization. There is a strict separation between privately organized religious activities and public social activities in the movement. Core members of the movement are supposed to share conservative moral and religious values, and in this respect it can be said that the movement turns its back on Dutch society; however, there is no evidence of indoctrination of students in the boarding schools. The schools that are associated with the movement are strongly oriented toward academic success and seem to promote rather than hinder integration of Turkish Muslims into Dutch society.[29]

The Dutch government sent the report to Parliament in December 2010 with its own conclusion that can be paraphrased as follows: parents of children who bring them to schools associated with the Gülen Movement are free to do so because of freedom of religion and freedom of choice. However, the Gülen Movement shows a lack of transparency in its organizational structure and an introverted or withdrawn attitude.[30] This is in itself not contrary to

28. Text of the questions and the answers (in Dutch) can be found on the Internet in Tweede Kamer der Staten-Generaal, *Vergaderjaar 2008–2009, Aanhangsel van de Handelingen: Vragen gesteld door de leden der Kamer, met de daarop door de regering gegeven antwoorden,* 33–37 and 519–21.

29. Martin van Bruinessen, *De Fethullah Gülenbeweging in Nederland. Een rapport opgesteld op verzoek van de Minister voor Wonen, Wijken en Integratie* [The Fehullah Gülen Movement in the Netherlands. A report on behalf of the Minister of Living, Neigborhoods, and Integration] (Utrecht: Universiteit Utrecht, 2010), 75.

30. "Een naar binnen gekeerde houding." Original (Dutch) text in Tweede Kamer

Dutch law, and therefore there is no reason to intervene; yet, there is some reason for heightened attention to indications of social pressure on parents (of students in boarding schools associated with the movement). Upon hearing this conclusion, some members of Parliament motioned to stop any state support of Gülen-related organizations because, as one of the representatives of Geert Wilders's Freedom Party stated, "the Gülen Movement has Islamization as its purpose."[31] The motion went nowhere but the movement was publicly associated with the nightmare of a society dominated and regulated by Islam.

In 2012 a government organization for social scientific research reported that Turkish communities in the Netherlands tend to be more introverted and withdrawn from general society than other minorities. Even though the Hizmet Movement was not mentioned in the report, *Nieuwsuur*, another program on current affairs broadcast on Dutch public TV, aired a news item on the Gülen Movement and its boarding houses, where students receive homework assistance. One of the students told a reporter that he had to watch films that picture the history of Islam as a series of clashes with other civilizations. The journalists also interviewed a Turkish politician who is a member of one of the Provincial Councils. When asked about his relation to some of the "houses of light," he answered evasively, but then the journalists confronted him with a number of public documents showing his name as chair of a foundation that manages a sizeable number of such houses. A few days later, the politician had to resign as member of the Provincial Council.

The strategy in the two news broadcasts is strikingly similar: they suggest that the Gülen Movement is a widespread and secretly operating organization that promotes an anti-Western form of Islam and obstructs integration by fostering a climate of withdrawal from and resistance to core values of Dutch society. Mem-

---

der Staten-Generaal, *Vergaderjaar 2010–2011 kamerstuk 32500–VII nr. 71: brief van de Minister van Binnenlandse Zaken en Koninkrijksrelaties d.d. 14 december 2010.*

31. "[D]e Gülenbeweging [heeft] islamisering als doelstelling," in Tweede Kamer der Staten-Generaal, *Handelingen vergaderjaar 2010–2011 vergadernummer 36,* Motie Van Klaveren 74 (32500 VII).

bers of the Hizmet are evasive about their relation to Fethullah Gülen, which justifies skepticism about their honesty and makes plausible the suggestion that they might be secretly promoting an Islamic society.

On March 21, 2013, Turkish Prime Minister Recep Tayyip Erdoğan of the AK Party went on a state visit to the Netherlands. One of the points of discussion between Erdoğan and the Dutch government was the so-called Yunus affair. Yunus is the name of a child of Turkish parents in the Netherlands. Having received signals of possible child abuse, the Dutch Youth Welfare Council decided to place Yunus with a foster family. However, in this case the foster family happened to be a lesbian couple. This case brought to light one of the well-known differences between what is perceived as "Western" and "Islamic" cultural values: Yunus's parents did not agree to placement with this particular family because they did not live according to norms acceptable to Islam. Dutch welfare organizations, on the other hand, said that they did not look at sexual or religious preferences, only at what would be best for the child. Back in Turkey, the placement of Yunus in a Dutch lesbian family caused quite a public commotion, and Erdoğan promised to discuss with the Dutch government that Turkish children should be placed in "straight" Muslim foster families. However, the Dutch minister of social affairs — who was the vice prime minister as well — was not pleased with Turkish interference in a matter between a child born in the Netherlands and Dutch child welfare organizations, one that had been arranged according to the Dutch customs and laws.[32] So in both countries there was quite an outcry over the values and customs of the other, and it caused a public show of disagreement between the two prime ministers during the state visit.

Two weeks later, the highly regarded Dutch newspaper *NRC Handelsblad* printed a reconstruction of this Yunus affair, in which it asserted that the Gülen Movement instigated this crisis between

32. Information in this paragraph is from *NRC Handelsblad* (Rotterdam), March 21, 2013.

the two countries. The uproar in the Turkish media was caused by *Zaman*, one of the biggest Turkish newspapers associated with the Hizmet Movement, according to the paper.[33] The journalist who wrote the story discovered an event concerning child welfare at the Islamic University of Rotterdam in November 2012.[34] The journalist claimed the event was connected with the Gülen Movement as well. At this meeting, one of the scholars in the Islamic studies program is said to have spread the rumor that Dutch welfare organizations "give away thousands of Turkish Muslim children to Christian families." While the purpose of the meeting and the ongoing publicity by *Zaman* was clearly to incite more Turkish families in the Netherlands to apply as foster families, it was construed by the journalist as an anti-Dutch and perhaps even anti-Christian event.[35] Yet the fact that the journalist mentioned the Gülen Movement as the source of the clash is no coincidence, since the article was published the day after the resignation of the Dutch politician of Turkish origin over his relation to the boarding houses. In fact, the same newspaper contained the two news items, plus a third article that gave background information about Gülen as "a man with mighty friends." Yet there is more: on the very same day, the Dutch vice prime minister was set to attend the official launch of a new Dutch-language version of the *Zaman* newspaper. He had clashed with Prime Minister Erdoğan, who at that time seemed to be positive about Gülen and the people he inspired.[36] However,

33. *NRC Handelsblad*, April 9, 2013.

34. The Islamic University of Rotterdam (English website: www.islamicuniversity.nl, accessed June 7, 2014) was founded in 1997 by Turkish Muslims living in the Netherlands. It received accreditation by NVAO, the Dutch and Flemish accreditation organization for a master's progam in Islamic Spiritual Care in 2010, and a bachelor's program in Islamic Theology in 2013. The university is closely associated with the Nurcu Community, not the Hizmet Movement. On the relationships between Said Nursi and Fethullah Gülen and between the two communities, see chapters three and four.

35. Later publications, in October 2013, accused Prof. Ahmet Akgündüz, the rector of the Islamic University of Rotterdam, of anti-Christian (and anti-Alevi) statements. This is another case in which Turkish political tensions were the source of negative publicity in the Netherlands.

36. Until the end of 2013, the general opinion among scholars was that the Gülen Movement seemed to associate itself closely with the AK Party and its Prime Minister

because of the "controversial nature of the Gülen Movement" the Dutch vice prime minister decided to cancel his attendance at this event. This, of course, was a big victory for the politicians and the journalists who like to suggest that a dangerous form of Islamism lurks behind the Gülen Movement in the Netherlands.

Strange as these allegations may seem to people with more than a superficial knowledge of Fethullah Gülen and the organizations he inspired, it is important to analyze this form of critique of the Gülen Movement, and to understand its motives. In fact, in almost all chapters of this book, I will have to come back to these criticisms and try to show how they misinterpret the religious motivations of Fethullah Gülen and the nature of the network of volunteers who are inspired by his thoughts while doing their service work. In fact, those of us who sympathize with Hocaefendi but try to be independent scholars at the same time, have to weigh the evidence time and again, especially if large institutions and considerable amounts of money are involved. In this respect, American sociologist Helen Rose Ebaugh, who can be characterized as largely sympathetic to the Hizmet, has recently mapped the voices of the critics and answered their objections in an insightful way by giving details of the financial sources of the movement.[37]

I have phrased this question — summarized in the proverbial Turkish question, "Where does the water for the mill come from?" — for myself ever since I was invited to an event organized by the Hizmet Movement in Istanbul in 2004 with all my expenses paid by the movement. Checking the movement's financial sources was one of the motives that made me investigate this particular Islamic group further, in order to see whether I could accept these trips. I have come to the conclusion that I can pair my scholarly

Erdoğan, after a long history in which it did not want to identify with one particular political party. Yet an ongoing investigation into some allegations of corruption by members of the AKP government led to unexpected allegations against the Hizmet Movement by Prime Minister Erdoğan. More about this at the end of the next chapter.

37. Helen Rose Ebaugh, *The Gülen Movement: A Sociological Analysis of a Civic Movement Rooted in Moderate Islam* (Dordrecht: Springer, 2010), 115–28.

independence with my sympathy for the movement, as long as those who organize scholarly conferences about Fethullah Gülen and the movement he inspired are open to criticism, even though they may not always like what they hear. At the occasion of one of the first conferences on the Hizmet Movement that I attended in 2005, I gave a paper on Gülen's concept of interreligious dialogue in which I made a few fairly critical remarks. For instance, I said that I disagreed with both Gülen and *Nostra Aetate* that we should forget the past in Christian-Muslim encounters. Although not everyone appreciated this criticism – some told me that I had to make more effort in studying the works of Hocaefendi – the paper was published in-house by the movement and has been featured on several websites.[38] Similarly, Joshua Hendrick, who has written a rather critical study about the Gülen Movement, was invited to present his book at a conference organized by Rumi Forum in 2013.[39] I remember vividly that Hendrick said that if the movement would take its engagement in dialogue seriously, it needed to invite those who were demonstrating against the movement in front of the building where we had our conference. Unfortunately but also understandably, the conference organizers did not follow up on this, but at least he was allowed to give his dissenting opinion. At that same conference, I expressed the opinion that the Hizmet Movement should stop talking about itself and start addressing the wider field of interfaith engagement through service. David Tittensor, another scholar who recently published a study about the movement as a "House of Service" has the following critical observation: "I find the routine production of in-house academics that write on the Movement (some of whom do not declare their

38. Pim Valkenberg, "Fethullah Gülen's Contribution to Muslim-Christian Dialogue in the Context of Abrahamic Cooperation," in *Islam in the Contemporary World 1: The Fethullah Gülen Movement in Thought and Practice*, Conference Proceedings November 12–13, 2005, Rice University, Houston, Tex., 1–10 (Somerset, N.J.: Tughra Books, 2009). The paper can also be found on some of the websites devoted to Fethullah Gülen in English: www.fethullahgulenconference.org/houston and http://en.fgulen.com/conference-papers/the-fethullah-gulen-movement-i (both accessed June 9, 2014).

39. Hendrick, *Gülen*.

position) along with the Movement-sponsored conferences about itself and its leader, Fethullah Gülen, deeply problematic and ultimately counterproductive."[40]

At the same time, Tittensor, in spite of these critical words, does not hide his admiration for the modern interpretation of Islam and the fruitful approach to education in the Hizmet Movement. I can echo both his critical words and his admiration from my experiences that started in the Netherlands, with my Muslim partners. I appreciate the fact that members of the Hizmet are continuously taking new initiatives and invited me to collaborate, thus counteracting the traditional idea that it is always Christians who take the lead in dialogue initiatives. Later, when the political situation made it more difficult to continue initiatives in the spirit of multiculturalism, and when the Hizmet Movement needed to rethink its position in Dutch society, its members started a process of revisiting their longtime goals. In the process, they discovered that further professional and academic education and openness are the two main ingredients for a better integration into Western culture.[41] I am aware that these initiatives by Muslims contain an element of *da'wa* or invitation to their faith, which might cause many Christians to shy away from such initiatives. But as a Christian theologian I am convinced that we have a mission of our own, and that the two missionary faiths can work together as long as they allow one another to bring their convictions openly to the table in a nonaggressive way.

As concerns the question, "Where does the water for the mill come from?" I can only endorse the conclusions that Ebaugh draws in her book.[42] I will come back to this matter in chapters five and six.

While Ebaugh's perspective can be dismissed as being too sympathetic to the movement, this is certainly not the case with

40. Tittensor, *The House of Service*, x.

41. This was the conclusion of the presentation mentioned in note 24 of this chapter. For a short report, see http://www.turkishreview.org/YnYYZ/newsDetail_openPrintPage.action?newsId=223598 (accessed May 28, 2014).

42. Ebaugh, *The Gülen Movement*, 83–107.

Turkish political scientist Hakan Yavuz who gives an elaborate explanation of the arguments of the "Critics of the Movement."[43] Even more critical is sociologist Joshua Hendrick, who considers the ambiguity displayed by the Hizmet as an organizational strategy.[44] Despite his deep suspicion of the movement's alleged goals, he still admits that he does not view the movement as "inherently threatening to the structural integrity of Turkish society; to U.S. education, or to Turkish-U.S. relations."[45]

THE ACADEMIC STUDY OF DIALOGUE: COMPARATIVE THEOLOGY

As the contributions by Ebaugh, Yavuz, and Hendrick show, most academic studies written about Fethullah Gülen and the movement he inspired have thus far been of a social scientific nature. Therefore, I think it is important to explain why I think that it is not only necessary to approach the man and the movement from a theological point of view, but also that it is useful to do so from an explicitly Christian perspective. My basic claim here is that a theological approach is able to bring to light some of the theological convictions that enabled Gülen and the Hizmet Movement to renew Islamic faith by service. Moreover, I am convinced that a comparative form of theology, in which I consider not only the Muslim sources involved but also my own Christian theological background, helps to see the renewal of faith by service in a new light—a light that might be relevant not only for Muslims but also for Christians.

As a scholar working in the field of Christian-Muslim dialogue, my main task is to study the two religious traditions in hopes of gaining a better insight into the way in which the interaction between these traditions may lead us on our way to God. After my first encounters with young Turkish Muslims inspired by Fethullah

43. Yavuz, *Towards an Islamic Enlightenment*, 221–42.
44. Hendrick, *Gülen*, 32.
45. Ibid., x.

Gülen, I used my sabbatical leave in the fall of 2004 to write a book about Muslim-Christian dialogue and theology in the context of Abrahamic partnership.[46] In fact, this book was an investigation of the theological and spiritual backgrounds of my partners in dialogue and was written to be a contribution to a form of God-talk in which Muslims and Christians may share their traditions as mutual incitements to a broader understanding of God. This mutual incitement is beautifully expressed in the Qur'ān when Prophet Muhammad is addressed as follows, in the context of disputations between the "Scripture People" (*ahl al-kitāb*):

> We have sent down to you (O Messenger) the Book with the truth (embodying it, and with nothing false in it), confirming (the Divine authorship of, and the truths that are still contained in,) whatever of the Book was revealed before it, and guarding over (all the true teachings in) it. Judge, then, between them by what God has sent down (to you), and do not follow their lusts and fancies away from the truth that has come to you. For each (community to which a Messenger was sent with a Book), have We appointed a clear way of life and a comprehensive system (containing the principles of that way and how to follow it). And if God had so willed, He would surely have made you a single community (following the same way of life and system surrounded by the same conditions throughout all history); but (He willed it otherwise) in order to test you by what He granted to you (and thereby made you subject to a law of progress). Strive, then, together as if competing in good works. To God is the return of all of you, and He will then make you understand (the truth) about what you have differed on.[47]

This text from the Qur'ān helps me as a Christian comparative theologian to delve into the sources of my own tradition and to find similar texts about "mutual emulation" in some of St. Paul's letters, mainly at places where he is confronted with the question of the rejection of his message about Jesus Christ by many Jews while quite a number of non-Jews seem to accept this message. Paul speculates that maybe God wanted the gentiles to accept the

46. See Valkenberg, *Sharing Lights on the Way to God.*

47. Qur'ān, *al-mā'ida* 5:48; interpretation according to Ünal, *The Qur'ān*, 246.

message first, in order to make the Jews jealous and eager to accept it at a later stage. This "Qur'ānic-Pauline model of spiritual emulation"[48] helped me to understand how theological and spiritual masters of the Islamic tradition could offer guidance to some of the Muslims inspired by Gülen, and how they can become lights for Christians on their way to God as well. But in order to do so, I needed to read Fethullah Gülen in the light of the broader Muslim tradition. I am thus interested in an "intertextual" reading in which texts are read "backwards" to connect them with their basic sources. As I will show later in this book, the most evident sources of Gülen's works are the writings of Said Nursi and Jalāl ad-Dīn Rūmī. This is apparent from the fact that Gülen often quotes them, and that they function as sources of inspiration for Gülen's followers as well—one can often see books by the three authors side by side in bookstores and publisher's lists. Yet at a less apparent level the basic sources for Gülen and Nursi and Rūmī are the Qur'ān and the *hadith* literature, since they want to write in the tradition of Muslim thought.

My preference for such an intertextual reading may have originated in my own doctoral research in which I tried to read Thomas Aquinas, the great medieval theologian, as an interpreter of Scripture.[49] I came to the conclusion that the systematic theological works of Aquinas are, in fact, shaped by their relation to the Scriptures. The research for this thesis made me aware of the possibility that the influence of sources in a particular text can of course be determined by the number of explicit quotations of this source in the text, but more often the presence of the source can be discovered at a deeper level by showing how the source determines the very structure and phrasing of the text. When a source is really influential, the author of the text will often not quote the text as an external source, but use the language of the source and only

48. Valkenberg, *Sharing Lights on the Way to God*, 158.

49. Wilhelmus Valkenberg, *Words of the Living God: Place and Function of Holy Scripture in the Theology of St. Thomas Aquinas*, Publications of the Thomas Instituut te Utrecht 6 (Leuven: Peeters, 2000).

allude to it implicitly since he (or she) assumes that the readers of his (her) text will be able to discover the references to the source in the allusions. This, however, presupposes a thorough knowledge of the source and its particular phrasings, in my case the Latin *Vulgata* text of Scripture, in order to discover its presence at the background of Aquinas's theological works. Often, though, the link between source and text is not a direct one since Aquinas did not read the Scripture in isolation from the tradition of the church fathers and the medieval theologians, whose writings were to a large extent part of a long commentarial tradition. Often Aquinas read the Scripture through the eyes of the fathers or the later glossators.

In my research, I try to read the works of Fethullah Gülen as a Christian comparative theologian, looking for relationships between these works and the larger Muslim tradition, but I am aware as well that my reading originates from a specific interpretation of the Christian tradition that codetermines my theological acumen. This has three important consequences. In the first place, the comparative theologian works with two theological traditions, but in a different way. The Christian comparative theologian remains rooted in the Christian tradition and will therefore start from the assumption that God has revealed Godself in the sources of that tradition. Yet at the same time, the comparative theologian leaves open the possibility that God can reveal Godself through other sources as well. This implies that, while I do not accept the Qur'ān as a revelation of God that has superseded the revelation of God in Jesus Christ, I do accept that Muslims consider the Qur'ān to be God's revelation for them, and, moreover, I accept that this source often leads them to serve God in an admirable way as well. Furthermore, in principle I accept the possibility that God can use the Qur'ān to correct my ever-deficient understanding of Jesus Christ. This may sound radical, but it was already the position of Nicholas of Cusa in his *Cribratio Alkorani* shortly after the conquest of Constantinople by sultan Mehmet II in 1453.[50]

50. See Pim Valkenberg, "Learned Ignorance and Faithful Interpretation of the Qur'ān in Nicholas of Cusa (1401–1464)," in *Learned Ignorance: Intellectual Humility*

The second consequence is that my reading of Fethullah Gülen is intertextual in a double sense. I try to read him in the light of the Muslim tradition, which means that I relate his texts to some of the texts written by Said Nursi and Jalāl ad-Dīn Rūmī, since Gülen refers to their texts in his own works. I also try to read him in the light of the broader tradition of Islam, not only the Qur'ān and the *hadīth* literature to which Gülen frequently refers in most of his works, but also the (Maturidi) theological and (Hanafi) legal tradition that he acknowledges as his own. The other form of intertextuality is that I read Gülen against the background of my own Christian theological tradition, which determines my way of interpreting his texts. In order to do so as well as possible, I have to become aware of this background in order to see where it helps me to read Gülen properly, but also to recognize where it skews my vision and shows my bias in reading him as non-Muslim.

The third consequence is that I read Gülen with a special approach that has been determined by my own theological education. This means that I will have other preferences, will pose different questions, and will notice different things than others. My theological education has been formed by Thomas Aquinas and more specifically by the special God-centeredness in Aquinas's theology. I have always been struck by the fact that Aquinas shows this God-centeredness in so many of his texts, and I have the basic conviction that precisely this God-centeredness helps me in understanding Islam in general and Fethullah Gülen in particular. In my readings of the Islamic tradition, I have recognized this God-centeredness in the writings of Al-Ghazali, Said Nursi, and also Fethullah Gülen. This is one of the reasons why I would find it difficult to write solely about Fethullah Gülen and his movement. If I understand Gülen well, he would be the first to say that the movement is not Fethullah's movement but a movement of volun-

---

among Jews, Christians, and Muslims, ed. James L. Heft SM et al., 34–52 (New York: Oxford University Press, 2011); Pim Valkenberg, "Sifting the Qur'ān: Two Forms of Interreligious Hermeneutics in Nicholas of Cusa," in *Interreligious Hermeneutics in Pluralistic Europe*, ed. David Cheetham et al., 27–48 (New York: Editions Rodopi, 2011).

teers who are ultimately driven by devotion to God. Let me give a characteristic quotation: "Muslims continually seek the approval of God; this is the greatest gain of all."[51] Seeking God's approval or God's pleasure is for Fethullah Gülen the only criterion for what is worthwhile and what is not. This characterizes his person and his movement as oriented toward the service of God. And therefore I think that it does more justice to his person and to his work if we discontinue speaking about "the Gülen Movement" but try to speak about "the faith-based service movement inspired by Fethullah Gülen," or shorter, "the Hizmet [service] Movement."

One of the characteristics of such a comparative theology is that it is much more interested in the particulars of religious traditions than in general sayings that do not seem to be related to any religious tradition at all.[52] In this sense, comparative theology runs counter to a modern tendency in the theology of religions that can be characterized as pluralism.[53] Many advocates of this pluralist position think that different religions are slightly different ways to reach the same ultimate end, and therefore the details within these traditions – for instance, the question as to whether Jesus Christ died on the cross for the wellbeing of humankind (Christianity) or not (Islam) – do not matter much, as long as we are aware that all religions bring us from self-centeredness to reality-centeredness.[54] Contrary to this pluralist position, comparative theologians say that differences do matter and that precisely these differences make interfaith dialogue worthwhile. Yet such a comparative theological reading is not unproblematic if it goes against a tendency in Gülen's own work to stress general similarities rather than specific differences. If it is true that Gülen at a

51. M. Fethullah Gülen, *Toward a Global Civilization of Love and Tolerance* (Somerset, N.J.: The Light, 2004), 52.

52. See Francis X. Clooney, SJ, *Comparative Theology: Deep Learning across Religious Borders*, (Chichester, U.K.: Wiley-Blackwell, 2010), 14.

53. See Paul Knitter, *Introducing Theologies of Religions* (Maryknoll, N.Y.: Orbis Books, 2002), for a full discussion of contemporary models in the Christian theology of religions.

54. This is, in a nutshell, the position of John Hick, *An Interpretation of Religion: Human Responses to the Transcendent* (London: MacMillan, 1989).

certain moment of his life has begun to shift his discourse from a more specific discourse steeped in the Islamic tradition to a more general discourse that appeals to a broader public, my analysis will be able to shed more light on his earlier works than on his later works. At the same time, I think that such an analysis is needed in order to bring to light some of the basic presuppositions in Gülen's later works. My analysis will also show that the shift from a more specifically Islamic to a more general mode of discourse is true to a lesser extent than I assumed it to be when I began to read some of Gülen's works. From a comparative theological point of view, I can only understand the full interreligious impact of his discourse if I read his more general thoughts against the background of his more specific references to the Islamic tradition. Nor is this a specific characteristic of comparative theological research, since I think that every biography or scholarly analysis of Fethullah Gülen and the movement he inspired will have to retrace his thoughts to their origins. In my own theological research, I did something similar when I wrote my master's thesis about the radical feminist theologian Mary Daly and reconstructed the sources of her theological thinking by going back to Paul Tillich and Thomas Aquinas. In a similar way, I could understand the theological language of one of my predecessors at the Catholic University of Nijmegen (now Radboud University), Edward Schillebeeckx, OP, by tracing his roots back to – once again – Thomas Aquinas. And finally, as I noted earlier, my Ph.D. was about the roots of Aquinas himself in the Scriptures of Christianity. But I have also experienced that persons who are confronted with such a "retrograde" interpretation usually do not like the results, since they prefer to see themselves as reformers or progressives rather than in continuity with the past. I can see that it would not make much sense for the faith-based service movement that Gülen inspired to resort to a more explicit Islamic form of discourse, since this would diminish its chances of building bridges to other movements and societies.

Yet I want to make two final observations here. In the first place, in my encounter with supporters of the Hizmet Movement,

I have seen how Islam is a very important and powerful motivating force in the personal lives of those who are inspired by Gülen, and this is certainly the case with Fethullah Gülen himself; so every analysis of this movement should take this rootedness in faith into account. In the second place, a more explicit reference to the Islamic roots of the movement would help to avoid some of the critiques that the movement has a hidden agenda. When members of the Hizmet Movement abandon any reference to the Islamic faith in their public discourse while maintaining this faith at the same time as a very important principle in their private lives, they display an ambiguity that is often perceived as a source of potential deceit and lack of transparency by politicians and the public media, as we have seen in some of the examples from the Netherlands in this chapter. It may also have given rise to allegations that the Gülen Movement has plans to surreptitiously introduce Muslim *shari'ah.* I am convinced that this imputation seriously misreads Gülen's discourse and the intentions of those he inspired – but I can see how the Turkish political situation has occasioned moments of secrecy in the Hizmet Movement and led to obligatory insinuations by its secularist and nationalist opponents. In a Western context in which openness and transparency are much more important, it would be good if the community would serve God and humankind by being less nervous about its religious identity.

2

TURKEY BETWEEN THE OTTOMAN EMPIRE AND THE EUROPEAN UNION

THIS CHAPTER aims to describe some of the most important social and political contexts that shed light on the life and works of Fethullah Gülen, whose works will be discussed in the next chapter. The rise of the network of faith-based service communities inspired by Gülen is not an isolated phenomenon, since it fits in a series of events that can be characterized as the renewal of public religious life and the rise of political Islam in Turkey.[1] During his extended residence as a journalist and scholar in Turkey, Rainer Hermann has observed the traces of what he calls a "new cultural war" in Turkey, not dissimilar from the famous *Kulturkampf* in nineteenth-century Germany.[2] One of the most important changes characterizing Turkey at the beginning of the twenty-first century is the rise of an Anatolian middle class that has a much more positive approach to the traditional values em-

1. Angel Rabasa and F. Stephen Larrabee, *The Rise of Political Islam in Turkey* (Santa Monica, Calif.: RAND Corporation, National Defense Research Institute, 2008).

2. Heinz Kramer, *A Changing Turkey. The Challenge to Europe and the United States*, (Washington, D.C.: Brookings Institution Press, 2000), 70; Rainer Hermann, *Wohin geht die türkische Gesellschaft? Kulturkampf in der Türkei* (Munich: Deutscher Taschenbuch Verlag, 2009).

bodied by Islam than the state elite associated with Mustafa Kemal's secular republic. In this respect, the national fame of Gülen's Hizmet Movement in the 1990s was an early sign pointing to the possibility of the landslide victories of the Justice and Development Party (Adalet ve Kalkinma) in 2007 and 2011, since both organizations have so much in common.[3] This has been true even though tensions between them seemed to be developing in 2013. While there is no official relationship between the Hizmet and the political party, there is an important similarity in convictions that Berna Turam describes as an "organic continuity" with a cooperative attitude as its major characteristic.[4] It is significant to note that Gülen and his most important supporters embraced the values represented by the AK Party and its leader Tayyip Erdoğan, while they always kept its precursors – the Islamist parties led by Necmettin Erbakan – at a greater distance than its secularist antagonist, the CHP. Ahmet Kuru concludes that the movement inspired by Gülen "recently … largely dropped its neutrality principle and supported the AK Party in the national elections of July 22, 2007."[5]

Rainer Hermann writes that the AK Party represents the periphery that was excluded from political power for a long time under the centralist government.[6] He describes the power of this new phenomenon using the widespread metaphor of "Anatolian tigers" (Anadolu kaplanları): the provincial entrepreneurs who paired a strong work ethic to a conservative Muslim worldview. Thanks to Turgut Özal's opening to a free market economy, they were able to expand their businesses and enlarge their political influence.[7]

3. Ahmet T. Kuru, "Changing Perspectives on Islamism and Secularism in Turkey: The Gülen Movement and the AK Party," in *Muslim World in Transition: Contributions of the Gülen Movement* (London: Leeds Metropolitan University Press, 2007), 140–51. More recently, M. Hakan Yavuz, "The Clash of Political Visions: The Military and the JDP," in *Towards an Islamic Enlightenment: The Gülen Movement* (New York: Oxford University Press, 2013), 198–220.

4. Berna Turam, *Between Islam and the State: The Politics of Engagement* (Stanford, Calif,: Stanford University Press, 2007), 13.

5. Kuru, "Changing Perspectives on Islamism and Secularism in Turkey," 148.

6. Hermann, *Wohin geht die türkische Gesellschaft?* 125.

7. Ibid., 101.

Since the same Anatolian entrepreneurs form the financial backbone of the Hizmet Movement, it makes sense to talk about a specific contribution of Anatolian Islam as Fethullah Gülen does in some of his recent interviews.[8] Among the characteristics of such an Anatolian form of Islam is its tolerance.[9] For Gülen, Anatolian Islam as a term is more or less interchangeable with Turkish Islam to indicate a tolerant, modern, and strongly spiritual (Sufi) form of Islam.[10] Mentioning the Asian countryside of the Turkish Republic also has the advantage of pointing to its long history in which many cultural influences were amalgamated.

Another reason to refer to "Anatolia" is that it may be strange to refer to "Turkey" as the most important political identity that determines the context of Gülen's works, because "Turkey" is the name of a secular republic founded in 1923. Since Gülen was born more than fifteen years after the declaration of the republic of Turkey, of course he refers to this reality in most of his writings. Yet at the same time he is well aware that many of his ideas are connected with the past history of the area. The Ottoman Empire that ended in the years before the First World War probably forms the most important part of this memory, but there are reminiscences of an earlier history as well when Gülen refers to "Anatolian Islam." On the one hand, the mindset of Gülen clearly reflects his origin in eastern Turkey, and the social and religious conservatism of the movement that he inspired matches better with Anatolia than with Ankara or Istanbul. On the other hand, one of the meanings of "Anatolian Islam" for Gülen is that it – unlike Iranian or other forms of Islam that can be associated with strongly politicized religion – fosters openness and relationships with other peoples and cultures. "Gülen has written about an Anatolian Islam that differs from Arab Islam in its tolerance and openness to dialogue with all

8. See the series of interviews in Nevval Sevindi, *Contemporary Islamic Conversations* (Albany, N.Y.: State University of New York Press, 2008).

9. Bülent Aras, "Turkish Islam's Moderate Face," *Middle East Quarterly* 5, no.3 (1998): 23–31.

10. Ihsan Yilmaz, "State, Law, Civil Society and Islam in Contemporary Turkey," *The Muslim World* 95 (2005): 397.

segments of society, including other religions and sects."[11] In that sense, it is no coincidence that nowadays Gülen's supporters can be found in Istanbul and the Western world. Moreover, as I will explain in the next chapter, Gülen's discourse may sometimes have a national or even patriotic orientation, but at other times it may be strongly universalistic. So, the notion of "Turkey" in Gülen's writings has multiple connotations that are connected with the different phases in the history of this region.

Bernard Lewis opens his *The Emergence of Modern Turkey* by stating, "[t]he name Turkey has been given to Turkish-speaking Anatolia almost since its first conquest by the Turks in the eleventh century—given, that is, by Europeans. But the Turks themselves did not adopt it as the official name of their country until 1923."[12] The name Anatolia, on the contrary, brings with it a much wider historical perspective, evoked by the Anatolianist movement associated with Atatürk that tried to establish the Turkish origin of ancient peoples such as the Sumerians, the Trojans, and the Hittites.[13] In using the name Anatolia, we look at the Asian main part of the country rather than at the smaller part on the European continent, and that is in line with the consciousness of most Turks who stress their kinship with central-Asian peoples rather than their shared history with the inhabitants of the Balkans. The creation of Ankara as the new capital of the Turkish republic instead of Istanbul seems to underline this orientation toward an Anatolian rather than an Ottoman past.[14]

Because of the double relatedness in Gülen's works and the thoughts of his supporters to both the Anatolian origins and the Western horizon of the Turkish people it makes sense to describe these historical backgrounds in more detail. Since the histori-

11. Jenny White, *Islamist Mobilization in Turkey: A Study in Vernacular Politics* (Seattle: University of Washington Press, 2002), 111.

12. Bernard Lewis, *The Emergence of Modern Turkey*, 3rd ed. (New York: Oxford University Press, 2002), 1.

13. Lewis, *The Emergence of Modern Turkey*, 3.

14. Douglas A. Howard, *The History of Turkey* (Westport, Conn.: Greenwood Press, 2001), 4.

cal legacy of the area is not without relevance for the present-day dialogue between Muslims and Christians, I will pay attention to these aspects as well.

ANATOLIAN CIVILIZATIONS

The oldest remnants of civilizations in present-day Anatolia are found in excavations at Çatal Hüyük in the Konya Plain (about 7000 BCE) and Hacılar in the Lake District (about 5400 BCE). But the first large-scale civilization to emerge is the Hittite kingdom between 2000 and 1250 BCE. Centered around Kanesh (present-day Kültepe) and Hattusa (Boğazköy) in northeast Anatolia, the Hittites established contacts with the Greeks and the inhabitants of Troy (present-day Hisarlık). Because they did not leave much archeological evidence behind, the centuries after the collapse of the Hittite kingdom are described as a "Dark Age."[15] New evidence indicates the emergence of the Phrygians, Lydians, Ionians, and – a bit later – Medes and Persians. The era between 500 and 330 BCE is marked by the continuous rivalry between the Persians and the Greeks and the rise of Macedonia along the Aegean Sea. It was the Macedonian king Alexander the Great who would cross the Hellespont in 334 BCE to destroy the Persian Empire and in doing so change the map of world history.[16]

Thanks to Alexander, the Hellenistic culture began its dominance in large parts of Asia, and in the Anatolian plains this led to considerable cultural centers such as Smyrna (Izmir), Pergamum, Ephesus, and Miletus. In Roman times – two centuries before and three centuries after the beginning of the Christian calendar – these centers developed into independent city-states in western Asia Minor. It was in these regions that many of the earliest Christian communities developed. In the New Testament, we hear about Saint Paul's travels through the region, and he is believed to

15. Richard Stoneman, *A Traveller's History of Turkey*, 5th ed. (Northampton, Mass.: Interlink Books, 2009), 22.

16. Ibid., 53.

have written letters to the churches in Ephesus and Galatia. Revelation, the final book of the New Testament, is usually ascribed to someone closely associated with the author of the Gospel according to John. It begins with an interesting series of seven letters addressed to the churches in western Asia Minor, to wit Ephesus, Smyrna, Pergamum, Thyatira, Sardis, Philadelphia, and Laodicea.[17] The John of Revelation identifies himself as someone who lived in exile in the Roman penal colony of Patmos, an island in the Aegean Sea, because of his proclamation of the word of God and his testimony to Jesus.[18] The Christian tradition believes that John the Evangelist lived in Ephesus where he wrote his famous Gospel, the most profound theological interpretation of Christ as the word of God – in the Greek tradition, John is called "the theologian." This Gospel tells how Jesus at the cross established the future relationship between John and Mary, the mother of Jesus, with the following words: "When Jesus saw his mother and the disciple there whom he loved, he said to his mother, 'Woman, behold, your son.' Then he said to the disciple, 'Behold, your mother.' And from that hour the disciple took her into his home."[19]

When I visited Ephesus in the summer of 2009, together with some friends invited by Rumi Forum's Maryland branch, I noticed that there were quite a few signs indicating the location of the House of the Virgin Mary in Ephesus, and that it was a place of pilgrimage for Western tourists and Christian faithful, among whom three popes may be counted: Paul VI in 1967, John Paul II in 1989, and Benedict XVI in 2006. This place (also called Panaya Kapulu, after the Greek designation – *Panhagia* – of Mary) is of some significance for Muslims as well, since the mother of Jesus has an important place in the Qur'ān and is mentioned there even more often than in the New Testament, as our Muslim guide remarked with some emphasis. On the basis of the New Testament and later

17. See the book of Revelation, chapters 1:4 to 3:22, in the New Testament of the Christian Bible.

18. Revelation 1:9.

19. John 19: 26–27.

church history, I was expecting an equal attention to vestiges of Saint John, since another Greek name for the region, *hagios theologos*, pointed to the importance of the memory of his name, but of course John does not get the same attention in the Qur'ān and is therefore less relevant for Muslims.

Another sign near Ephesus pointed us to an old story that connects Christians and Muslims as well: the cave of the seven sleepers, where Christians who are said to have fled into a cave in order to escape persecution in the third century slept protected by God for a few centuries to awake in an empire where Christianity had become the state religion. This story of the *ashāb al-kahf* is mentioned in the Qur'ān as well where they are praised as strong believers in the one true God.[20]

Asia Minor is still full of remnants of the period in which Christianity was the dominant religion. The European part of Istanbul contains many buildings dating back to the old city of Constantinople where Constantine the Great made Christianity a lawful religion (*religio licita*) after his conversion to the cross of Christ in the battle of the Milvian Bridge (324). Almost immediately, he tried to settle the debates on the right relationship between Christ and God at the first ecumenical council in the imperial palace in Nicaea (Iznik). Emperor Theodosius did not only make Christianity the state religion, but he organized a second ecumenical council in Constantinople (381) where the Nicene Creed was confirmed. The five following ecumenical councils all took place in the area of present-day Turkey: Ephesus (431), Chalcedon (451), Constantinople (553 and 680), and again Nicaea (787).

Of course, Constantine ordered a church to be built in the center of his empire; this simple wooden Roman basilica was destroyed after thirty years during riots, and a second church fell to the same fate a century later. Emperor Justinian ordered the construction of the building that we now know as Hagia Sophia (Ayasofya) in 532. After its completion in the unbelievably short time of five years, it

20. Qur'ān, *al-Kahf* (18), 9–22.

served as a Christian church dedicated to Hagia Sophia (Holy Wisdom) for almost a millennium, and as a mosque for almost half that time until the new Turkish republic converted it into a museum in 1935. In a certain sense, the interior of the Ayasofya summarizes three important periods in Turkish history: a first period in which Christianity emerged as the main religion in the Byzantine empire; a second period after the conquest of Constantinople by Sultan Mehmet in 1453 when Islam became the dominant religion in the city; and a third period in which church and mosque were literally secularized – that is, withdrawn from use as a sacred space – to fulfill a new function as a museum. Religious people – Christians and Muslims together – will count it as a loss that this sacred building no longer functions in a religious context, but at the same time it should be said that this secular context makes it possible for Muslims and Christians to walk together through the building, admiring mosaics and calligraphies together. Yet it also leaves an aftertaste of dissatisfaction that the building is no longer used to glorify God as it was meant to do by Christians and Muslims alike.

Similar feelings of admiration and amazement about an unexpectedly impressive past mixed with sadness at the seemingly irretrievable loss of its original function came over me when I visited the remnants of Christian culture in Cappadocia. This region in the middle of Anatolia, with Nyssa (Nevşehir) at its center, and Caesarea (Kaisari) to the east, was an important place for developments in Christian monastic life and theology. Christian theologians are familiar with the "Cappadocian Fathers," Saints Basil the Great, Gregory of Nyssa, and Gregory of Nazianzus, who lived in the fourth century and were very important in the development of Trinitarian theology. The famous churches and monasteries that were carved out of the rocks in the neighborhood of Nevşehir and Göreme date from the final centuries of the Byzantine era, before the Selcuks would become the most important political power in the region. Christians still were able to live their lives and practice their religion under Muslim rule, but the mutual population exchange – some historians use the term "mutual deportation" or "agreed mutual expulsion"—between the new Turkish republic and Greece in 1923 practically ended the Christian presence in Turkey outside of Istanbul and the region of the Suryani (Syrian Orthodox Christians) along the Syrian border. Just like the Hagia Sophia, the region of Cappadocia lost its focus and its holy places became an open air museum. In its relation to non-Muslim communities, the nascent Turkish republic adopted the heritage of the Ottoman Empire in which non-Muslim citizens were tolerated but segregated.[21] In a radicalization of this segregation, the Greek-Orthodox citizens of Anatolia had to leave their houses and churches, while their ethnic and religious brothers and sisters in Istanbul and Thrace were allowed to stay.

The first influence of Turkish people in the territory that was later to receive their name becomes visible at the beginning of the eleventh century when the Selcuks, one of the Turkish tribes in Central Asia, extended its influence westward through Persia and Armenia to include Caesarea (Kaiseri) and Iconium (Konya). Having defeated the Byzantines in the battle of Manzikert (Malazgirt) in 1071, the Selcuks established an empire that came to be known as the Sultanate of Rum, after the traditional name for the Byzantines or east Romans. This name became also the familiar epithet of the most famous Sufi poet, Jalāl ad-Dīn Rūmī, who lived in Konya in the thirteenth century when it was the capital of the Selcuk Empire. In his case, the name only indicates the place where the great tradition of the Mevleviyya order originated, since Jalāl ad-Dīn himself was born in Balkh in present-day Afghanistan and traveled together with his father Bahā al-din Valad and his family from Khorasan to Konya where they arrived in 1221.[22] In Konya, Rūmī had his transforming encounter with Shams al-Dīn Tabrizi and in Konya he wrote his famous poems until he migrated to his Beloved on December 17, 1273. Soon after his death, his son Sultan Valad initiated the building of a dome over the remains

21. Lewis, *The Emergence of Modern Turkey*, 14.

22. Franklin D. Lewis, *Rumi: Past and Present, East and West. The Life, Teachings and Poetry of Jalāl al-Din Rumi.* (Oxford: Oneworld, 2003), 77.

of Jalāl al-din and his father Bahā al-din. This building, known as the *Kubba-i Hadra* (the Green Dome) still serves as a sacred place in memory of Rūmī, his family, and his followers, although it was transformed – once again – into a museum after the closing of the Sufi lodges in 1925.[23]

Meanwhile, Constantinople as capital of the Byzantine empire was threatened by the crusaders from the West, who wanted to express their zeal for Christ by not only attacking the Muslims who held possession over the region where he had lived but the Christians of the Eastern churches as well. The fourth wave of crusaders succeeded in capturing Constantinople in 1204, and count Boudewijn van Vlaanderen (Baldwin of Flanders) became the first Latin Emperor of Constantinople. After some years, the Byzantine emperors succeeded in regaining authority, but this time it was threatened by new powers, first the Mongols and later the Turkomans under Osman. In 1280, Osman established a new dynasty, the Osmanlıs, in the West known as the Ottomans. After the Selcuks, they were the second Turkish tribe from central Asia to establish an empire in Anatolia.

THE OTTOMAN EMPIRE

The Ottoman sultan Mehmet II, also known as *Fatih*, the "opener" or conqueror, finally succeeded in capturing Constantinople in the year 1453. For the Muslims in Anatolia, this meant that an important supply route for the crusaders was finally cut off, but for the Western Christians in Europe, it meant the beginning of a new threat that would remain until the siege of Vienna in 1683. The Ottoman Empire began its steady expansion in prosperity and relative religious freedom thanks to the *millet* system, according to which every ethnic and religious minority could be governed by its own authorities under the overall command of the sultan.[24] The sultan showed his ultimate power by conscripting some Chris-

23. Lewis, *Rumi: Past and Present, East and West*, 427.
24. Stoneman, *A Traveller's History of Turkey*, 134.

tian boys and bringing them to court, where they formed a special "collection" or devşirme poised to be trained as the elite military rank of the Janissaries (Yeniçeriler). In their turn, these Janissaries had the potential to become a military and political power that threatened the authority of the Sultan – one of the reasons for the increasing instability of the Ottoman Empire.

The time of Süleyman the Magnificent (1520–66) is generally seen as the artistic apogee of the Ottoman Empire, not least because of Sinan the famous architect of, among other works, the Süleymaniye Mosque. Meanwhile, in Europe, the phrase "the Turks" was used for the first time to indicate this new political reality, but it was an unfriendly label for a people perceived as a Muslim threat to the religion and culture of Western Europe, as can be read in the sermons and letters of, among others, Martin Luther and Desiderius Erasmus. However, once the Ottoman Turks had to break up their siege of Vienna, relations between the Ottomans and the West began to improve, and the so-called Tulip Period in the eighteenth century indicates the affinity between the Ottoman and the French ideals of enlightened administration and rococo art. While the Ottoman Empire was not as strong as its grandeur seemed to suggest – the famous metaphor tells about the long decline of the "Sick Man of Europe" – France and England did not allow Russia and Austria to profit from its long illness. In this respect, Sina Akşin mentions Ibn Khaldun's theory according to which a new state reaches its natural end after four generations. The Ottomans, however, "did not come to their 'natural' conclusion, because there was no sufficiently powerful nomadic force to strike the deathblow. The European Great Powers were reluctant to carve up the empire in case another of their number should capture İstanbul and gain control of the strategically vital Bosphorus and Dardanelles Straits, and therefore they did not allow the Ottoman state to collapse but were content to exploit it."[25]

25. Sina Akşin, *Turkey from Empire to Revolutionary Republic. The Emergence of the Turkish Nation from 1789 to the Present*, trans. from the Turkish by Dexter H. Mursaloğlu (New York: New York University Press, 2007), 16–17.

After the Greek war of independence and the loss of Egypt it was clear that the army needed to be reconfigured, and this led to the end of the Janissaries. Mustafa Reşit Paşa, who had served as ambassador in Paris and London and as foreign minister, was able to convince Sultan Abdülmecit I that further reforms were needed. In 1839 the *Tanzimat* (Reorganization) was proclaimed to representatives of the European states, asserting, among other things, equality between Muslims and non-Muslims.[26] This was followed by the abolishment of the poll tax on non-Muslims in the Imperial Rescript of 1856. Such equality between Muslims and non-Muslims was a betrayal of the Islamic values of the empire in the eyes of the so-called Young Ottomans who began to push for a constitutional monarchy. The Young Ottomans argued that the values of "Islamism" should be more important than the values of "Turkism;" yet, some decades later, the Young Turks would reverse this argument. Meanwhile, Abdülhamit II adopted the constitution shortly after his accession to power in 1876, but he disbanded Parliament less than two years later.

During these years, the empire did not suffer only a long conflict with Russia over the area of the Balkans, but an uprising of the Armenian province as well.[27] Because of Abdülhamit's autocratic regime, and because of the rising financial problems of the empire, a number of young officers in the Ottoman army stationed in Macedonia and Edirne began a revolt in 1908 that would lead to major changes and the birth of the modern state of Turkey. Their focus was on Turkey as a nation rather than on the ideas central to the Ottoman government. Consequently, they called themselves the "Young Turks" and their first demand was the restoration of

26. Akşin, *Turkey from Empire to Revolutionary Republic*, 28.

27. Whether or not the fierce Ottoman (and later Turkish) reactions to the Armenian pursuit of independence can be called a "genocide" is still severely contested in present-day Turkey — as became evident once again when a subcommittee of the U.S. House of Representatives, in March 2010, voted 23–22 in favor of labeling the Ottoman handling of Armenian resistance between 1915 and 1923 a "genocide" — but most historians do not hesitate to talk about the "massacres." See Howard, *The History of Turkey*, 70; Stoneman, *A Traveller's History of Turkey*, 164.

the 1876 constitution. When the sultan granted this request, the Young Turks participated in the government under the name of the Committee of Union and Progress (CUP). The political situation grew tense because of losses of territory in Bosnia and Crete, a new Armenian uprising in eastern Anatolia, and a counter revolution by an extremist religious party. Some of the Young Turks – an officer named Mustafa Kemal among them – marched to Istanbul and convinced Parliament to depose the sultan. The CUP was now in power, but the international situation grew worse with the Balkan wars (1912–13) and the First World War (1914–18), in which Turkey was on the losing side. As Stoneman argues, "the loss of territory acted as a spur to ideas of Turkish nationalism, which were vigorously promoted by the writer and scholar Ziya Gökalp (1876–1924)."[28] Mustafa Kemal became famous as a general at Gallipoli where the British navy was not able to continue its first success in invading the Dardanelles. In the end, however, the Ottoman Empire had to surrender to the Allies, and more particularly to the British who occupied Istanbul in November 1918. The sultan wanted cooperation with the Allies, but had to dissolve Parliament because of the resistance of the Young Turks who began to organize their opposition in eastern Anatolia. Meanwhile, the Greeks profited from the terms of the upcoming Treaty of Sèvres (1920) that divided the Near East along the lines of an earlier agreement between France and Great Britain, to claim parts of western Anatolia and to invade Izmir and the surrounding area. Since the unrest between Greeks and Ottomans occasioned the British threat to occupy the entirety of Anatolia, the Ottoman government reacted by asking Mustafa Kemal – named Atatürk, the father of Turks, from 1934 on – to restore order and to enforce disarmament according to the 1918 armistice. He landed in Samsun on May 19, 1919, a date which, as Atatürk, he would later make his official birthday and a national holiday.[29] He organized

28. Ibid., 169.

29. Stoneman, *A Traveller's History of Turkey*, 175.

the struggle for independence by proclaiming the Declaration of Amasya that called for a national congress in Erzurum. This congress drafted the National Pact, a document that would later be adopted by Parliament in Istanbul and would become the manifesto of the nationalists. While the government in Istanbul tried to outlaw the nationalists as traitors and enemies of the faith, many members of Parliament fled to Ankara in order to join the Grand National Assembly convened by Mustafa Kemal as its president. When the Ottoman government accepted the term of the Sèvres treaty, the nationalists returned the accusation of treachery.

THE TURKISH REPUBLIC

Between 1920 and 1922 the nationalist troops began a series of battles against the Greek invaders of western Anatolia and against the Armenians in the northeast. According to most historians, all parties committed atrocities against innocent civilians, disturbing the relations between Turkey on the one hand and Greece, Armenia, and Russia on the other hand for decades, until relations improved under the new Turkish government in recent years. In October 1922, the nationalists abolished the sultanate and took over the government in Istanbul. In the same month, they took part in the peace conference of Lausanne in Switzerland. A year later, in October 1923, Ankara became the new capital of the Turkish Republic. Two heroes of the independence war became president and prime minister: Mustafa Kemal and Ismet Inönü – named after the place where he stopped the Greek invasion. From the very beginning, Mustafa Kemal, later called Atatürk, sought to establish the new republic on principles that differed significantly from the Ottoman state. While he could not abolish the influence of Islam as the established religion, he tried to curtail its public influence by banning some of its most visible signs, such as the Arabic script and call to prayer, the caliphate, the *fez,* and the veil. The French model of strict separation between religion and the state, known as *laïcité* (*laiklik* in Turkish) was adopted, and the state was to be built on a nationalist foundation according to the ideas of Ziya Gökalp. After a Kurdish uprising in 1924, the Republican People's Party became the only party to rule the people. After Atatürk's death in November 1938, Inönü became his successor as president, and he established a strict interpretation of the nationalist and secular principles of Kemalism as the leading ideology of the state.

It was in this situation that Fethullah Gülen was born and raised as a Turkish Muslim. Islam was the accepted religion of the large majority in the country, but the religion was not allowed to have any influence on public policy. Islamic education was seen as backward and Islamic organizations were either forbidden or viewed with suspicion. Said Nursi, whom we will later meet as one of the major intellectual and spiritual guides of Fethullah Gülen, was invited to address the Parliament of the new Turkish republic, but when he discovered that the majority was not interested in his proposals for a revival of Islam under the new government, he withdrew from politics to focus on his spiritual life and writings.[30] Fethullah Gülen avoided any direct involvement in politics as well, but generally speaking he tends to view the different forms of government favorably because of an inborn tendency to avoid conflicts and to prefer collaboration to opposition.[31] Nevertheless, some of the volunteers I met in the Hizmet Movement seem to prefer the past of the Ottoman Empire to the present of the Turkish republic, since they proudly display the maps and symbols of the empire in their homes. As Jenny White

30. Sükran Vahide, "Bediüzzaman Said Nursi and the *Risale-i Nur,*" in *Globalization, Ethics and Islam. The Case of Bediuzzaman Said Nursi*, ed. Ian Markham and Ibrahim Ozdemir (Burlington, Vt.: Ashgate, 2005), 16.

31. He is quoted (in Çelik, *The Gülen Movement*) to have said: "The worst government is better than the absence of a government, because the absence of a government will lead to anarchy and insecurity." Gülen therefore will not easily support rebellions, even if they are ventured in the name of Islam. A recent example of this is Gülen's reaction to the "flotilla incident" in the spring of 2010. In a sharp contrast to Turkey's Prime Minister Erdoğan's reception of the Turkish flotilla leaders as heroes when they returned from an Israeli prison, Gülen said that they should not have tried to break Israel's sea blockade of Gaza without the permission of the Israeli authorities. See Joe Lauria, "Reclusive Turkish Imam Criticizes Gaza Flotilla," *Wall Street Journal*, June 4, 2010.

says about them: "[l]ike other Islamists, the Fethullahçılar use Islam and the Ottoman past to symbolically bridge contemporary ethnic and sectarian diversity."[32] This does not imply that they would not be loyal citizens, but they combine an overt loyalty to the symbols of the Turkish republic with a more private loyalty to some of the values associated with the Ottoman Empire. In this respect, Berna Turam talks about "different levels of front and back stages in the movement."[33] While most of the schools associated with Gülen display "Atatürk corners" to show their loyalty to the founding father of the republic of Turkey, in their private sites many members of the Hizmet community display books and maps referring to the Ottoman period and its values.[34]

In 1946 the multiparty system was reintroduced in Turkey. Four years later, the new Democratic Party won the elections, and Adnan Menderes became prime minister. The Democrats withdrew some of the radical secularism that characterized the RPP's Kemalist heritage, and reintroduced religious instruction in all schools. During the reign of the Democratic Party, Turkey joined NATO and it applied for membership in the European Economic Community. However, the country's economic situation worsened and demonstrations and riots occasioned the military to intervene with the first of a number of coups in 1960. A Committee of National Unity took over the government and institutionalized a national security council, "a body dominated by the military and entrusted with ensuring that the government's domestic and foreign policies were in line with the basic tenets of the Kemalist revolution, particularly secularism."[35] The leaders of the Democratic Party were executed in 1961 and Inönü reclaimed the status of prime minister. In 1965, however, the Justice Party – an offshoot of the Democratic Party – regained power under Süleyman Demirel who took a more liberal course while remaining on speaking terms with the military.

32. White, *Islamist Mobilization in Turkey*, 111.

33. Turam, *Between Islam and the State*, 59.

34. Ibid., 62.

35. Rabasa and Larrabee, *The Rise of Political Islam in Turkey*, 36.

Again, the economic situation grew worse and the RPP accused Demirel of forsaking the principles of Atatürk which is, as Çetin argues, the gravest accusation possible in Turkish politics.[36] Political violence by radical socialists, Kurds, and Islamists erupted again, and in 1971 the military took control to impose martial law and dissolve some of the radical political parties.

This unstable political situation was the context in which Fethullah Gülen first served in the military (1961) and later started his career as a teacher and preacher (*vaiz*) in Edirne (1964) and Izmir (1966). As will be described in the next chapter, he started to set up meetings in coffee houses, to gather money to provide for the needs of students, and to teach them in summer camps and at other locations. As several supporters of the Hizmet told me when I interviewed them in Izmir, the military coup of 1971 made it difficult to continue this work, since forces in the police and the military were suspicious of prominent Muslims who were accused of undermining the secular principles of the state. In fact, Gülen was arrested with some of his supporters in 1970 and held in prison for six months.[37]

In the 1970s the most important politicians were Bülent Eçevit, who headed the reorganized Republican People's Party, and Süleyman Demirel. They alternated in forming governments, but Necmettin Erbakan also succeeded in gaining some political power with his National Order Party based on strong Islamic convictions and values. A new political factor was the Turkish invasion of Cyprus in 1974 and the consequent partition of the island. Once again, the economic situation worsened, and inflation rose together with political violence. For the third time, the military intervened in 1980 to restore order and to combat the antinational forces. This time, Islam was seen as a good defense against communism and other leftist ideologies.[38] One of the generals was appointed president, and all political leaders were banned from ac-

36. Çetin, *The Gülen Movement,* 27.

37. Ibid., 30.

38. Rabasa and Larrabee, *The Rise of Political Islam in Turkey,* 37.

tive politics for some time. During these years, Gülen held posts as imam and preacher in different places in the Aegean region, and he was able to provide opportunities for students to come together and live in an atmosphere of service and piety. In 1976 he returned to Izmir to become imam and preacher in the mosque of Bornova, near one of the biggest universities in Turkey. His sermons and public religious conversations (*sohbetler*) drew the attention of large crowds, and many more listened to his words on audio cassettes. During the time of the military coup, however, Gülen took a leave of absence because of his health situation, and in 1981 he retired from preaching.

After the military allowed parliamentary elections once again in 1983, the newly formed Motherland Party under Turgut Özal came into power. Özal was an economist who succeeded in reforming Turkish finances along the lines of free market economy. Political stability and economic gains increased and tourism became an important source of income. Moreover, in 1987 Özal applied for full membership in the European Union. One of the most important consequences of economic and political liberalization was the growth of a new class of entrepreneurs from Anatolia, the so-called Anatolian tigers mentioned at the beginning of this chapter. Özal took a more tolerant approach to religion as well, and under his governance, "Muslim groups and brotherhoods were given greater freedom and were allowed to finance the construction of private schools and universities."[39] Moreover, he became the first Turkish prime minister "to publicly fulfill the religious obligation of pilgrimage to Mecca."[40] These were very favorable conditions for the Hizmet Movement to develop in, and the movement was able to build its first schools and media outlets during these years. On a more personal note, some of the persons I interviewed in Izmir said that Özal sometimes came to listen to Gülen's sermons. While Gülen was no longer active as *imam* and

39. Ibid., 39.
40. Kramer, *A Changing Turkey*, 63.

hatip,[41] state authorities asked him to resume preaching, with the special right to preach in any mosque. This happened in 1989, the year that Özal became president. Gülen alternated between preaching in Istanbul and Izmir during two years, and his sermons were attended by unprecedented numbers of listeners who often repeated their experiences by playing the cassettes and videotapes that were assembled on these occasions. However, some of these sermons caused controversies and some radical fringe groups tried to assassinate Gülen in 1990.[42] While Gülen withdrew again from public preaching, the movement associated with his name began to play a more visible public role through its media publications (newspapers, radio, and TV), and dialogue organizations. The Journalists and Writers Foundation that coordinated many initiatives for public dialogues in Turkey was founded in 1994. After the fall of the Soviet Union, the movement spread its influence outside of Turkey as well, founding a number of schools in a number of the central Asian republics that were ethnically related to the Turks.

In 1993 Özal died suddenly and Demirel became his successor as president; shortly after that Erbakan's Welfare Party (Refah Partisi) won the 1995 elections and he attained the position of prime minister. For the first time siince the founding of the Turkish republic, an Islamist party was in charge. Erbakan profited from anti-Western sentiments provoked by the rejection of Turkish membership in the European Union in 1989, and by the suffering of the Bosnian people in the Balkan wars with Serbia.[43] Yet Erbakan failed to fulfill the expectations of his Islamist followers and angered secularist forces as well, so much so that the military intervened once again by proposing, in the National Security Council on February 28, 1997, a list of recommendations, to save the secular identity of the republic. After an initial refusal,

41. An *imam* is a person who leads the prayers; a *hatip* is a person who gives the official sermon, *hutpe* in Turkish. Religious schools that prepare for these functions are called *imam-hatip* schools in Turkey.

42. Çetin, *The Gülen Movement*, 43.

43. According to Rabasa and Larrabee, *The Rise of Political Islam in Turkey*, 43.

Erbakan had to retreat in what has since become known as the February 28 Process, often termed a "soft coup" or "postmodern coup" by the military.

This "silent coup" was the reason for a debate in the camp of those who wanted to pursue an Islamist agenda yet were facing the boundaries set by the secular powers dominant in the army. Now that the Welfare Party was forbidden, they founded the Virtue Party (Fazilet Partisi) and began to embrace a number of Western political values. Some of them wanted to push the democratization process further and began to argue that a more circumspect strategy would be necessary to reach the goals of promoting Islamic values without a direct confrontation with the protectors of republican values. These "reformists" included Recep Tayyip Erdoğan and Abdullah Gül. When the Constitutional Court dissolved the Virtue Party in 2001, they founded the Justice and Development Party (Adalet ve Kalkınma Partisi or AK Party) that would become very successful in subsequent years. The more traditional Islamists around Erbakan founded another new party, the Felicity Party (Saadet Partisi) that would not be as successful.

TURKISH POLITICS AND THE HIZMET MOVEMENT

Meanwhile, Fethullah Gülen and the people supporting him became the most important targets of counter propaganda. As Berna Turam suggests, "the major area of contestation between the state and the Gülen movement has been education," since, because of the number and the influence of the schools founded by supporters of Fethullah Gülen, these schools were seen as a threat to the secular identity of the Turkish state.[44] The military dismissed many among its ranks who were accused of being members of Gülen's organizations. One of the arguments was that Gülen would pursue a hidden agenda, which would be consistent with

44. Turam, *Between Islam and the State*, 67.

the strategy of *taqīya* (dissimulation of one's faith): for the greater public, Gülen would act as if he would endorse Western, democratic values, but in speeches to his own followers he would urge them to wait patiently until they could introduce *sharī'ah*. A videotape of one of Gülen's sermons shown on a TV channel in 1999 suggests such a form of dissimulation: he seems to encourage his followers to infiltrate the ranks of power and to work silently until the time has come to seize power.[45] While Turam gives some examples of these anti-Gülen shows in the public media, it seems that an entire anti-Hizmet industry has developed in the past years.[46]

The development of these imputations against Gülen and the people he inspired are connected with the mounting political tensions in Turkey, and with the growing influence of both the Justice and Development Party and the Hizmet Movement in the years since 2007. In the concluding pages of this historical survey, I want to pay some attention to this situation and its consequences for the Hizmet in Turkey and abroad.

In February 2010, a number of leading army officers were arrested on allegations of planning another coup against the AK Party government. Some journalists suggested that Gülen and his supporters were behind these actions. Soner Cagaptay, for instance, wrote that "[A]ll shots against the military are now fair game, including those below the belt. The force behind this dramatic change is the Fethullah Gülen Movement (FGH), an ultraconservative political faction that backs the ruling Justice and Development Party."[47] Elsewhere, the same journalist talks about the "power-hungry Gülenists who are working to infiltrate the secular

45. Kramer, *A Changing Turkey*, 67

46. See Turam, *Between Islam and the State*, 80–83. From the perspective of an insider, Dogan Koç has developed an analysis of the most important critical voices in his *Strategic Defamation of Fethullah Gülen*; an analysis of the political trials against Gülen can be found in James Harrington, *Wrestling with Free Speech, Religious Freedom, and Democracy in Turkey: The Political Trials and Times of Fethullah Gülen* (Lanham, Md.: University Press of America, 2011).

47. Online article on ForeignPolicy.com, dated February 25, 2010; accessed through www.cagaptay.com/6993, March 3, 2010.

institutions."[48] Cagaptay reasons that the "Gülenists," who were purged from the military in 1990, made a comeback to purge the military from power ten to twenty years later, with the AK Party as their allies. A well-known self-proclaimed Islam-watcher in the United States, Daniel Pipes, talks about the Gülen Movement as the "Islamist ally" of the AK Party, and warns that the military will be turned into a "Gülenist institution" while the country in its entirety may "slide towards Islamism."[49] As John Esposito, professor of religion and international affairs and of Islamic studies at Georgetown University remarks, these are suggestions that come from hardline secular elites and persons in the military forces who do not perceive Gülen and his supporters as a conservative religious movement, but as an Islamist political clique. While this is understandable against the background of the severe struggle between secularist and religious forces with catch phrases such as Ergenekon and Balyoz, Esposito suggests that we are not watching "a showdown between secularists and so-called Islamists or the demise of the secular state, but a process of normalization and the maturing of Turkey's democracy, institutions and the rule of law."[50]

While Pipes and Cagaptay suggest that "the Gülenists" associate themselves with both the Welfare Party (RP) and the AK Party, scholars who have researched the relationships between these institutions say that there is a clear distinction between the Islamist course of Erbakan's parties on the one hand and the much more moderate and cooperative course of Erdoğan's political party and the faith-based service movement founded by Gülen on the other. Turam, like Esposito, remarks that the old phrase stating that there is a "clash of civilizations" between secularism and Islamism in Turkey, seems to be outdated since "the Gülen Movement and

48. Article for *Newsweek,* February 26, 2010; accessed through www.cagaptay.com/6994, March 3, 2010.

49. Online article for *National Review Online,* dated March 2, 2010; accessed through www.danielpipes.org/8009, March 3, 210.

50. See http://www.huffingtonpost.com/john-l-esposito/the-crisis-in-turkey_b_482829.html, accessed March 13, 2010.

the AK Party," although organizationally independent from one another, have a stylistic element in common: "Both have displayed similar cooperative attitudes, as opposed to confrontational ones, towards the secular Turkish Republic."[51]

Now that the February 28 Process has showed that any direct agenda of Islamization of Turkish society would not be tolerated by the defenders of the secularist inheritance of Atatürk, the more cautious and cooperative strategies of Gül and Erdoğan are becoming more and more influential at the beginning of the twenty-first century in Turkey. While the Virtue Party (FP) and later the Felicity Party (SP) were opposed to collaboration with the ruling elite, and to the process of application for membership in the European Union, the founders of the Justice and Development Party (AK Party) were in favor of collaboration with moderate defenders of secularism – to be distinguished from the more militant form of laicism that does not allow any public role for religion – and of Western values such as democracy and human rights. As we saw at the beginning of this chapter, the AK Party – just like Fethullah Gülen and his supporters – is often associated with the new liberal market economy that brought the "Anatolian tigers" a combination of wealth and piety, a phenomenon that is sometimes characterized as "Islamic Calvinism."[52] Although Gülen has never explicitly endorsed a political party, it is a well-known fact that most of his supporters were involved in the AK Party since both organizations embodied values that can be characterized as religious, conservative, and democratic, much like the Christian Democrats in many European countries such as Germany and the Netherlands. Yet, while the AK Party gradually came to power, Fethullah Gülen did no longer play a public role in Turkey, since he was among the most prominent targets of the "February 28 process," and was alleged to have "organized a movement to change the secular government."[53] The trial against Gülen was officially opened in 2000

51. Turam, *Between Islam and the State*, 13.

52. See Hermann, *Wohin geht die türkische Gesellschaft?* 102.

53. Ebaugh, *The Gülen Movement*, 32.

and the charges were dismissed by the High Criminal Court in 2006.[54] Yet at that time, Gülen was no longer in a position to resume his public role, since his medical situation had forced him to go to the United States, where he has lived since 1999.

Meanwhile, in Turkey, the AK Party became the biggest political party in the 2002 elections, and since only two parties were represented in Parliament, it received almost two-thirds of the seats in the National Assembly. The party gained most of its votes from recent migrants in the working-class areas on the outskirts of urban centers: mostly pious and socially conservative blue-collar workers. The elections of 2007 brought the AK Party an even greater number of supporters: the 34 percent of the votes they received in 2002 grew to an amazing 47 percent in 2007, and even 50 percent in 2011.[55] Rabasa and Larrabee conclude: "the support it received from different social groups gives the AK Party the attributes of a center-right party. It has managed to blend cultural preferences typical of the right with social-economic policies that are generally associated with the left and that are favored by the electorate as a whole."[56] The outcome of this process is that the AK Party has emerged as the champion of a number of values such as freedom and openness that are usually associated with the West rather than with Islamist parties. Consequently, the AK Party has developed as a party that embraces the desire to become a member of the European Union, despite its former hesitancy on this issue.[57] The so-called Copenhagen Criteria that the EU has developed to be able to determine the extent to which Turkey is ready to apply for full membership, however, still cause quite a number of debates in Turkish political circles. The CHP (Cumhuriyet Halk Partisi, or Republican People's Party), once the champion of a Western orientation in Turkish politics, is becoming more and more skepti-

54. Harrington, *Wrestling with Free Speech . . .*, 117.

55. Tittensor, *The House of Service*, 49.

56. Rabasa and Larrabee, *The Rise of Political Islam in Turkey*, 50.

57. See Ali Çarkoğlu and Barry Rubin, *Turkey and the European Union: Domestic Politics, Economic Integration and International Dynamics* (Portland, Ore.: Frank Cass, 2003).

cal about the European Union, and anti-European voices can still be heard in other parties as well. Yet most observers are convinced that Turkey's future is best served when it can regain its function as a bridge between the West and the world of Islam. The AK Party is certainly trying to open up to both sides, but it still meets with a lot of mistrust not only in the Arab world and in Europe, but also in Turkey.

Although the AK Party seems to be the party in power right now in Turkey, this power certainly does not go undisputed. Defenders of the secularist heritage frequently express their fear that the party will change the very structure of the Turkish republic by introducing laws and rules that embody an Islamist agenda. Since such a move would be against the constitution, they have several times seized the opportunity to build suspicion against the AK Party. In 2008, a petition to close down the party as nonconstitutional was introduced to the Constitutional Court, and it was only rejected by a one-vote majority.[58] This petition is indicative of growing tensions in Turkish society, where secularist powers try to outlaw the ruling majority party, while strong forces in this party find reasons to suspect many military and judiciary authorities of conspiring against the state. This tension between the democratically elected government and persons in the military, security, and judiciary forces who sometimes collaborate with criminals, gives Turkish society a grim outlook, characterized in the expression "deep state" (*derin devlet*) that suggests that underneath the visible structures of government a deeper layer of power exists that pursues its own objectives. This means that some members of the government may use members of certain "gangs" to accomplish particular aims.[59]

Some evidence for this "deep state" surfaced in the so-called Sursurluk scandal. In November 1996, after a car accident near Sursurluk, police discovered evidence for relationships between persons in the police, ultra-nationalists, and organized criminals. An

58. Tittensor, *The House of Service*, 49

59. Çetin, *The Gülen Movement*, 271.

investigation by a parliamentary commission brought to light that certain politicians instigated nationalists and criminals to commit certain actions that would destabilize Turkish society and pave the way for a military coup. More recently, in January 2008, the Turkish police arrested 33 members of Ergenekon, an ultranationalist clandestine organization, on the charge of plotting a series of attacks against intellectuals such as the Nobel Prize winner Orhan Pamuk, in order to prepare a military coup. These ultranationalists, collaborating with members of the security forces and organized criminals, were not only concerned about a possible form of Islamic government, but they were also concerned about political concessions that were being considerd to get Turkey ready for a possible membership of the European Union, including proposed better relations with Greece, Armenia, and the Kurdish people.[60] In later waves of arrests, army generals and police officers were detained and indicted in connection to Ergenekon and, in 2010, the *Balyoz* (Sledgehammer) coup plan.

The political situation has changed considerably since the AK Party and Prime Minister Erdoğan have been able to extend their power base after being successful in a slate of elections in 2011 and again in 2014. However, the demonstrations in Gezi Park next to Taksim Square in Istanbul at the end of May 2013 brought a new set of tensions. The rather harsh words of Erdoğan for what seemed to be a nonpolitical protest against plans for a shopping mall in the central part of Istanbul betrayed a tendency toward authoritarianism in the eyes of many political observers.[61] The impression that the ruling party might have gained too much power was reinforced by allegations of corruption in the government later that year. Again, Prime Minister Erdoğan reacted ferociously, and this time he pointed at Gülen as the culprit. As *The Guardian* stated in a news article: "The power and the influence of the elderly cleric

60. Information provided by Sarah Rainsford, BBC News, Istanbul (http://news.bbc.co.uk/2/hi/europe, accessed June 2, 2010).

61. See BBC News Europe, June 7, 2013 (http://www.bbc.com/news/world-europe-22753752, accessed June 12, 2014).

is the defining issue of Turkish politics. Recep Tayyip Erdoğan, the prime minister, has declared war on Gülen – previously a key ally of his conservative, Islamic ruling party – following the eruption of a corruption scandal in December that implicates the government, the prime minister's closest associates and his family."[62] As the quotation makes clear, the clash between the Prime Minister and the Hizmet Movement came as a surprise because they have been considered as close allies for a long time, and yet M. Hakan Yavuz, writing before these events, makes an observation that may explain some of the budding opposition between the AK (or Justice and Development) Party and the Hizmet Movement:

> In spite of this new alliance confronting a common enemy, there are several policy areas over which the Gülen Movement and the JDP are in conflict. Some important JDP ministers are not happy with the involvement of the Gülenist activists in policy making. Prime Minister Erdoğan, who is not a follower of the Gülen Movement, and does not want to share power with it, seeks to maintain some distance from it by supporting ... two outspoken critics of Gülen.[63]

According to this analysis, influential members of the AK Party appreciate the combination of social liberalism and religious conservatism of the Hizmet Movement, but they do not want members of the movement too openly involved in politics. Since I am not a political scientist, I do not want to speculate further about the causes of this clash. It might simply be true that the Hizmet Movement has become too powerful, just like the AK Party. But perhaps the movement tends to foster the values of democracy, human rights, and transparency more than the politicians do.[64]

62. Constanza Letsch on behalf of the *Guardian,* February 9, 2014, http://www.theguardian.com/world/2014/feb/09/turkish-police-fethullah-gulen-network, accessed June 12, 2014.

63. Yavuz, *Toward an Islamic Enlightenment*, 217.

64. This is the basic message in several interviews given by Hocaefendi Fethullah Gülen about this clash, both in the *Wall Street Journal,* January 21, 2014, and on BBC World Service News, January 27, 2014. Moreover, *Today's Zaman* published a long interview in its issues of March 16–19, 2014.

We have considered two different ways in which tensions in contemporary Turkish politics influence the media attention to Fethullah Gülen and the people he has inspired. In the first place, there is the traditional secularist voice in Turkish politics that sees the man and the movement as a possible ally of Islamism. Yet in most recent days, influential politicians in the AK Party have started to sketch the "Gülenists" as "power-hungry infiltrators" as well. In the first chapter, we discussed how this tension in Turkish politics explains some of the anti-Gülen press campaigns in the Netherlands. Often it seems that the success of schools founded by members of the Hizmet Movement was at the basis of the negative news. We now need to look at the situation in the United States, and we will see that there is a similar history of anti-Gülen and anti-Hizmet propaganda on the Internet as well.

Even though he is an insider from the Hizmet Movement and therefore his involvement is somewhat debatable, social scientist Doğan Koç has carefully researched all forms of negative publicity on Fethullah Gülen in both Turkish and English.[65] He comes to the conclusion that a sizeable part of the negative publicity is indeed a form of defamation, "the deliberately slanderous or libelous injury of another's good reputation."[66] Concerning the negative publicity in English, Koç mentions six different negative claims: Gülen secretly tries to introduce an Islamist ideology; like Ayatollah Khomeiny, he lives in exile but will return to create a theocratic regime; he wants to overturn the Turkish government and establish an Islamic state; he wants to restore the Ottoman Empire and a universal Caliphate; his movement is secretly infiltrating into the Unites States; he is training an Islamist militia in the United States.[67] Some of these strategic defamations are not very specific and echo other forms of Islamophobia, such as the Internet pieces written by self-proclaimed Islam-watchers in the U.S., for

65. Doğan Koç, *Strategic Defamation of Fethullah Gülen. English vs. Turkish* (Lanham, Md.: University Press of America, 2012).

66. Koç, *Strategic Defamation of Fethullah Gülen*, 1.

67. Ibid., 23–28.

instance, Daniel Pipes.[68] Other Internet bloggers are much more specific, however, and therefore require some special attention, even though their claims are plainly outrageous. Paul Williams, for instance, describes Gülen as "the most dangerous Islamist on planet earth," who lives in his "mountain fortress in Pennsylvania" where he lays the foundations of a future universal Caliphate.[69] He suggests that Gülen is surrounded by an army of *jihad* warriors who are trained in armed combat, and that the network of schools (*madrassahs,* he calls them) that he controls serves to train young men to become instrumental in the Islamization of the Western world. Williams blames Gülen for openly endorsing pluralism and dialogue while secretly promoting the establishment of Islamic states, in Turkey but in the Western world as well. Even though I have never heard of Paul Williams apart from his weblogs on Gülen, he claims to have a Ph.D. in theology and the names of the websites on which he publishes suggest an engagement with a conservative interpretation of Christian traditions.[70] Since he claims to have specializations in medieval history, comparative religion, Catholic doctrine, and Islam, his take on Gülen is of some concern to me, since his approach, which starts from principles I might want to endorse, leads to such an infamous result.

Some of the insinuations of writers such as Daniel Pipes and Paul Williams are quite shocking; while insiders such as İhsan Yilmaz[71] and outsiders such as John Esposito[72] were quick to show

68. See "Crisis in Turkey," at www.danielpipes.org, dated March 2, 2010 (accessed March 3, 2010).

69. Articles by Paul Williams, www.familysecuritymatters.org, dated April 7, 2010, and www.thelastcrusade.org, dated April 28, 2010 (accessed May 7, 2010).

70. Information retrieved from the Facebook page of Dr. Paul L. Williams, accessed on June 12, 2014. For more information about Paul Williams and some of the lawsuits filed against him by others, see Koç, *Strategic Defamation of Fethullah Gülen*, 50–52.

71. See "Jane's Gülen movement analysis: an Orientalist misreading," *Today's Zaman*, February 8 and 9, 2009; accessed through www.todayszaman.com, December 11, 2009.

72. See "The Crisis in Turkey?" www.huffingtonpost.com, dated March 2, 2010 (accessed July 21, 2010). Maybe the best refutation of Williams's claims comes from

that these insinuations originate in the mind of the beholder and have nothing to do with the life and works of Hocaefendi himself, doubts are likely to linger in the minds of those who are less informed. That is why it is so important to be able to access and to judge the words and the works of Fethullah Gülen from the point of view of someone who is not primarily interested in a political movement, but who wants to understand what Gülen has to say and how this is related to the future of Christian-Muslim relations. In my opinion, Australian theologian Greg Barton has given us the best analysis, indicating where the suggestions of many pundits may touch on some reality, but mainly showing how Gülen cannot be considered a "hidden Islamist" by any scholarly standard.[73]

A few years ago, I compared Gülen and the movement he inspired to the contemporary Muslim reformer Tariq Ramadan.[74] While I was not aware at that time of any allegations against Gülen of the kind described above, Ramadan had been the object of very similar accusations in France and elsewhere for some time, and he even had his entrance visa to the United States revoked under the Bush administration in 2004, a time when I had hoped to work with him at the University of Notre Dame. Catholic theologian Gregory Baum puts these similarities into a broader perspective:

> According to Ramadan, the renewal movement is having a profound influence upon Muslim communities in the countries of East and West. Muslims are grateful to find in the movement an emphasis on rationality, on personal freedom and on doing God's will in the world. Because theologians of *al-nahda* [Islamic renewal movement] want to remain faithful to the Quran

local journalist Dan Berrett who established in the *Pocono Record Writer* of April 18, 2010, that the observations by Williams were not true and not endorsed by any of the neighbors of the retreat where Gülen lives in Pennsylvania. (See www.poconorecord.com, accessed June 2, 2010). See also Koç, *Strategic Defamation of Fethullah Gülen*, 51.

73. Greg Barton, "Progressive Islamic Thought, Civil Society, and the Gülen Movement in the National Context: Parallels with Indonesia," in *Islam in the Contemporary World 1: The Fethullah Gülen Movement in Thought an Practice,* Conference Proceedings, November 12–13, 2005, Rice University, Houston, Tex. (Somerset, N.J.: Tughra Books, 2009), 224–70.

74. Valkenberg, *Sharing Lights on the Way to God*, 321–27.

and insist that their rereading of the Quran, while new, is sanctioned by tradition, they are sometimes accused by secular commentators of being fundamentalists in disguise. This has happened to Ramadan many times. In my study of the Turkish religious thinkers Said Nursi and Fethullah Gülen, brilliant representatives of the Islamic renewal, I have discovered that this also happened to them. Even though they defended democratic pluralism in theological terms, they were suspected by secular politicians of being Islamists in disguise, plotting to create an Islamic state.[75]

Even though there are, to my mind, more differences than similarities between Ramadan and Gülen, some of these parallels might be related to a similar heritage, since Ramadan compares the position of his grandfather Hasan al-Banna, the founder of the Muslim Brotherhood in Egypt, to the position of Said Nursi in Turkey: both were renewers on the basis of a solid return to the Qur'ān, but they were opposed to Salafism, literalism or fundamentalism, and most of all, they were focused on education as the basic medicine for the distressful situation of Muslims in the modern era. Being students of Hasan al-Banna and of Said Nursi, respectively, Ramadan and Gülen might have a similar point of departure, and both made the transition to the Western world, even though their opponents are able to spread suspicions about them as well. In the first chapter of this book, I told how in my native country, the Netherlands, the Gülen movement was subjected to insinuations and questions in Parliament in 2008 and again in 2010. Meanwhile, Tariq Ramadan was dismissed as advisor to the local government of the city of Rotterdam, and as visiting professor at the Erasmus University, also in Rotterdam, in August 2009 on the basis of similar questions and insinuations. In my country of residence, the United States, Ramadan was not admitted to his position at the University of Notre Dame in 2004 by the Bush administration because of the Patriot Act, and between 2004 and 2006 Gülen was almost denied his permanent residency in the United States because of allegations against him.[76]

75. Gregory Baum, *The Theology of Tariq Ramadan: A Catholic Perspective* (Notre Dame, Ind.: University of Notre Dame Press, 2009), 56–57.

76. See Harrington, "Gülen's Immigration Case in the United States: Intersection

So, apparently, the position of a renewer of the spiritual lives of many Muslims evokes contradictory opinions. These opinions become louder and more shrill to the extent that the political situation becomes more tense, as is the case in Europe and certainly in Turkey nowadays. Not so long ago, the interests of the European Union and of Turkey seemed to converge, but in recent times critics have become louder on both sides. Even though all the major political parties that are represented in the Turkish Parliament are in favor of future EU membership, the support for this membership seems to have waned in public opinion since the Copenhagen summit of 2002.[77] Government leaders in some major European countries such as Germany and France have indicated their resistance in the last couple of years against Turkey joining the European Union. In such a climate of growing uncertainty, some observers think the AK Party is turning away from the West to orient itself to the world of Islam once again. In this context, Fethullah Gülen certainly emerges as a religious leader who favors continuing the long tradion of Turkish or Anatolian Islam, but at the same time intends to build bridges to the Western world. In his recent interviews, Gülen indicates that this is one of the convictions that he still upholds while Erdoğan seems to shy away from notions such as human rights and the "democratic values of the European Union."[78] At the end of his investigation of the clouds of suspicion hanging over the Gülen Movement, Greg Barton observes: "Modern Turkey is unique in the Islamic world (with the exception of the former Soviet Union and China which overlap the edges of the Muslim world) in its aggressive, totalizing approach to secularism and secularization. There is no question that the Gülen Movement

of the U.S. Government and Turkey's Military," in *Wrestling with Free Speech, Religious Freedom, and Democracy in Turkey*, 133–44. Gülen applied for permanent residence in October 2002 and was finally granted this status in October 2008 after refusals in 2004 and 2006. By way of comparison, I applied for permanent residence status in 2007 and received it within a year.

77. Çarkoğlu and Rubin, *Turkey and the European Union*, 249.

78. Quoted from the *Wall Street Journal* (online version), January 21, 2014 (accessed January 24, 2014).

is deeply critical of the positivistic character of Turkish secularism. But to argue that it is opposed to secularity and democracy is to misread the movement by projecting the dark anxieties and phobias of the more militant elements of the republic onto precisely the sort of movement that offers Turkey's (and the entire Muslim world's) best hope of uniting Islam, modernization, and secular, liberal democracy."[79] Likewise, Ebaugh, after having interviewed a sizeable number of critics of the "Gülen Movement," comes to the following conclusion:

> In summary, therefore, I am respectful of the fears expressed by the Kemalists that Turkey's history of secularism might be threatened and overthrown by an authoritarian leader with a strong following and replaced with the type of Islamic state that exists in Iran. However, the critics present no empirical data relating their fears to actual events and behaviors associated with Mr. Gülen or members of his movement. Likewise, the empirical data (e.g., interviews, field visits, review of records and documents) that I gathered over the past 12 months related to the Gülen movement do not substantiate the accusations and fears expressed by critics of the movement.[80]

As I wrote before, it is possible to dismiss Barton and Ebaugh as perhaps too involved in the movement to be completely impartial. But even rather critical observers such as Hakan Yavuz and Joshua Hendrick come to the conclusion that most of the criticism of the Gülen Movement "far too often treads into the waters of conspirational fantasy and xenophobic alarmism."[81]

Let me end this chapter with two small pieces of evidence that confirm Ebaugh's statement. They form a fraction of the many indications that I have gathered and that guide my opinion that the Hizmet Movement is theologically trustworthy. For me as a Christian theologian, that means that I need to consider it as a possible instrument of God's grace and that the Catholic Church needs to take Hizmet members seriously as the Muslims they profess to be.

79. Barton, "Progressive Islamic Thought . . . ," 265.
80. Ebaugh, *The Gülen Movement*, 122.
81. Hendrick, *Gülen*, x.

The first piece of evidence is Gülen's comment on the flotilla incident in June 2010, mentioned earlier in this chapter: the fact that he did not endorse the way his Turkish compatriots had organized their help to the Palestinians in the Gaza Strip, but instead blamed them for entering the coastal zone without asking approval from the Israeli authorities, is a clear indication that Gülen does not think (let alone behave) along the lines of political radicalism, as those who critique him allege, even though he would probably have had much support in Turkey if he had done so. He is more concerned about the rights of "the others" even if these others are Israeli citizens.

The second story that I remember vividly is the testimony of a police officer from Orange County, California, at Pepperdine University on December 5, 2009, when the participants at the conference "East and West Encounters: the Gülen Movement" organized by the University of Southern California and Pacifica Institute in Los Angeles visited its campus in Malibu. He told us that his wife had an Armenian background and that her family was very suspicious of all Turkish people, but that the Pacifica Institute in Los Angeles reached out to several Armenian families, telling them that they wanted to listen to their stories. The fact that there were Turkish citizens who wanted to hear his story instead of defending their case first, convinced him that Fethullah Gülen must be a bridge builder instead of a secret defender of Turkish nationalism and Islamism. His remarks formed an endorsement of what another Armenian had said during the opening of the conference two days earlier, namely that the Turks inspired by Gülen are serious about dialogue and that they pave the way for better relations between nations and religions in the future.[82]

82. Zeki Saritoprak describes the last testimony in his report of the conference in *Today's Zaman*, December 10, 2009 (see http://fethullahgulen.biz/press-room/columns/3573-impressions-from-the-gulen-conference-in-los-angeles.html, accessed August 23, 2010).

3

THE LIFE AND WORKS OF M. FETHULLAH GÜLEN

WHEN ONE WANTS to write about Muhammad Fethullah Gülen in English, the first challenge one encounters is that no comprehensive critical study of his life and works has yet been written.[1] The situation may be somewhat different in Turkish – for instance, Ali Ünal's portrait describes some of the basic intellectual dimensions of his person – but there is no internationally acclaimed biography that one could take as point of departure.[2] Editions of Gülen's books usually contain short biographies but these are not based on independent critical research. The same holds true of the biographical materials in publications that introduce Gülen to a wider audience, such as the booklet *Understanding Fethullah Gülen* or the several websites in English that bear his name.[3] These publications and websites are usually based on a few autobiographi-

1. His official first name is Muhammad, but Gülen is usually known by his middle name, Fethullah. On book covers, his name is written as "M. Fethullah Gülen." When I was interviewing some of his friends in Izmir, I asked them why Gülen never uses the name Muhammad, and their answer was that it has to do with his humility: he wants to avoid the claim that his name could be put on a par with that of the Prophet of Islam.

2. Ali Ünal, *M. Fethullah Gülen. Bir Portre Denemesi*, (Izmir: Nil yayınları, 2002).

3. *Understanding Fethullah Gülen* has been published by the Turkish Journalists and Writers Foundation without a place and year of publication, but it covers materials up to and including 2009. The oldest website dedicated to Gülen in English is www.fethullahgulen.org. Another website is http://www.en.fgulen.com (both accessed June 13, 2014).

cal pieces of information in Turkish, such as *Küçük Dünyam* ("My Small World"), an interview that Gülen gave to Turkish journalist Latif Erdoğan. This is true even of the otherwise very commendable website of the Gülen Institute based in Houston, Texas.[4]

At the same time, there is a rapidly growing number of studies about Gülen since organizations that are part of the Hizmet Movement started organizing a number of scholarly conferences on his person and inspiration about ten years ago. The websites devoted to Fethullah Gülen in English usually contain a list of papers presented at these conferences.[5] Almost all conference papers, however, are short and rather impressionistic; since they lack knowledge of the broader array of historical and literary sources, they cannot be considered authoritative interpretations of the person and work of Fethullah Gülen. My own book is no exception to this rule, and therefore I have to rely on some of the scholars who have been able to read the original sources in Ottoman Arabic and Turkish, and to place them in the context of twentieth century Turkish history.

A second reason for the rather fragmentary state of research on the person and the works of Fethullah Gülen is that most scholars writing from a sociological point of view are more interested in the so-called Gülen Movement than in the person who proposed the basic ideas that inspired this movement. Again, my book is no exception since I will discuss the Hizmet Movement in the second part of the book, but as I wrote before at the end of the first chapter, it is always good to go back to the sources in order to explain a new phenomenon, certainly in the world of Islam. Consequently, this chapter looks at the life of M. Fethullah Gülen and gives an analysis of his major works within the limits of what is possible for a scholar who has only a basic grasp of the Turkish language. The brief description of the social and political situation of Turkey in the twentieth century, given in the previous chapter, will be use-

4. See http://www.guleninstitute.org/about-gulen/fethullah-gulen.html (accessed June 13, 2014).

5. http://www.en.fgulen.com/conference-papers and http://fgulen.com/en/gulen-movement/conference-papers (both accessed June 13, 2014).

ful to understand certain characteristics of the ideas of Gülen and the faith-based service movement he inspired a little better. The fourth chapter aims at a more profound understanding of these ideas by considering the main sources of Gülen's theological ideas: the Qur'ān, Jalāl ad-Dīn Rūmī, and Said Nursi. These three chapters together will enable us to give an analysis of the main characteristics of the faith-based service movement in chapters five and six, and to compare them with similar phenomena in Christian religious movements in the final chapter.

The most reliable scholarly introductions to the life and works of Fethullah Gülen have been written by a small number of scholars who were able to read his works in their original language. However, they were mainly interested in political or sociological analyses of the so-called Gülen Movement, and therefore their writings about Gülen are fairly short and introductory. To my knowledge, M. Hakan Yavuz has been one of the first scholars to introduce Gülen to the English-speaking public as part of his book on Islamic social movements.[6] He describes two other Islamic social movements that are important as sources for Gülen's ideas as well: the Naqshbandi (Nakşibendi) Sufi order and the Nur Movement, the followers of Said Nursi. In the line of this historical approach, Yavuz writes about Gülen and his followers as "a neo-Nur movement." Yavuz, who studied political science in Turkey and the United States, wrote another short description of both the Nur Movement and the Gülen Movement in a volume that he edited together with the founding director of the Center for Muslim-Christian Understanding at Georgetown University, John L. Esposito.[7] The volume is the result of the very first conference on Gülen in the United States, hosted by Georgetown University. Bekim Agai, who studied the movement in Albania, Turkey, and

6. M. Hakan Yavuz, *Islamic Political Identity in Turkey* (New York: Oxford University Press, 2003).

7. M. Hakan Yavuz, "Islam in the Public Sphere: The Case of the Nur Movement" and "The Gülen Movement: The Turkish Puritans," in *Turkish Islam and the Secular State: The Gülen Movement*, ed. M. Hakan Yavuz and John L. Esposito (Syracuse, N.Y.: Syracuse University Press, 2003), 1–47.

Germany, published the most comprehensive study about Gülen and his "educational network" in 2004.[8] He published this version of his Ph.D. at the University of Bonn in the German language but he has published interesting contributions in English as well.[9]

While Yavuz and Agai to my mind have written the most important early publications about Gülen and his faith-based service community, five somewhat later studies, published between 2007 and 2010, look at the movement from the perspective of the social sciences: the perspective of sociology in the cases of Berna Turam, Mehmet Enes Ergene, Muhammed Çetin, and Helen Rose Ebaugh; and the perspective of intercultural studies in the case of Gürkan Çelik.[10] Whereas Ergene, Çetin, and Çelik write from the inside perspective of members of the Hizmet Movement, Turam and Ebaugh write from the perspective of outsider social scientists, even though Ebaugh sometimes tends to share the perspective of the insiders.

After I had finished the first version of this manuscript, three more studies written by social scientists became available to me. Again, these are social scientific studies written by outsiders who are more interested in the Gülen Movement as a social phenom-

8. Bekim Agai, *Zwischen Netzwerk und Diskurs: Das Bildungsnetzwerk um Fethullah Gülen (geb. 1938): Die flexible Umsetzung modernen islamischen Gedankenguts*, Bonner Islamstudien 2 (Schenefeld: EB-Verlag, 2004).

9. Bekim Agai, "The Gülen Movement's Islamic Ethic of Education," in *Turkish Islam and the Secular State: The Gülen Movement*, ed. M. Hakan Yavuz and John L. Esposito (Syracuse, N.Y.: Syracuse University Press, 2003), 48–68; Bekim Agai, "Discursive and Organizational Strategies of the Gülen Movement," in *Islam in the Contemporary World 1: The Fethullah Gülen Movement in Thought and Practice*, Conference Proceedings, November 12–13, 2005, Rice University, Houston, Tex. (Somerset, N.J.: Tughra Books, 2009), 47–59. Agai now works at the Goethe University in Frankfurt, Germany, where he organized a conference on Islamic Theology in September 2014.

10. Berna Turam, *Between Islam and the State: The Politics of Engagement* (Stanford, Calif.: Stanford University Press, 2007); Mehmet Enes Ergene, *Tradition Witnessing the Modern Age: An Analysis of the Gülen Movement* (Somerset, N. J.: Tughra Books, 2008); Muhammad Çetin, *The Gülen Movement: Civic Service without Borders* (New York: Blue Dome Press, 2009); Gürkan Çelik, *The Gülen Movement: Building Social Cohesion through Dialogue and Education* (Delft: Eburon, 2010); Helen Rose Ebaugh, *The Gülen Movement: A Sociological Analysis of a Civic Movement Rooted in Moderate Islam* (Dordrecht: Springer, 2010).

enon than in the spiritual and theological backgrounds of the faith that inspired Hocaefendi to form the Hizmet. Yet the studies by Hakan Yavuz, Joshua Hendricks, and David Tittensor give us fresh perspectives as well since they tend to be more critical than the earlier studies.[11] This is especially interesting in the case of Turkish political scientist M. Hakan Yavuz who has at times shown a rather critical distance to the movement and can therefore be seen as one of the most impartial and knowledgeable observers of Gülen and the Hizmet Movement.[12]

Apart from these more substantial contributions, more than a hundred shorter studies have recently been published in the form of conference proceedings. As was discussed before, most of these papers have been published in-house by publishers allied to the Hizmet Movement, and they are often replicated on websites associated with the name of Fethullah Gülen. Even though these are not official (peer-reviewed) publications, I will use some of them for additional evidence in the next chapters, especially if they have been presented at conferences that I have attended as well.[13] In recent years, some selections of conference papers have been published in edited volumes with reliable academic publishers. This is the case with some of the papers from conferences in London and Rotterdam (both 2007), in Los Angeles (2009), and also at the University of Maryland at College Park (2010).[14] The first confer-

11. M. Hakan Yavuz, *Towards an Islamic Enlightenment: The Gülen Movement* (New York: Oxford University Press, 2013); Joshua Hendrick, *Gülen: The Ambiguous Politics of Market Islam in Turkey and the World* (New York: New York University Press, 2013); David Tittensor, *The House of Service: The Gülen Movement and Islam's Third Way* (New York: Oxford University Press, 2014).

12. Yavuz seems to be disappointed about certain developments in the so-called Gülen Movement since his most recent comments on Gülen and his followers are often quite negative. For instance, in the *New York Times* of June 12, 2010, he is quoted as comparing the movement to the Catholic Opus Dei organization, their common point being the will to be in power. Hendrick gives a similar analysis as he considers the movement as a way to improve one's social and economic standing.

13. This is the case with conferences organized by the Hizmet Movement in Houston (2005), Rotterdam (2007), Washington D.C. (2008 and 2013), Potsdam, Germany (2009), and Los Angeles (2009).

14. For the London and Rotterdam conferences, see Paul Weller and Ihsan

ence at Georgetown University also resulted in a peer-reviewed publication that was mentioned earlier in this chapter.[15] I know of some plans for publications that have not yet been completed as well.

When reviewing the recent literature on Fethullah Gülen and the Hizmet Movement, we can say that there is a rapidly increasing number of interesting scholarly approaches, yet there is no sufficient basis for a comprehensive biography, nor for a comprehensive overview of Gülen's works and their sources. So much of this chapter and the next one on Gülen's sources covers new ground.

A SHORT BIOGRAPHY OF FETHULLAH GÜLEN

One of the consequences of the scarcity of critical research is that both 1938 and 1941 are frequently indicated as the year of Gülen's birth. On the one hand, most new editions of books written by Gülen and the websites in his name mention 1941 as the year of his birth, but older editions still have 1938. In two books published in 2003, M. Hakan Yavuz gives two different dates as well.[16] As Agai explains, most authors mainly refer to autobiographical data given by Gülen himself in the interview with Latif Erdoğan, "My Small World," published in Turkish in 1994.[17] Some of the older sources indicate November 10, 1938, as the date of Gülen's birth, which

Yilmaz, eds., *European Muslims, Civility and Public Life: Perspectives On and From the Gülen Movement* (New York: Continuum, 2012). For the Los Angeles conference, see Sophia Pandya and Nancy Gallagher, eds., *The Gülen Hizmet Movement and Its Transnational Activities: Case Studies of Altruistic Activism in Contemporary Islam* (Boca Raton, Fla.: Brown Walker Press, 2012). For the University of Maryland conference, see Ori Z. Soltes and Margaret A. Johnson, eds., *Preventing Violence and Achieving World Peace: The Contributions of the Gülen Movement.* Washington College Studies in Religion, Politics, and Culture, 4 (New York: Peter Lang, 2013).

15. Yavuz and Esposito, *Turkish Islam and the Secular State: The Gülen Movement,* mentioned in footnote 7.

16. Yavuz gives 1938 in *Turkish Islam and the Secular State: the Gülen Movement,* 20, and 1941, in *Islamic Political Identity in Turkey,* 180.

17. Agai, *Zwischen Netzwerk und Diskurs,* 122.

would coincide with the death of Mustafa Kemal Atatürk, the founder of the secular republic of Turkey, and would therefore be a highly significant date for the birth of a new approach to Turkey. In official materials published by the Turkish government, however, the year of birth is 1941.[18] Gülen's English website now gives April 27 as the date.[19] Joshua Hendrick discusses this as one of the "strategic ambiguities" in the Gülen Movement. He presents information from one of Gülen's closest students and personal biographers, stating that Gülen was born in 1938 but that his parents only registered his birth three years later. He then concludes: "an academically rigorous biography of Fethullah Gülen would need to account for the *social construction* of Fethullah Gülen, which would necessitate a focus on the contradictions, ruptures and imperfections that constitute all of human life."[20] In other words: the followers of Fethullah Gülen can construct the events of his life in a manner that suits their particular goals; only a critical biography will be able to separate the historical facts from the social constructions.

Muhammad Fethullah Gülen was born in Korucuk, a small village in the region of Erzurum in northeast Turkey. His parents taught him to memorize the Qur'ān and to pray, and they told him many stories about Prophet Muhammad.[21] When Gülen was ten years old, his father became an imam in the village of Alvar. He was educated at home and later at the local *madrasa* where he studied with the local imams. One of his teachers, the grandson of famous local imam Muhammed Lütfi, introduced him to the Sufi path in the tradition of Jalāl ad-Dīn Rūmī and Yunus Emre. Some sources say that Gülen became acquainted with the followers of Said Nursi as well. We will come back to the influence of both Rūmī and Nursi on Gülen in the next chapter of this book.

18. Ibid., 125.

19. www.fethullahgulen.org/fethullah-gulen-life-chronology, accessed July 10, 2009.

20. Hendrick, *Gülen*, 71–72.

21. Yavuz, *Islamic Political Identity in Turkey*, 180.

Yavuz draws attention to the specific form of Islam in northeast Turkey at the time: the region of Erzurum was a contested area between the Ottoman Empire, Russia, and Iran. The region harbored many refugees, and the memory of several bloody battles lingered.[22] These circumstances created a conservative and defensive form of Islam in which Russian communism was seen as the archenemy, while the Turkish state was seen as the main defender of Islam. This "nationalism and statism"[23] characterizes not only Said Nursi, but Fethullah Gülen in the first phase of his life as well.

Gülen did not pursue the usual education for an imam in Turkey. In order to do so, he would have had to follow the professional education for an *imam–hatip*, which comprises seven years of secondary education before the graduate can be admitted to higher theological education at the university level.[24] Gülen only attended the *madrasa* in his home town, and he received the traditional *ijāza* or license to teach, but he did not pursue any secondary education.[25] Yet he passed the examination for *vaiz* (preacher), organized by the Directorate of Religious Affairs (*Diyanet İşleri Başkanlığı*), at the comparatively young age of seventeen and therefore was awarded the license to preach. Since Gülen was not an imam but a *vaiz*, he was often not attached to a particular mosque, but had the opportunity to preach in different mosques.

22. The contested nature of this memory comes to the surface in the allegations against Turkish writer and 2006 Nobel Prize winner Orhan Pamuk, whose 2005 remarks about the mass killings of Armenians and Kurds were seen as antipatriotic. Although the charges against Pamuk were dropped, some politicians in the European Union saw the process as evidence that Turkey was not ready to join the EU.

23. Yavuz, *Islamic Political Identity in Turkey*, 181.

24. One of the bones of contention between several secular and religious powers in Turkey nowadays is whether the *imam–hatip* school gives entrance to university education in general or only to theological studies. The secular powers in Turkey want to confine graduates from the *imam–hatip* schools to theological studies in order to limit their access to more important nonreligious jobs.

25. When Gülen applied for permanent status as a resident alien ("green card" holder) in the U.S. on the basis of his exceptional educational abilities, this lack of formal education was held against him by some "Islam-watchers" in the U.S. But the government finally accepted Gülen's exceptional status in 2008 and he was allowed to remain in the U.S.

Gülen began preaching and lecturing in Edirne in the European part of Turkey, in 1959. During his years in Edirne, he fulfilled his military service as well. In 1966, he began to teach at the Kestanepazarı complex in Izmir, Turkey's third-largest city, where he soon began to attract students. In most of his preaching and teaching in Izmir, he utilized Said Nursi's ideas on ethics and the natural sciences. Although he never met Nursi, Fethullah Gülen adopted not only his ideas but also major characteristics of his ascetic lifestyle.[26] Something of this lifestyle and the personality behind it is visible in the many photographs that portray Gülen in the company of several figures of authority and famous persons.[27] The pictures show a very modest man with an almost diffident look and the absence of a Western tie. Gülen is quite aware of the symbolic character of his public personality: not only in his words but also in his behavior he is the model for his followers. They recognize in Gülen what Gülen himself recommends in the Prophet, who was someone who practiced and represented what he preached.[28] And so is Gülen for those who follow him as volunteers in the Hizmet Movement.[29]

M. Hakan Yavuz divides the life of Fethullah Gülen and the movement that bears his name into three periods. The first period began when Gülen was appointed to the Kestanepazarı Qur'ān School to teach courses on Islamic sciences in 1966. In this period, he began building his own network and spreading his own ideas, most explicitly when he started to set up summer schools and student dormitories in 1969. Yavuz characterizes Gülen's ideas as religiously conservative and nationalist but at the same time open to Western ideas such as democracy, capitalism, and tolerance.[30]

26. Yavuz, "The Gülen Movement: The Turkish Puritans," 20.

27. See, for instance, *Fethullah Gülen: Advocate of Dialogue,* compiled by Ali Ünal and Alphonse Williams, trans. Ali Ünal (Fairfax, Va.: Fountain Publications, 2000), 381–86; M. Fethullah Gülen, *Essays, Perspectives, Opinions*, compiled by the Fountain (Rutherford, N.J: The Light, 2002), 65–72.

28. Fethullah Gülen, *Love and the Essence of Being Human* (Istanbul: Journalists and Writers Foundation Publication, 2004), 106.

29. Gülen, *Essays, Perspectives, Opinions*, 8.

30. Yavuz, "The Gülen Movement: The Turkish Puritans," 21.

Consequently, the Gülen Movement is nourished by a combination of modern and premodern ideas. Several researchers note a difference, however: while Gülen himself is open to changes in gender relations and thinks that wearing headscarves is primarily a cultural and hardly a religious matter, his followers tend to be more conservative and practice a quite rigid segregation of the sexes.[31]

In this first period, Gülen concentrated on gathering his students into a religious community with the aim of forming them into a new generation of pious but modern Muslims. These first followers of Gülen developed their own forms of community in the *dershanes* of the followers of Said Nursi, and in the *ışık evleri* (houses of light) of the new movement, where university students came together to pray and to discuss social issues. They focused their attention on developing an adequate Muslim ethics and on reconciliation between Islam and science. Yavuz argues that the atmosphere in these houses or dormitories was very much influenced by Sufi ascetism, although Gülen is not a Sufi in the strict sense of the word; he rather is "A Sufi in his own way."[32] The moral perfection at which these communities aimed required a life of strict discipline and self-sacrifice.[33] In this period, Gülen's points of view were mainly in line with the ideas of the *Nurculuk*, the followers of Said Nursi, and the two groups often shared the same institutions. Yet Gülen did not want to be identified as a follower of Said Nursi, since his belonging to this particular group would prevent other groups from inviting him to participate in their activities.[34]

In this period, education emerged as the most important subject in Fethullah Gülen's worldview. His way of building a new generation of morally superior human beings may be called a re-

31. Agai, "The Gülen Movement's Islamic Ethic of Education," 56; Yavuz, "The Gülen Movement: The Turkish Puritans," 29.

32. Zeki Saritoprak, "Fethullah Gülen: A Sufi in His Own Way," in *Turkish Islam and the Secular State: The Gülen Movement*, ed. M. Hakan Yavuz and John L. Esposito (Syracuse, N.Y.: Syracuse University Press, 2003), 156–69.

33. Yavuz, "The Gülen Movement: The Turkish Puritans," 34.

34. Agai, *Zwischen Netzwerk und Diskurs*, 145.

newal movement in the world of Islam that refers back both to the times of Prophet Muhammad and to his followers. Gülen's modernist form of Islam differs from what is generally known as *salafiyya* Islam because the reference to the "Pious Forebears" (*al-salaf al-sālih*) is not used to impose a form of Islamic law, but to create a new and better generation of Muslims.[35] This future community is characterized by a combination of Muslim ethics, modern sciences, and modest personal behavior; in this combination it seeks to be a sign of light in modern societies. During this first period, Gülen began using the notion of *hizmet* (service) to characterize his movement more and more, and even to such an extent that Hizmet became the shorthand description for his movement.

It can be argued that two of the most important forms of religious discourse in the life and works of Fethullah Gülen originated in this period in Izmir. The first form of religious discourse is the lesson (*ders*) in which students receive instruction on basic religious texts from an elder brother or *abi*. Gülen would transform this form into the *sohbet*, a "conversation" between friends, mainly about religious subjects. These lessons and conversations take place in the educational context of the "houses of light" as places where students live and study together. These study houses and dormitories function as a source of spiritual renewal, nourished by a strong sense of community (*cemaat*) and by the common reading of spiritual texts, mainly the Qur'ān and Said Nursi's *Risale-i Nur*.[36] The second form of religious discourse is the sermon (*vaaz* or *hutpe*). Before he was ever known as a writer, Gülen became famous first and foremost as a public speaker, and his sermons were his most important method for educating a general public. In this respect, Ergene points out that Gülen fits into a long oratory tradition in Islam.[37] Similarly, Yasin Aktay writes that the spiritual au-

35. For the notion of the Pious Forebears and the different ways in which this notion can be used in the world of Islam, see Asma Afsaruddin, *The First Muslims: History and Memory* (Oxford: Oneworld, 2008), 148–99.

36. Agai, *Zwischen Netzwerk und Diskurs*, 142.

37. Ergene, *Tradition Witnessing the Modern Age*, 10.

thority of Fethullah Gülen was mainly based on his preaching, and that verbal communication is his usual way of addressing his supporters in the Hizmet Movement.[38] In this respect, the oral rather than the written nature of religious communication in the early Hizmet Movement fits into a pattern that starts in early Islam; as the very term *Qur'ān* or "Recitation" points out, the first revelations received by Prophet Muhammad were transmitted orally rather than in written form.[39]

IZMIR AND THE ORIGINS OF THE HIZMET MOVEMENT

The analysis of the goals and the nature of the Hizmet Movement in chapter five of this book will show that it was almost entirely shaped as a faith-based service movement in the period during which Gülen worked in Izmir. This is the reason that I decided to go to Izmir in order to become more familiar with some of the major aspects of Gülen's work as imam, teacher and *hatip* (preacher) at that time. More specifically, I wanted to know more about the sermons that made Gülen famous in this period. Many supporters of Hocaefendi have told me that his sermons moved them to join the Hizmet Movement, and that they still like to listen to them. As far as I can see, this aspect of Gülen's life and works has not been studied much, mainly because of language barriers; Gülen's sermons are well-known in Turkey, but they have not been translated into other languages. They have been edited into book chapters and in this form they can more easily be studied, but of course one misses the specific nature of the oratory tradition

38. Yasin Aktay, "New Media Figures and Instruments of Religious Authority in Turkey: Understanding Gülen and his Religious Leadership," in *Islam in the Contemporary World 1: The Fethullah Gülen Movement in Thought and Practice*. Conference Proceedings November 12–13, 2005, Rice University, Houston, Tex. (Somerset, N.J.: Tughra Books, 2009), 303.

39. See Ingrid Mattson, *The Story of the Qur'ān: Its History and Place in Muslim Life* (Malden, Mass.: Blackwell Publishing, 2008), especially chap. 3, "The Voice and the Pen," 76–136.

mentioned above. As far as I know, Lynn E. Mitchell is the only theologian who has drawn attention to the importance of Gülen's sermons in a comparison with the Christian "Clapham Circle" for the Gülen conference in Washington, D.C.[40] In the final chapter of this book, I will try to clarify the importance of Gülen as preacher by a similar comparative approach, but in this chapter I want to give the floor to testimonies from some of his supporters in Izmir about his preaching, and I will connect that with their views on how exactly the origin of the movement associated with Gülen came about.[41]

I was fortunate to meet Necdet İçel, the main preacher (*vaiz*) in Izmir, after the Friday afternoon prayer in the Şadırvan Mosque in the center of Izmir. Unfortunately we missed most of his *vaaz* since someone misunderstood the name of the mosque where he was to preach. When we arrived at the right mosque, he had just finished his *vaaz* but I was able to witness the afternoon prayer at the back of the mosque, behind a platform where the *müezzin* and the prayer leaders were seated.[42] After the prayer, we drank a cup

40. Lynn E. Mitchell, "M. Fethullah Gülen: A Preacher of Piety and Integrity of Action: A Study in Analogy Between the Gülen Movement and the Clapham Circle," in *Islam in the Age of Global Challenges: Alternative Perspectives of the Gülen Movement*, Conference at Georgetown University, Washington, D.C., November 14–15, 2008 (Washington, D.C.: Rumi Forum, 2008), 534–60.

41. These excerpts from interviews conducted in Izmir in the first full week of August 2009 may contain imprecisions because I wrote down the text in Dutch after translation from the Turkish by my friend Alper Alasağ. A year later, I have translated my notes into English for this book. I have not checked all the details because I find it more important to let the memories of some of Gülen's supporters in Izmir speak in the form in which they remembered the facts. This may lead to some redundancy, yet I hope that one of the advantages of this book will be that it gives some testimonies about the characteristics of Gülen's life that his oldest friends and students still remembered after all these years. Since they gave me permission to quote from the interviews, I use their full names.

42. A *vaaz* (Arabic: *wa'z*) is a catechetical sermon (literally, a warning or admonishment) that is often preached before the Friday afternoon prayer. The difference between a *vaaz* and a *hutpe* (Arabic: *khutba*) is that the latter is integrated into the Friday afternoon prayer, is more formal and ceremonial in style than the *vaaz*, and begins with an elaborate prayer in Arabic. In the *vaaz*, the preacher can elaborate more on specific topics, and he may sit down instead of standing as he does while

of tea with İçel, but since many people wanted to talk to him, he invited us for breakfast on Sunday morning at his house. Our conversation during breakfast centered on the importance of preaching and the model of Fethullah Gülen. Necdet İçel was born in Korucuk in 1955, and grew up in an era in which religion gradually became more important after the 1960 coup. He tells about his first meeting with Gülen as follows:

At that time Diyanet (the Department of Religious Affairs) did not have many preachers at its disposal; one of the best was Yaşar Tunagür who was a very charismatic preacher in Izmir. Many people travelled long distances in order to listen to him, even from Korucuk people hired a bus to go. In 1965 Tunagür obtained a position as assistant-director of Diyanet, and when I (İçel) came to say farewell to him, he had to cry but promised that he would send someone better than himself. Tunagür knew Fethullah Gülen from the time that he was *müftü* (mufti) in Edirne, while Gülen was imam there. So he knew that he would send another charismatic preacher to Izmir. I went with my family to the Şadırvanaltı Mosque in the center of Izmir where Gülen preached.[43] Until that time, some people used to cry in the mosque, but the preacher himself never cried – but Gülen did cry himself, and therefore he was known as "the crying preacher." He cried when he talked about the Prophet and about his Companions, and he also cried when he discussed the sad situation in the world of Islam. After his first festive prayer and sermon, people went to introduce themselves to Gülen, and they wanted to kiss his hand, but Gülen withdrew his hand out of humility. Since I was only ten years old at that time, I was allowed to kiss Gülen's hand, and since I came from a village named Korucuk as well, Gülen kissed me on the head and invited me to attend the Qur'ān-school after I finished my elementary education. Later Gülen

proclaiming the *khutba*. In Turkey, the *vaaz* is probably more important than in other Muslim countries, because knowledge of Islam had declined for a long time in the Republic, and the *Diyanet* used to prescribe the contents of the *khutba* while a preacher was more often free to give his own elaboration during the *vaaz*. Notes from my conversation with Alper Alasağ, Izmir, August 5, 2009; see also Patrick Gaffney, *The Prophet's Pulpit: Islamic Preaching in Contemporary Egypt* (Berkeley: University of California Press, 1994), 32.

43. Gülen was appointed as head of the Qur'ān-school at the Kestanepazarı Mosque, but he was assigned the duty to preach in different mosques in the Egean region as well.

came to visit the village since he was allowed to preach in the region. He came by bus because he has a very simple and austere lifestyle.

When asked to explain the difference between Gülen and most other preachers, Necdet İçel answered that most preachers carry big books with notes when they give a *vaaz*.[44]

Tunagür was the first preacher who prepared his sermons very well and did not need all these papers. Hocaefendi also preached without notes, but he was different from all others in that he never spoke badly of unbelievers, or the government, or anyone. He tried to talk not about how bad people are but about how good Islam is. In the second place, he was very well prepared. For one *vaaz* he used to read 500 pages in the original sources. In the third place, most preachers tell a lot of beautiful stories, but they do not live accordingly. But Hocaefendi only told stories that were in keeping with the way he lived. For instance, when he told that he was often awake and praying during the night because of the suffering of human beings, we knew that this was the case indeed. In the fourth place, Gülen was an eminent *hafız*. He knew the Qur'ān by heart when he was seven years old, and a volume of poetry by Mehmet Âkif Ersoy when he was eleven. He also memorized Ibn Hajar's dictionary of the Companions, which is an enormous task because of the literary quality of this work. Gülen was trained in the Sufi way, and it is a habit among Sufi preachers to often recite poems. This is what Gülen does as well. Once I travelled with him to Erzurum, and he was constantly reciting poems during the journey. So he has a fabulous memory and he does not need to react to what others say since he has enough to say himself. In the fifth place, humility is characteristic for Hocaefendi. Other preachers like to be invited to important festivities, but Gülen always hopes that someone else will be invited. For instance, during the *hafız* ceremony in 1967 everyone wanted Gülen to speak, but he declined since the *müftü* was present as well. This is *ikhlās* (sincere devotion): if someone else can speak the truth, it is better to give the floor to him. In the same way (sixth point) Gülen does not like to get presents or to be invited for dinner. When he was the director of the Qur'ān-school he was entitled to eat with the others, but

44. In the interview, Necdet İçel gave a very systematic answer in which he explained one point in which Gülen, together with Tunagür, differed from other preachers, and eleven points in which Gülen differed from all others.

he did not want to do so since others paid for the dinners. In the seventh place, others begin to discuss an issue during their sermons, but they stray from their subject. Gülen, on the contrary, begins and ends with the same subject matter. No one is able, like Gülen, to discuss an issue systematically during 15 or 30 *vaazlar*. That is why it is so easy to print the sermons as parts of Gülen's books. A next characteristic is that many people came to record his sermons on audio cassettes. Sometimes, there were 50 people recording at the same time. There is an audio industry with sermons in Turkey, others have their sermons recorded as well, but Gülen's sermons are the most famous. In the ninth place, Gülen was a renewer in what he discussed during his sermons. No one wanted to preach about Darwin and the theory of evolution, but Gülen has done it. The same is true (tenth point) with his audience: Gülen always wanted to preach not only for Muslims but also for people without faith. He was able to preach in an academic environment because he had enough intellectual background for it, and he really wanted to reach out to the faculty. Finally, Gülen did not leave immediately after his sermons, but he stayed and talked with the people. He visited them outside of the mosque as well, he went to different places in order to reach out to people. That is the reason why his preaching formed the basis of the Hizmet Movement that took its origin in Izmir.[45]

After this interview concentrating on some of the characteristics of Fethullah Gülen as a *vaiz* (preacher), I want to give the floor to some of Gülen's first companions in Izmir. They have told me how they met Gülen, what their impression of him was, and how the movement that we now know as the Hizmet Movement originated in the years after 1965 in Izmir.

Gürbüz Dönmez is a businessman who owns a furniture store and is – thanks to Gülen's suggestions – involved in the relationship between Turkey and Uzbekistan. He told me that he went regularly to the Kestanepazarı Mosque in Izmir.

At that time, in 1965–1966 Yaşar Tunagür was the imam of that mosque, and he was a very good preacher. People loved him and were very sad

45. Interview with Necdet İçel in his house near Izmir, on August 9, 2009. (Additions within parentheses are mine.)

when Tunagür became deputy head of Diyanet, the Directorate of Religious Affairs in Ankara. Tunagür, however, promised them: "I will send you someone who will be able to let you forget me." He knew Gülen earlier in his career, and because of his new function he had the power to appoint Gülen as his successor. When he came to Izmir, I invited him to my home, and Gülen gave a *sohbet* (religious instruction) there. Many people came and they were impressed by his personality. He was a very charitable person and had a warm personality, but the difference with others was that he was a man of action as well. When he came to Izmir, Gülen participated in the movement of followers of Said Nursi. He read Nursi's works with the people and gave his own interpretation. But that was not what was special about him; he was a very active man and he wanted us to go out and to serve other people. Taking care for others, becoming active in helping, that was what Hocaefendi taught us. One of the things that Gülen learnt from Said Nursi was that ignorance is the source of all evil, so he was very keen to look at education. Izmir was a city with a number of universities, but most of the students were atheists, therefore God showed his mercy by sending Gülen to the city. It was the combination of his personality and his energy that made him outstanding. He always wanted to meet people, and he invited me to go with him to meet other religious personalities. He always wanted to know what problems were bothering people, and he tried to give answers, in words but in deeds as well. This is how he got involved in educational projects: people showed their needs and he tried to answer with love and peace. He engaged himself without expecting to get anything back; he did it out of love for God, in the way of the Prophet.[46]

I interviewed Yusuf Pekmezci in the office of his household goods shop in one of the market halls in the center of Izmir. He was a member of the board of the Qur'ān-school when Gülen was appointed as its director and as preacher in several mosques.

When I first heard Hocaefendi preaching, we were both in our mid-twenties, but it was immediately clear to me that Gülen was an important man of piety, vision and knowledge. He did not only teach and preach, but he lived according to what he said. He tried to reach out to all people, with-

46. Interview with Gürbüz Dönmez, Izmir, August 5, 2009.

out any discrimination. He went to the coffee houses in order to reach out to young people.[47] At that time, there were many students in Izmir, and many did not have any religious background. But Gülen really tried to get in contact with them, to see what their questions were, and how he could help them. He gave *sohbetler* in these coffee houses, visited all of them in 1½ year. He began to help students by finding places to live for them, by trying to find scholarships for them, or furniture, or books and food. This is how we got involved in his educational projects. At the beginning, in 1966, there were only three of us who tried to help him, but gradually more people became involved and Gülen visited other places as well to get more supporters. Together we founded an association, which later became the "Foundation for Students in Secondary and Higher Education." We began to rent buildings and boarding schools for these students. Those who could pay were supposed to do so, but those who could not pay did not have to. Gülen himself did never receive any money, he never ate with the students in order not to live at their expenses. When he drank a glass of water, he insisted on paying for it. He began to organize summer camps as well, and tutoring and coaching classes. Everything was for free, it was paid from the *zakat* money.

When the Soviet Union fell apart, Gülen asked Pekmezci to become involved in Kazakhstan, where he owns a factory and is involved in some of the schools of the Hizmet network. He stated that Gülen's most important characteristic of was that he loved everybody, without making any distinction between believers and nonbelievers.

He used to say that we even had to love the communists. But he had a preference for the youth, since their future was important to him. That is why he began to ask them about their needs. His actions were simply responses to their needs. If a student needed accommodation, we started renting buildings, but during the first three years we could only rent one house and one boarding school. Later on, more people became involved and we also went to other cities to tell what we did. In the 1980s we could

47. At this moment in the interview, Pekmezci showed me a photo from 1968 featuring Gülen in discussion with a number of students. This part of the interview reminded me of Jan van Kilsdonk (1917–2008), a Dutch Jesuit priest who was famous as a student chaplain in Amsterdam for his method of "pastoral presence," which implied that he used to frequent bars in order to talk with students about the important things in life in an atmosphere that made it easier for them to open their hearts.

add a school to the accommodations, Yamanlar Koleji. Gülen was a student of Said Nursi, but he wanted to reach out to everybody, yet he did not want to become a leader of an organization. God's pleasure and the benefit of humanity – that was the only thing that counted for him.[48]

I met Zeki Sakman thanks to his son-in-law Ali Yurtsever, the former president of Rumi Forum in Washington, D.C., who was at that time in Izmir between jobs. Sakman told me that when Fethullah Gülen came to Izmir, there was already a group of students who read the writings of Said Nursi, and Gülen was willing to share his belief and to continue teaching the works of Said Nursi.

In the beginning, Fethullah Gülen acted more as a friend than as a leader. As a person, he was different because of his intensive prayer life, and also because he cared about the rights of other people. He would never use food of other people, or sleep in their beds even though he had the right to do that. He was always very tidy and clean despite the fact that he was not married. His humbleness was remarkable. These were the virtues that made us follow him. He really cared about young people, and he would go to the coffee shops to explain about God's religion. That is why he began to give education an important place. At that time, we would give our usual *zakat* but Gülen told us that we should do more. He started fundraising meetings, and he started convincing us that we should donate more. We did so because he was utterly trustworthy. The first thing that we did was to open a house and later a dormitory in the Bozyaka neighborhood, in 1976. It is important to have such dormitories, because if you take away a child from his house, he needs to have teachers and *abiler* (elder brothers; mentors). The most important thing is that Gülen was entirely trustworthy because he did what he said, and therefore the parents trusted him. Therefore, people started to give their things to the Hizmet and he began visiting more people to facilitate new initiatives. That is how the Hizmet grew. He taught us that we should always live in dialogue and peace with others.[49]

We spent almost a full day with Mehmet Küçük, a teacher at an advanced school for studying and memorizing the Qur'ān. Together

48. Interview with Yusuf Pekmezci, Izmir, August 6, 2009.

49. Interview with Zeki Sakman in his house in Izmir, August 9, 2009. The interpreter for this interview from Turkish to English was Rana Yurtsever.

with a friend, Mehmet Portakal, he showed us the mosque and the Qur'ān-school where Gülen was appointed as director in 1965.

At that time, Hocaefendi was 27 years old. While the Qur'ān-school is located next to the mosque, Gülen lived in a small cabin in the corner next to the school. It was not much more than a place where he could lie down, and he lived in extreme austerity. He did not eat with his students and did not use their water or bathroom facilities. We were among the first group of students guided by Gülen in the Kestanepazarı Qur'ān-school, and as a group we still come together every year. That year, the class had 99 students, 30 of whom proceeded in their studies to become imams, while most of the others went into business. Gülen was very active and very watchful as director; he was always present and it seemed that he never slept. He taught all subjects, English included, and gave private lessons to a group of 33 students who mastered the Qur'ān so well that they were able to teach their teachers in secondary education. On Thursdays, he would teach *ahlak* (ethics), and he would point out that the ethical principles of all religions are the same. The Qur'ān-school is still located next to the mosque, but the *imām*-academy moved to a different place.[50] At that time, we could start Qur'ān-school when we were 11 years of age, but later the government changed the required age to 14 years,[51] after elementary school and two years of secondary school.[52]

Mehmet Küçük also showed us the place outside of the town where Gülen organized summer camps during which he continued his teaching. Mehmet attended this camp in 1968.

50. When we visited the Kestanepazarı Mosque, the building of the Kestanapazarı Foundation, and the bookstore underneath the mosque, I did not see any visible reference to Fethullah Gülen, although I saw photos of founders, donors, and other imams of the mosque. This is — in my opinion — a very important indication of the nature of the Hizmet Movement that Gülen inspired, which I will discuss in chapter five: there is no "Gülen Mosque," but the relations between the Hizmet and a local mosque are personal rather than institutional. In this case, Mehmet Küçük formed the personal link between the Hizmet and the mosque, but the Kestanepazarı *vakfi* and the Qur'ān-school do not have an institutional link with Fethullah Gülen and his supporters.

51. This restriction was changed by the AK Party government in 2011 and currently there is no age limitation for the Qur'ān-schools in Turkey.

52. Interview with Mehmet Küçük and Mehmet Portakal at several locations near the Kestanepazarı Mosque and Qur'ān-school, Izmir, August 7, 2009.

Gülen brought sixty students in two big tents, while he slept in a small tent alongside them. The second year we built small sheds, the remnants of which can still be seen at this place. We did not have food, but people from the village supported us. Some of us had to work during the summer, but Gülen gave money to our parents so that we could follow his lessons, saying: "This is what you do if you want an *'ālim* (scholar) in your family." At that time, the political situation was rather tense, there were a lot of anarchists and communists around, and moreover the police did not allow religious meetings, therefore we had to be on guard in case someone would come and harm us. In the beginning, only students from the Qur'ān-school came, but later other students from the Dokuz Eylül University joined them.[53] Gülen used to give *sohbetler* (religious lessons) in the neighborhood of the university, and during one of these conversations, one of the students who sympathized with the "grey wolves" (an ultra-nationalist political group) said: "We should kill all communists." Another student replied: "If you had done that yesterday, I wouldn't be sitting here next to you." Gülen often uses this story to tell that he often learned more from his students than they learned from him. During these summer camps, Gülen did not only teach Qur'ān, grammar, Arabic and *takallum* (conversation) but he taught the contents of the works of Said Nursi, however, without telling them that Nursi was his source, since his works were banned by the military authorities.

When asked how Gülen was different from other Muslim preachers and teachers, Mehmet mentioned two characteristics.

In the first place, Gülen acted according to his words, he was absolutely reliable. In the second place, he never said anything negative about anyone. When he heard that an atheist had died, he started to cry and said "We missed a chance with this person." There is also the story about one of his sermons in the Şadırvan Camii (Mosque) when he fainted while crying because of the many children that died in the wars. So he reacts very strongly

53. Dokuz Eylül means "September 9" in Turkish. This university is the largest university in Izmir. The date refers to the day on which the Greeks were driven away from Izmir in the independence war of 1922. Since the university was founded in 1982, I am not sure if the reference to this university is entirely correct but in later years Gülen was *imam-hatip* of Bornova Mosque (see interview with Mehmet Yildiz) and he had many contacts with university students in those years.

if something bad happens, that is part of his loving-kindness for the entire humanity.[54]

Mehmet Eldem is a jeweler who met Fethullah Gülen in 1974. It was a difficult time because of the military coup in 1971. For a few years, Gülen could not organize any conferences, this became possible only in 1973. The reason why Eldem got involved in the movement was that Gülen lived the life that he preached.

He embodied Prophet Muhammad's character of *al amīn*, the trustworthy one. He had a very broad horizon and he forsaw developments in the future, but he was patient until his students could understand what he meant. If someone is so trustworthy during fourty years, it seems that God's support is with him.[55]

Mehmet Yildiz is a teacher who showed us the Bornova Mosque in Izmir where Gülen worked as a preacher during four years from 1976 onward. Bornova was the site of a big university and many students were activists at that time.

Gülen was already famous as a preacher, and the square in front of the mosque was filled with people a few hours before Hocaefendi preached his *vaaz* on Friday afternoon before the prayer. I must confess that I found something in Gülen's sermons that I never experienced again: one part of knowledge; one part of *ruh* (spiritual presence); one part of action; and one part of tears. On Friday evenings, Gülen used to give his *sohbet* and many students would come to listen, even from other cities where they tried to copy Gülen's dormitories and other educational institutions. Politicians like Turgut Özal came to listen to his sermons as well.

Yildiz met Gülen for the first time in 1972 when he was twelve years old and came to Izmir for his studies. He lived in Guzelyalı, one of the first dormitories founded by Gülen's supporters near the bay in Izmir. Since everyone was talking about this man, Yildiz decided to go to a mosque and listen to one of his sermons. Gülen was cry-

54. Interview with Mehmet Küçük (continued) at the place where Fethullah Gülen held summer camps at the end of the 1960s outside of Izmir, and in the office of Mustafa Duğral's furniture store, Gaziemir (Izmir), August 7, 2009.

55. Interview with Mehmet Eldem, Özbek (Urla), August 5, 2009.

ing during this sermon, and everyone was crying with him. At first Mehmet Yildiz did not understand what was happening, but gradually he opened his heart and started to follow Gülen and listen to his sermons, wherever he went: to Edremit (1972–75) and later Manisa (after 1975). Between 1977 and 1980 Gülen gave his sermons in Bornova Mosque, but the military coup in 1980 ended this. Many *vaazlar* (plural of *vaaz*) and *sohbetler* (plural of *sohbet*) from these years have been taped, and one can still find these tapes nowadays.

People came to him with all sorts of questions, and he asked them to put these questions on paper, and he would draw some of these papers from the stock and answer the questions. For instance, there was a biology professor at the university who doubted that faith and natural sciences could go together, but Gülen showed him how that could be done.

When asked to mention a specific characteristic of Fethullah Gülen, Yildiz mentioned his humility. He never wanted to live off someone else's purse, for instance, he always wanted to pay for his own water and medicines. Mehmet Yilmiz gave the following example:

At a certain moment, Gülen went to Burdur to pick up some soldiers who were to be set free, but it took some time so we had to spend the night in the mosque. It was very cold but Gülen did not want to make fire unless we would leave some money in the imam's box. The day after, the imam used this as an example: the country will not be lost as long as there are people who anonymously leave their gifts. Another characteristic is that he took everyone seriously, including children. He did not care about material things, but he always wanted to open his heart for everyone. This is something that is still useful for me as a teacher: Gülen has taught me to respect everyone, and my students give me good feedback because of that. Also, Gülen has taught me how to connect religion to the natural sciences, this is very important in today's world.[56]

Ahmet Gürkan is a businessman who came to know Fethullah Gülen when he was nine years old. His father had invited Gülen to give a *sohbet* in his house, and a group of twenty people came to participate in this event.

56. Interview with Mehmet Yildiz, Bornova (Izmir), August 8, 2009.

At first, my grandfather was hesitant about Gülen, but when he heard him speaking about the function of the skin, he was convinced and let me organize this *sohbet*. Later on, I stayed in the first dormitory that was founded in the Bozyaka neighborhood by the Akyazılı Foundation. I began my studies to become an imam but never finished them. During these years, I went to hear a number of sermons by Gülen, who often used topics from the natural sciences and — later — economics in his sermons and his *sohbetler*. I also participated in a summer camp that Hocaefendi organized under quite primitive conditions, and I remember that Gülen dug the hole for the latrine himself, encouraged by the children.[57]

It is good to compare these stories with the story of two friends who joined the Hizmet community much later. Cemal Yavuzer, the owner of a restaurant and his friend İhsan Taşpinar, who owns a shoe factory, met Hocaefendi in 1990 when they went to a *sohbet*.

One of the most remarkable things at that time was that Gülen talked about humanity in its entirety; he clearly had a global horizon while the movement at that time was only active in Turkey. Gülen was always ahead of people, he was thinking about projects that seemed impossible, but very often they turned out to be possible thanks to his stimulating energy. We do not have many resources but Hocaefendi has taught us to love all human beings without discrimination since we are Muslims. Because we have love for humanity, we can do a lot with scarce resources.

When the Soviet Union was disbanded, Gülen began to focus on the new republics that had a common origin with Turkey; he asked some of his supporters to go to these countries and see whether it would be possible to start schools there. He also stressed the importance of encounter as an objective of intercultural and interreligious dialogue.

Cemal and his friend participate in a circle of businessmen, and they are members of the board of an association that takes care of a number of educational projects. They meet in a *sohbet* four or five times every week, and sometimes they organize a *sohbet* for an

57. Interview during a dinner at the house of Ahmet Gürkan with his wife, Senai Özyaşar, and their daughter, Buca (Izmir), August 6, 2009.

entire day. They invite a theologian to come and give a lecture, or they watch Gülen on a video. They talk about one of his sermons or about one of his books, or they talk about what they have read on Gülen's website. Individually they also regularly listen to Gülen's new sermons and *sohbetler* through the Internet site Herkul.org. They recently visited Gülen, because they still miss him, yet they think that it is better for humanity that Gülen now resides in the U.S., since this makes his influence more universal. When I asked about Gülen's role in their lives, they said they could see that something has changed.

> When he was still in Turkey, Gülen was both an inspirator and a model. Now he still inspires us, but his life is different from ours since he becomes more and more centered on God in a daily rhytm that is built around *namaz* (prayer). His main inspiration for us now is that spiritual life is centered not on words but on the experience of love for the whole of humankind.[58]

SPREADING GÜLEN'S IDEAS

The second phase of Gülen's life was marked by an expansion of the ideals formulated in the first phase. Because of the changing political context in the beginning of the 1980s, Gülen began developing close ties with state institutions and became a nationwide public figure in the 1990s. The Hizmet began to spread its ideas through newspapers, journals, and radio and TV broadcasts. The privatization of the education system in 1983 gave Gülen's sponsors ample opportunity to implement his educational ideas in a great number of private schools (*dershanes*), beginning with Turkey but in later years in countries in central Asia and southeastern Europe as well. The most important difference between these new schools and the traditional religious schools is that religion is *not* an integral part of the curriculum in these schools.[59] The promi-

58. Interview with Cemal Yavuzer and İhsan Taşpinar, Izmir, August 7, 2009.
59. Agai, *Zwischen Netzwerk und Diskurs*, 150.

nence of the sciences, together with the absence of religion made it possible for the movement to build bridges toward other groups in Turkish society. While his religious ideas remained largely conservative, Gülen's political outlook became quite liberal, emphasizing democracy, freedom of the press, and a free market economy.[60] In his preaching Gülen began to emphasize the moral values of Islam and the model of Muhammad as a liberal, open-minded, bridge-building person. Gülen's openness started to include Western values and other religions as well. The notions of dialogue, peace, and tolerance between religions, cultures, and civilizations became more and more a central dimension of Gülen's message.[61] This combination of traditional Muslim spirituality and modern Western values explains the great attraction of the movement that Gülen inspired for many socially and economically prominent persons in Turkish society. In the 1990s the movement was very successful in attracting private funding for public and educational activities, so much so that a recent analysis argues that the Journalists and Writers Foundation is now the most powerful civil foundation in Turkey. Hakan Yavuz concludes that Gülen's followers used the market economy and the mass media to establish what he calls "an unprecedented Islamicization of the public sphere" in Turkey.[62]

One of the principles of Gülen's political ideas was that it is good to collaborate with the government, if they leave enough space for religion, and that it is not good to actively oppose the government in the name of Islam. This explains why the Hizmet Movement has generally agreed with the policy of the different Turkish governments since 1980, even if they were led by military and secularist forces. Although Gülen supported the government, secular forces suspected him of secret opposition against the secular nature of the republic, and they took him to court but never succeeded in getting him convicted. While Gülen was no longer

60. Yavuz, "The Gülen Movement," 38.

61. The compilation *Fethullah Gülen: Advocate of Dialogue* is clearly meant to show this dimension of Gülen's works to the larger public.

62. Yavuz, "The Gülen Movement," 42.

active as an official preacher and imam, he gave many sermons to his followers in which he urged them to accept the constitution of the country and to abandon protest movements in favor of Islamic principles. When Turgut Özal's administration came into power in 1987, Gülen openly promoted its policies and he made a tour around the country, supporting the government's initiatives in a series of sermons that attracted large numbers of listeners; he became the "Muslim preacher of liberalism."[63]

Some scholars have observed that after 1992 Gülen adapted the style of his discourse, now that he no longer acted as an official preacher. His main channels of discourse became the modern media that allowed him to reach out to a larger public. His ideas are now mainly spread through a number of media outlets that are part of the Hizmet network: TV and radio channels, newspapers, periodicals, and publishing houses. He still refers to the basic Muslim sources, such as Qur'ān and *hadīth* literature, but he quotes Western scientists, philosophers, and writers as well.[64] From 1994 to 1999 he became one of the most well-known public figures in Turkey. Since, however, the open display of religion in the Turkish public scene once again led to a counterattack by the military elite in their "soft coup" of February 28, 1997, it became harder for the Hizmet to steer a middle course between the forces of secularism and those of Islamism. Presenting themselves as heirs of Kemal Atatürk's secularization, forces in the new government began to curtail the influence of Islam in the public sphere. Gülen justified the military campaign against radical Islamist groups, but he was attacked by voices in the media as a threat to the secular nature of the Turkish state. Gülen, who had succeeded in balancing secularist and Islamist powers until then, now became the target of accusations from both sides in the third phase of his life. The secularist leaders claimed that he was an Islamist-in-disguise, while some Muslim circles criticized his involvement in politics and ac-

63. Ibid., 38.
64. Agai, *Zwischen Netzwerk und Diskurs*, 157.

cused him of aligning himself with Western values.[65] Gülen and the Hizmet found a way out of this thorny situation by widening their vision while stressing their allegiance to the Turkish nation. The Journalists and Writers Foundation began to concentrate less on Islamic issues and more on building forms of consensus among important groups in Turkish society.[66] At the same time, Gülen mitigated some of the nationalistic overtones in his discourse in order to make room for a more liberal and global perspective. In Turkey, Gülen had met with a number of Jewish and Christian religious leaders, but in 1998 he went to Rome to visit Pope John Paul II. This visit generated a lot of publicity and goodwill, but some voices in Turkey said that it was a betrayal and a humiliation of true Islam.[67]

Not long after these events, Gülen withdrew from the Turkish public scene and left for the United States, where he has lived since 1999. Medical reasons seem to have been the major cause for this move, but some sources say that Gülen did not want to become the focus of another political process. In 2000 a warrant was issued for his arrest in Turkey, suggesting that he intended to organize Islamist antigovernment activities, but in 2008 the Turkish Supreme Court dismissed the charges against Gülen.[68] Some still insist that Gülen is a major Islamist threat, and that his return to Turkey would be similar to Ayatollah Khomeiny's return from France to Iran in 1979.[69] Others come closer to the truth when they point

65. For details about these contrasting accusations, see Doğan Koç, *Strategic Defamation of Fethullah Gülen. English vs. Turkish* (Lanham, Md.: University Press of America, 2012).

66. Yavuz, *Islamic Political Identity in Turkey*, 45.

67. See Çelik, *The Gülen Movement*, 123.

68. Çetin, *The Gülen Movement*, 103. Also, Harrington, *Wrestling with Free Speech*, 126.

69. This suggestion is made by Michael Rubin, a resident scholar at the American Enterprise Institute, and associated with the website Middle East Forum, in an article "Could There Be an Islamic Revolution in Turkey?" in *National Review Online*, April 14, 2008 (www.meforum.org/1882/turkeys-turning-point, accessed June 2, 2009). For a detailed critique of his argument, see Koç, *Strategic Defamation of Fethullah Gülen*, 47–50.

out that Gülen is no longer interested in politics, and that he tries to contribute to a better future generation of Muslims by a life of asceticism, prayer, and writing. In this way, he once again follows in the footsteps of the Said Nursi who withdrew from politics to write his masterful commentary on the Qur'ān, the *Risale-i Nur*. In his personal life, Gülen seems to follow the path of a Sufi teacher who lives a life of seclusion and asceticism, surrounded by a group of students who take care for his personal well-being. As the interviews earlier in this chapter indicated, those who are close to him mention his God-centeredness on the one hand, and his concern for the well-being of humankind in general on the other. As we will see in chapter five, this fundamental spiritual attitude can be summarized in two notions. The first notion is *rıza-i İlahi*, the pleasure of God as the sole goal of one's life, and *hizmet,* service to humankind as the way that leads to this goal. Although Gülen occasionally gives an interview, he does not care much about public appearances any longer. This might give some credibility to the opinion that his "exile" has mainly to do with his health, although we have seen that his humility might be a more important factor. But Gülen might also have foreseen what many Muslims nowadays think: that the future of Islam may be made not in the traditional heartlands of Islam, but in the West. Hakan Yavuz quotes from a private conversation with Gülen as follows:

> By visiting the States and many other European countries, I realized the virtues and the role of religion in these societies. Islam flourishes in America and Europe much better than in many Muslim countries. This means freedom and the rule of law are necessary for personal Islam. Moreover, Islam does not need the state to survive, but rather needs educated and financially rich communities to flourish. In a way, not the state but rather community is needed under a full democratic system.[70]

In this light, it is significant that Gülen's supporters now flourish in many countries in Europe, the United States, and Australia, where they have founded many institutions and continue to

70. Yavuz, "The Gülen Movement," 45.

organize a number of conferences on Gülen and his thought that bring together scholars from all over the world. While his personal voice is seldom heard, people who feel inspired by him are rapidly extending their influence in many countries in the world, partly through excellent schools and other educational institutions, partly through dialogue foundations, such as the organizations mentioned in the introduction to this book.

GÜLEN'S WORKS: AN ANALYSIS OF CONTEXTS AND DISCOURSES

These developments in the life of Fethullah Gülen can be connected to the different strands in the discourse that he developed in his works by using Bekim Agai's analysis of the network connected with Gülen.[71] In his book on the educational network inspired by Fethullah Gülen, Agai shows how this network extends to four different groups of people that coincide with levels of Gülen's discourse and activities. If one depicts this network as a series of concentric circles, one may represent the different partial networks within the major network by ellipses with different ranges.[72] The central circle represents the person of Fethullah Gülen who took the initiative for a number of different activities that aim at different levels of involvement in the community of his supporters. The first level (smallest circle around Gülen) is what is usually called the *cemaat*, a specific network that is ruled by a specific discourse determined by its founder.[73] Earlier in this chapter, some of Gülen's first supporters in Izmir told how he started to implement his own teaching activities – partly following the tradition of the students of Said Nursi – such as *ders* (common study of religious

71. I presented an earlier version of this section at the conference *Mapping the Gülen Movement* in Amsterdam, October 2010. For more details about this conference and its context, see the first chapter of this book.

72. Agai, *Zwischen Netzwerk und Diskurs,* 361.

73. Ibid., 53. An important book in Turkish from one of the most important voices in the movement: Ali Bulaç, *Din-Kent ve Cemaat: Fethullah Gülen Örneği* (Istanbul: Ufuk Kitap, 2007).

texts) and *sohbet* (group discussion on a religious subject). Moreover, he created a new context for this education, in apartments where a small group of students live (called houses of light or *ışık evleri*), in summer camps, and later in schools. The language of these discussions and lessons is typical of a *cemaat*: the network of Gülen's closest supporters and his first students.

The second level of the network around Gülen consists of members of the movement who are religiously inspired and who can therefore be addressed by using specific religious language, although this discourse is broader than the discourse that is typical for the *cemaat*. Agai mentions the readers of the religious and cultural magazine *Yeni Ümit* as an example. To this level of the network belong those whose religious motivations are in line with Fethullah Gülen, but who do not belong to the *cemaat* or community in the strict sense of the word.

The third level of the network functions mainly in Turkey since it appeals to the larger Turkish public by using positive references to national (Ottoman or Turkish) history and culture. There seems to be no religious motivation for the activities of the Hizmet network at this level because of the strong laicist tendencies in Turkish society. At this level, many students and teachers may want to enroll in the schools founded by the service communities, simply because they are among the best schools in Turkey, and because they form a bridge between traditional society and the modern sciences. If they know about Gülen, they might presume that he serves his country as much as God.

Finally, the fourth and widest form of network is the global network that has begun to develop during the last twenty years. Agai mentions examples of teachers who may often teach at schools in central Asia, founded by the service network without knowing about Gülen at all. For them, good education is simply the motivation to teach, but they have no idea where the inspiration came from.[74]

74. Ibid., 363.

When I first started to study the works of Fethullah Gülen in the Netherlands, I was mainly interested in the theological sources for some of the main ideas shared by the members of the Hizmet Movement. However, it turned out that many of the works translated into English did not refer to specific theological sources because they were directed at the larger public. I therefore tried to use the "retrograde" style of my comparative theological approach that I already mentioned at the end of the first chapter, in order to delve up older sources that might contain more references to Islam as a common ground between the author and his public. For some time I have thought that it would be possible – following Agai – to talk about a development in Gülen's thought from the smallest to the widest concentric circle. According to this hypothesis, Gülen's discourse would have started as an explicitly Islamic discourse aimed at the members of the *cemaat* or the wider community of Muslims, but would gradually have widened to include the entire Turkish community in the 1980s, and the whole of humankind in the 1990s. While much of this analysis is true, it suggests a development that does not do justice to the complexity of Gülen's discourse. On the one hand, the persons quoted in the interviews above clearly suggest that care for the well-being of the whole of humankind – and not only of the members of the *cemaat* or of Muslims – has been one of Gülen's distinguishing characteristics from the very beginning. On the other hand, an analysis of his most recent writings shows that some of these writings still presuppose an explicit knowledge of and engagement with the Islamic tradition. During my research in the summer of 2009, I took a sample of the most recent articles translated into English and published on Fethullah Gülen's website at that time.[75] While an analysis of the sources quoted in these articles shows that most articles do not presume any specific knowledge of Islam, yet some of them clearly presuppose such knowledge. Four meditations on *maulid an-nabi*, the birthday of the Prophet, written in March 2009, can be character-

75. See http://www.fgulen.org/gulens-works/recent-articles.html, accessed September 19, 2009.

ized as beautiful songs of mystical love that can only be appreciated by people who are deeply involved in Sufi spirituality.

The main thrust of my "retrograde" analysis is to do justice to a type of discourse that is seldom mentioned in recent publications about Gülen: his sermons and his *sohbetler*. It is important to pay attention to the form of discourse that was predominant during the origins of the Hizmet Movement in order to do justice to the full range of Gülen's intellectual and religious inspiration.

I have often noticed how some of my Muslim friends who are members of the *cemaat* read Gülen's texts but often find more spiritual nourishment in his sermons. When I drove with them from one place to another in Izmir, we usually listened to sermons by Gülen or recitations of the Qur'ān. This oral rather than written discourse was typical for the Gülen Movement between 1970 and 1983.[76] These admonitions (*vaazlar*) and conversations (*sohbetler*) are clearly directed to a group of followers (Agai's description of the *cemaat*), or at least to like-minded Muslims (Agai's second concentric circle). In that sense, they represent an internal or "esoteric" form of discourse in which the traditional language of Islam is presupposed as a means of communication between speaker and listeners; sometimes this is made explicit in quotations from the Qur'ān, *hadīth* or *fiqh*, but it is even there when no explicit references are given, since the speaker assumes that the average listener is able to grasp the basic references to the Muslim tradition. For this reason, we can distinguish it as a form of discourse in which a general knowledge of Islam – or a specific knowledge in the case of members of the *cemaat* – is assumed, and we can call this a form of "esoteric discourse," in contrast to a second form of discourse that has a more general scope and is aimed at a wider public, which we can call an "exoteric discourse."[77] In my research I want to empha-

76. Çelik, *The Gülen Movement*, 28.

77. I use the terms "esoteric" (meaning: primarily aimed at insiders) and "exoteric" (meaning: aimed at outsiders as well) in a descriptive sense, even though I realize that the word "esoteric" often carries negative associations. See also Marcia Hermansen, "The Cultivation of Memory in the Gülen Community," in *Muslim World*

size the role of the "esoteric discourse" in Gülen's life and works, not only because it relies more strongly on the religious sources of Gülen's thinking, but also because I have observed that this religious dimension is generally underestimated in publications about him. Therefore, I think that it is useful to give a list of the most important of these oral sources in order to show how they are still part of the written sources attributed to Gülen. Moreover, a list of the books published by Gülen in Turkish will show that many of them find their origin in these oral sources, and that only a minority of them has been translated into English. In other words: even though I do not know sufficient Turkish to prove my case convincingly, I am quite sure that the person who only reads Gülen's books in English will not get an adequate picture of the nature of his discourse.

The coherence between books and audio cassettes – or CDs and DVDs as contemporary equivalents – can easily be discovered when one enters one of the bookstores that sell Said Nursi's and Fethullah Gülen's works – among many other religious works, of course. During my time in Izmir I went to the local Nil bookstore where three bookcases displayed the works of Said Nursi, and three more the works of Fethullah Gülen. Yet next to these another bookcase displayed CDs and DVDs with Gülen's sermons. Indeed, in Turkish there is a close connection between Nil Yayınları, the firm that publishes Gülen's books in Turkish, and Nil Production which publishes his audiovisual materials, as a glance into the recent catalogue of available works in Turkish shows.[78] For someone who researches Gülen's sermons, the edition of the collected sermons (*Vaaz Külliyatı*) is the most important source. This collection contains a set of eleven DVDs and two sets of eleven CDs each with sermons by Gülen. An analysis of the table of contents of this collection shows the truth of Necdet İçel's assertion, quoted before

in Transition: Contributions of the Gülen Movement, Conference Proceedings, London, October 25–27, 2007 (London: Leeds Metropolitan University Press, 2007), 60–76.

78. I consulted the *2009–2010 Yayın Kataloğu*, the catalogue of works by Gülen that I received from Hüseyin Bingül when I interviewed him at the Akademi of the Kaynak Kültür Yayın Grubu (Kaynak Cultural Publishing Group) in Üsküdar (Istanbul) on August 11, 2009.

in this chapter, that Gülen often preaches in a very systematic way, and that he often discusses a specific theme in a long series of sermons. Gürkan Çelik affirms the importance of the sermons – and the same holds true for the *sohbetler* that are included in the *Vaaz Külliyatı* as well – as basis of many books: "Most of his series of sermons, talks, conversations, and public speeches were recorded and transliterated into text format and, with minor revisions, published as books."[79] Before discussing these books, however, I want to give an impression of the titles and the subjects of some of the sermons represented in this *Vaaz Külliyatı* collection.[80]

The first set of eleven CDs contains a series of thirty-six sermons preached in Bornova (Izmir) between 1975 and 1980. They are collected under the title *Minberden Yükselen Ses* ("The Rising Voice from the Pulpit") Next, there is a series of ten sermons preached in different places between 1976 and 1980 under the title *Gönül Dünyamızdan* ("From the World of Our Heart"]. Next, there is a series of forty *sohbetler* entitled *Bamteli* ("Keynotes") subdivided into "breathings from a foreign place," "spiraling thoughts," and "our values." The next CD contains twelve sermons on "the Afterlife," preached in the Bornova Mosque in 1977–78. The final series of thirty sermons is entitled "Questions and Ways Out" (again from the Bornova Mosque in 1976–77).

The second set of eleven CDs contains series of sermons on easily identifiable Islamic subjects, such as five series of combined *vaaz* and *hutpe* on pilgrimage (*hac*), five on destiny (*kader*), seven on prophethood (*nübüvvet*), eight on fasting (*oruç*), twenty on angels (*melekût Âlemi*), and twenty on prayer (*namaz*). Some other sermons are collected under the title "Anatolian sermons" and "Towards the Light." Most of these sermons were recorded in Bornova (Izmir) in 1977–79, but some go back to Gülen's preaching in Edremit (1973–74) and Manisa (1974–75).

79. Çelik, *The Gülen Movement*, 28

80. Translations of the Turkish titles are based on my conversations with Alper Alasağ in Izmir between August 4 and August 10, 2009. Once again, the titles in Turkish are often very poetic and my attempt at translation cannot do them justice.

The set of eleven DVDs mainly contains sermons preached by Gülen on Prophet Muhammad and his companions, given between 1989 and 1991during his last tour of the most important mosques in Turkey on behalf of the government. Some of the titles of these series of sermons are: "compositions from the heart," "holy persons on their ways of life," "the enlightened climate of the future," "waiting in hope," "endless light," and "engagement for renewal." Some DVDs contain *sohbetler* as well, for instance *sohbet-i Canan* ("Conversation on the Beloved") that contains materials from 1992–94. A series on "The last bringer of news concerning the unknown" even contains older materials (for instance Berlin 1977) and newer materials (from *Yeni Ümit* magazine, 2003).

While the CDs in the *Vaaz Külliyatı* collection give a decent impression of the oral tradition of Gülen's works, they are probably far from exhaustive. While they cover the period of Gülen's appointment in Bornova Mosque in Izmir (1976–80) rather well, there are only a few recordings of sermons from the period in which Gülen preached in Edremit and Manisa (1973–75). Moreover, the collection contains no sermons from his first years in Edirne (1964–66) and Izmir (1966–70). At that time his sermons probably were not yet recorded, or the contents of his sermons were communicated in a less professional way.[81]

The DVDs in the *Vaaz Külliyatı* collection give a fair impression of a second important period in Gülen's preaching, namely the years between 1989 and 1991 when he was approached by *Diyanet* to resume preaching, after eight years of silence, because of the political situation. Muhammed Çetin explains: "His license was reinstated to enable him to serve as an Emeritus Preacher with the right to preach in any mosque in Turkey. Between 1989 and 1991 he preached in Istanbul on Fridays and on alternate Sundays in Istanbul and Izmir in the largest mosques in the cities. His sermons drew crowds in the tens of thousands, numbers unprecedented in Turkish histo-

81. Çetin, *The Gülen Movement*, 71, refers to "thousands of audio and video cassettes."

ry. These sermons were videotaped and also broadcast."[82] Most of these sermons have been published more than once on video-CDs and some of them can be found on the Internet as well.[83] According to Mustafa Gokcek, Gülen's sermons in this period used more Sufi concepts than in his previous sermons. "In these sermons which lasted until 1992, rather than the basic concepts of faith, Gülen focused on the spiritual characteristics that an ideal Muslim community should carry. Besides portraying the heroic instances from the lives of Prophet Muhammad and his companions, he presented even more examples from the lives of early Sufis. The themes were more spiritual."[84]

While Gülen, to my knowledge, did not preach anymore after 1991, he still gives *sohbetler* that are recorded on DVDs and CDs. For instance, the *Nil* catalogue contains a number of cassettes entitled *Gurbet Soluklarι* ("Breathings from a foreign land"), or *Bamteli* ("Keynotes") with the subtitle *Amerika Notlarι*. They have been recorded at Gülen's present residence in Pennsylvania, and some are as recent as 2006.[85] This shows that the oral transmission of Gülen's conversations is not only limited to the formative period of the Hizmet Movement, but that it is a type of source that still has its significance for supporters of this movement. As some of Gülen's supporters in Izmir indicated, they like to listen to newer conversations by Gülen that are transmitted through www.herkul.org, a site based in the U.S. that still updates people in the Hizmet Movement about Gülen's newest audio recordings. The site is in Turkish, with English and Arabic versions as well, and it contains a section on "weekly sermons" that is regularly refreshed.[86]

82. Ibid., 43.

83. The VCDs can be found in the Nil catalogue on pages 26–41; the Internet sources can be found, among other places, on YouTube (last accessed on August 12, 2010).

84. Mustafa Gokcek, "Gülen and Sufism," in *Islam in the Contemporary World 1: The Fethullah Gülen Movement in Thought and Practice*. Conference Proceedings, November 12–13, 2005, Rice University, Houston, Tx. (Somerset, N.J.: Tughra Books, 2009), 305–11, 308.

85. See the *Nil* catalogue, pages 47–50.

86. http://www.herkul.org/this-week/ During my last visit, on June 17, 2014,

Before discussing the books written by Gülen, I propose to look first at some of the journals published by the Hizmet Movement, since they form, together with the *vaazlar* and *sohbetler*, the main sources of Gülen's books.[87] Most books published by Gülen have not been written directly as books, but have been edited by some of the older members of the Hizmet Movement at Gülen's suggestion. Since no scholarly study of this aspect of Gülen's work has been made as yet, my theory on its development and meaning is preliminary and open to further research. This research is especially needed since the several editions of Gülen's works usually do not include a preface in which the editors explain the method they followed in compiling the materials, nor do they give the date of the first edition.[88] Therefore, it is almost impossible to establish an exact chronology of the books written by Gülen, and this holds true both of the Turkish originals and of the English translations. One can be quite sure, though, that many of these texts go back either to oral materials such as the sermons and conversations that were discussed above, or to written materials such as Gülen's columns and essays in the journals that will be discussed now.

The oldest and the most popular of these magazines is *Sızıntı*. This Turkish title literally means "Seepage" or "Trickling down," which relates to the purpose of the magazine: to let knowledge concerning the relationship between religion and culture on the one hand and the natural sciences on the other hand trickle down to a wider public. Therefore, the subtitle in Turkish is *Aylık İlim-Kültür Dergisi* (Monthly Scientific-Cultural Magazine). Although this subtitle suggests a secular approach with culture and science as its main focus, a theological mind might associate the notion of "trickling down" with the tradition of revelation. The word that is used in the Qur'ān to describe the process of revelation, is

the most recent sermon translated into English was dated December 16, 2013. The Turkish version of that sermon was published on December 15, 2013.

87. Çelik, *The Gülen Movement*, 29.

88. The website www.gulenbooks.com (accessed June 17, 2014) gives a very nice display of some forty-five books by Gülen and books about the Gülen Movement, but it does not contain a chronology of these books.

nazala, which in its fourth verbal form means "to send down," and the same word is used for rain. So while God sends down God's revelation like rain, human beings try to pass on some of it to others, which is the basic meaning of the word "tradition."[89] While the majority of the contributions to *Sızıntı* discuss matters of science, education, and culture, Gülen's regular contributions refer to religion as well. The issue of August 2009 that was published while I was in Izmir, for instance, contains articles about the earth, education, migraine, Ottoman history, metals, plants, medical sciences, and pollen. In each issue Gülen writes two or three editorials, usually without an author's name. In the August 2009 issue, he contributed a meditation on the enduring cycle of light and darkness at the front of the magazine, and an article in the series "Emerald Hills of the Heart," about the Sufi concept of "Unveiling," in the middle.[90] Sometimes he also contributes a religious meditation on two pages with remarkable illustrations, but in this issue the meditation is given by Muammad Gökçin on Qur'ān 68:1 "Nūn! By the Pen and by the (Record) which (men) write."

Sızıntı was first published in 1979 as a popular magazine for students interested in the relationship between religion and science; it was followed a little later by a few other, more specialized magazines, such as *Yeni Ümit* ("New Hope") on religious sciences and culture, *Yağmur* ("Rain") on language, culture, and literature, and *Gonca*, a children's magazine.[91] *Sızıntı*, though, is the only magazine that is translated into other languages, such as English (*The Fountain*), German (*die Fontäne*), Russian (*Noviye Grani*), Spanish (*Cascada*), and Arabic (*Hira*). The English magazine, *The Fountain,*

89. My inspiration here is Thomas Aquinas and his idea of *revelata aliis tradere*, to hand down what is revealed to others as the basic task of the Master of Theology, but also of the Dominican friar. I will come back to this aspect in the last chapter.

90. "Işık-Karanlik Devr-i Dâimi," *Sızıntı*, August 2009, 314–16; "Mükâşefe," *Sızıntı*, August 2009, 338–39.

91. See the Turkish website of Kaynak publishers: http://www.kitapkaynagi.com/yayinevlerimiz.php (accessed August 13, 2010). For the U.S., subscriptions to the magazines can be made through https://www.antstores.com/Articles.asp?ID=138 (accessed June 17, 2014).

was first published in 1993, and its articles offer a fair reflection of its Turkish older sister. It is not a literal translation of the Turkish magazine, but it has a similar layout and it serves a similar purpose for members of the Hizmet Movement outside of Turkey. The issue of May–June 2009, for instance, opens with a lead article on "Satan and his contemporary followers" that was written by Fethullah Gülen.[92] Next follow articles in the fields of biology, mathematics, society, health, and language (in this case, an article about the translation of Sufi poetry). After an article about nature, a lengthy interview with Seyyed Hossein Nasr under the rubric "Matter & Beyond Talks" is followed by Gülen's contribution to "Emerald Hills of the Heart," in this case about *Taqwa* or Piety. The magazine continues with contributions on poetry, history, physics, medicine, engineering, belief, a book review, life sciences, and Q & A (questions and answers). Comparing the two periodicals, one gets the impression that very often Turkish contributions to *Sızıntı* are translated and republished later in *The Fountain.*

Very often, these contributions are published in book form as well. This process can best be followed with respect to Gülen's long series about key concepts of Sufism. For instance, his contribution on "Mükâşefe" in *Sızıntı*, August 2009, had been published before in part II of *Kalbin Zümrüt Tepeleri*, while its English translation can be found in the second volume of *Emerald Hills of the Heart*.[93] The contribution on "Taqwa" in *The Fountain*, May–June 2009 has been published before in the first volume of *Emerald Hills of the Heart*.[94] In these cases, the publication in book form preceded the publication in the magazine. The reason for this somewhat unexpected order – from book to magazine – is that *Emerald Hills of the Heart* is a carefully planned long-term project. Gürkan Çe-

92. A survey of the lead articles written by M. Fethullah Gülen can be found on the website of the magazine: http://www.fountainmagazine.com/index.php (accessed August 13, 2010).

93. M. Fethullah Gülen, *Emerald Hills of the Heart: Key Concepts in the Practice of Sufism, 2*, trans. Ali Ünal (Somerset, N.J.: The Light, 2004), 108–11.

94. M. Fethullah Gülen, *Emerald Hills of the Heart: Key Concepts in the Practice of Sufism, 1*, trans. Ali Ünal (Rutherford, N.J.: The Light, 2004), 45–49.

lik writes that Gülen in 1990 started a project to "simplify" Said Nursi's texts in order to make them accessible for the younger generation.[95]

> Periodically, the simplified text would be published in the *Sızıntı* and *Yeni Ümit* magazines, aiming thereby to eventually complete the whole *Risale-i Nur* collection. However, this initiative attracted much criticism from the Nursi groups in Turkey. They held that simplifying the text would result in losing its inner meaning and spirit. While disagreeing with them on this point, but seeking to avoid discord, Gülen abandoned this project. . . . Thereafter, Gülen decided on a different intellectual project, tracing the methodology of the concepts of Sufism (*tasawwuf*) and establishing its place within the foundations of Islam.[96]

This might explain why the entries on Sufi terminology are often published in book form before they are printed in the magazines. In the case of most other recent writings by Gülen, the situation is the other way around: some of his lead articles for *Sızıntı* are translated into English for *The Fountain*, and later published in book form as well.[97]

During my stay in Turkey in 2009 I was able to interview Hüseyin Bingül, one of the main translators and editors of Gülen's works for Tughra Books, an English imprint of Kaynak publishers. The interview took place at the Akademi, the intellectual center of the Hizmet Movement in Istanbul, and the location of its central publishing house.[98] Bingül told me that the lead articles of "*Sızıntı*" and *The Fountain* are often reprinted as book publications in se-

95. This goes back to Gülen's interview with Nuriye Akman that can be found on Gülen's website. See "Necip Fazil wanted to simplify the Risale-i Nur Collection," at: http://www.fethullahgulen.org/press-room/nuriye-akmans-interview/ (accessed August 28, 2010).

96. Çelik, *The Gülen Movement*, 33–34.

97. Many of these articles can be found on Gülen's website in English under "recent articles": http://www.fethullahgulen.org/gulens-works/recent-articles.html (accessed August 13, 2010) or http://fgulen.com/en/fethullah-gulens-works/1359-recent-articles (accessed June 17, 2014). Despite its name, the website http://www.gulenarticles.com/gulen (accessed June 17, 2014) does not contain articles by Gülen but articles about him.

98. Joshua Hendrick, *Gülen*, 28–29 describes the Akademi as "an all-in-one publishing house, think tank, library, theology center, meeting center, school and mosque."

ries such as *Fasıldan Fasıla* ("From Episode to Episode," 5 volumes) and *Cağ ve Nesil* ("Era and Generation," 8 volumes). I asked him about the process of publishing Gülen's works, and he explained that Hocaefendi in some cases takes the initiative to publish a book, for instance the books on Sufism. In other cases, some of the people who know his works very well compile a number of chapters and edit the materials into a book which is then presented to Hocaefendi. If he agrees, it is usually published under a somewhat poetic title suggested by Gülen himself, while the editors give the more prosaic subtitles. Sometimes Gülen wants to see and approve the final product, sometimes not. The English books are largely translations of Turkish books that contain materials that had their original form in articles in one of the magazines, or conversations with questions and answers (*sohbetler*), or sermons. Sometimes Gülen makes the selection himself because he thinks that this is what people need; sometimes it is suggested by editors who are among the older students of Hocaefendi, for instance Reşit Haylamaz who is the editor in chief of Kaynak publishing company.

Publishing Gülen's books started with Nil Publishing in Izmir between ten and twenty years ago; since that time many books have been published, also in English. The first publishing company was Fountain, later it changed to Light, and now the Hizmet Movement has Tughra Books and Blue Dome Press.[99]

This brings me to the book publications as the most important form in which the works of M. Fethullah Gülen are made accessible to the larger public. I will first discuss the books that have been translated into English, since the editors and translators consider them to be the most important works for the general public that is not able to read Turkish. After that, I will discuss the works in Turkish that have not been translated very briefly. If possible, I will indicate the source of these books.

Nil Publisher's catalogue for 2009–10 shows a total of forty-

99. Interview with Hüseyin Bingül, Akademi, Üsküdar (Istanbul), August 11, 2009.

five books in Turkish by Gülen on the list of this publisher only.[100] The list of books that is included in the first cassette with the eleven DVDs of Gülen's *Vaaz Külliyati* mentions seventy-six titles, but this listing includes a number of books with interviews and a number of books edited by others. The International Edition of the *Publication Catalogue* by Kaynak Publishing Group gives a fair idea of the numbers of translations of Gülen's works in other languages.[101] In its English section, under the imprint Tughra Books, the catalogue mentions fifteen books by Fethullah Gülen translated into English.[102] A few books published by others, such as the Journalists and Writers Foundation, and some older books that are no longer available need to be added to this list, so that the total number of books by Gülen translated into English will be about twenty.[103] A list of Gülen's books in Turkish and English on one of his websites mentions sixty-six Turkish and seventeen English books, so it is safe to assume that about a quarter of the Turkish books have been translated into English in recent years.[104] Another website gives twenty-two books by Gülen but this includes some smaller publications.[105]

100. Nil Yayınları, *2009–2010 Yayın Kataloğu*, 4–22.

101. My source is Kaynak Publication Group, *Publication Catalogue 09–10* which I obtained during my interview with Hüsey-in Bingül in Istanbul, August 11, 2009. This interview took place in a room in which all international editions of Gülen's work were collected, including a number of editions that were published by other publishing houses, so that the total number of translations will be higher than the translations mentioned in this catalogue. I supplemented the data from the Catalogue 09–10 with Internet data from http://www.kaynakpublishing.com/en/index (accessed June 17, 2014).

102. Most recent information obtained through http://www.tughrabooks.com/fethullah-gulen (accessed June 17, 2014). See also http://www.tughrabooks.com/public/digital/publication2014/#14.

103. This list does not include books about Gülen under the imprints Tughra Books and (for academic books) imprint Blue Dome Press (see www.bluedomepress.com, accessed June 17, 2014).

104. See http://fgulen.com/en/fethullah-gulens-life/about-fethullah-gulen/fethullah-gulen-in-short, accessed June 18, 2014. This list mentions publications up to and including 2010, but it does not mention titles that are no longer in print.

105. See http://fgulen.com/en/gulens-writings-and-other-publications (accessed June 19, 2014).

In order to get a sense of the international distribution of Gülen's books, it may be useful to mention that Kaynak's catalogue has separate sections for its Spanish, French, German, Russian, and Arabic imprints. These lists contain twelve books by or about Gülen in Spanish, the same number in French, sixteen in German, eight in Russian, and ten in Arabic (here with the author's full name: Muhammad Fethullah Gülen). Finally, the catalogue mentions works in twenty-nine other European, Asian, and African languages. Again, as an indication that this is not the full list of translations, the catalogue does not mention any Dutch translations, while I know of at least two translations published by the Islam en Dialoog foundation in the Netherlands.[106] It must be said that the quality of these translations is rather diverse; while the English translations are thoroughly supervised and of good quality, I remember that my first experiences with the Dutch translations were not very good.

Most scholars agree that the four books about basic concepts in Sufism probably contain Gülen's most original contributions. The four volumes were translated from the Turkish *Kalbin Zümrüt Tepeleri* as *Emerald Hills of the Heart: Key Concepts in the Practice of Sufism* between 1998 and 2010.[107] According to Çelik, it is "the only book he systematically authored, though the writing expanded to years and it was fragmentally published in the Turkish magazine, *Sızıntı*, and its English version, *The Fountain*.[108] The book contains

106. M. Fethullah Gülen, *De smaragden van het hart: basisconcepten van het Sufisme* (Rotterdam, 2002); *Profeet Mohammed: aspecten uit zijn leven* (Rotterdam, 2004). These are partial translations of Gülen's books on Sufism and Prophet Muhammad.

107. The bibliography at the back of this book contains Gülen's works in the editions that I used while writing this book. However, subsequent editions have been published by different publishing houses and do not contain indications about the first year in which the books were published. For instance, my copy of the first volume of *Emerald Hills of the Heart* was published by The Light in Rutherford, N.J., 2004; the second volume by the same publisher, but now based in Somerset, N.J., also in 2004. The third volume was published by Tughra Books, in Somerset, N.J. in 2008 and the fourth volume by the same publisher in 2010. Yet the original edition of the first volume of *Emerald Hills of the Heart* was, as far as I know, published in 1998. Tughra Books' Publication Catalogue for 2014 shows the four volumes together on page 17 (http://www.tughrabooks.com/public/digital/publication2014/#17/z).

108. Çelik, *The Gülen Movement*, 29–30.

a large number of references and footnotes, mainly to the Qur'ān and the authoritative collections of *hadiths*. Gülen tries to explain the basic concepts of the Sufi way in such a way that the average reader with some knowledge of Islam and some experience in mysticism may apply them fruitfully in her or his daily life. Gokcek says that Gülen began to write about these themes in 1990, which would coincide with the period in which Sufism was most important in his sermons.[109]

The volume on Prophet Muhammad was first published in Turkish as *Sonsuz Nur: Insanlığin Iftihar Tablosu* in 1993; it was translated into English – by Ali Ünal who translated many of Gülen's works – as *Prophet Muhammad: Aspects of His Life* in two volumes that were later combined in a revised version.[110] The book contains a large number of references to Muslim sources. It finds its origin in what Agai calls the *cemaat* discourse of Gülen: it has been transcribed from a number of sermons and conversations on Prophet Muhammad.[111]

Gülen has published a number of books in which he discusses the basic tenets of Islam. The book *Essentials of the Islamic Faith* was translated from the Turkish *Inancin Gölgesinde*.[112] It is a book in the style of Said Nursi, trying to demonstrate the existence of God from nature, and referring to a number of scientific observations. Gülen refers to the Qur'ān and sometimes to the *hadiths*, but to a number of Western scientists and philosophers as well. The two volumes of *Questions and Answers about Islam* were translated from the Turkish *(Asrın Getirdigi Terreddütler)* by Muhammad Çetin and first published in 2000.[113] The Turkish editions of these two vol-

109. Gokcek, "Gülen and Sufism," 307–8. The first volume in Turkish was published in 1994, the others in 2001, 2004, and 2008. English translations followed in 1998, 2004, 2008, and 2010.

110. M. Fethullah Gülen, *Muhammad, the Messenger of God: Aspects of His Life*, trans. Ali Ünal (Somerset, N.J.: The Light, 2005). Other editions may have somewhat different titles.

111. Çelik, *The Gülen Movement*, 31–32.

112. M. Fethullah Gülen, *Essentials of the Islamic Faith*, trans. Ali Ünal (Fairfax, Va.: The Fountain, 2000).

113. Revised editions: M. Fethullah Gülen, *Questions and Answers about Islam, 1*

umes, in 1983 and 1989/90, are among Gülen's oldest publications. The question and answer style seems to suggest that these books find their origin in the *sohbet* discourses of Gülen and his followers. Again, the style is reminiscent of Said Nursi, and there are quite a few references to Muslim sources. If Gokcek's theory is correct, that Gülen first concentrated on the essentials of faith in his sermons and religious conversations and only later included more Sufi materials in his sermons, the books about the essentials of Islamic faith would have their origins in the period 1982–90, before the books on Sufism that began to be published from 1990 onward.

The books about Muhammad and the Islamic faith seem to be directed primarily to Gülen's followers who are well-acquainted with the Muslim tradition. The titles and the styles employed are clearly congruous with traditional Islamic discourses. This type of discourse will be analyzed further in chapter five; it focuses on the members of the Hizmet Movement and presupposes an Islamic worldview. One of the consequences is that Islam is quite obviously presented as the best religion, a better religion than Judaism and Christianity. Some of Gülen's books show remnants of this way of thinking that would not fit very well with the more universal style prominent in his later texts.[114] For instance, twice Gülen seems to

(Somerset, N.J.: The Light, 2006); *Questions and Answers about Islam, 2* (Somerset, N.J.: The Light, 2005). The list of Gülen's books (see footnote 106) mentions 1993 as the original year of publication but I have not been able to verify that.

114. Some examples: the remarks on the distorted nature of Torah and Gospels in Gülen, *Essentials of the Islamic Faith*, 191; *Questions and Answers about Islam, 1*, 66 and 81; *Questions and Answers about Islam*, 2, 14 and 350; the negative remarks about Christians in *Muhammad, the Messenger of God*, 70–71 and 193; the defense of the Qur'ānic view of Jesus in *Essentials of the Islamic Faith*, 215; *Questions and Answers about Islam, 1*, 120 and *Questions and Answers about Islam*, 2, 128. Furthermore, his apologetic remarks about the marriages of the Prophet in *Essentials of the Islamic Faith*, 246, and *Questions and Answers about Islam, 1*, 130; his idea about Judaism and Christianity as nonnatural religions (*Questions and Answers about Islam, 1*, 47–48); the idea that "most of humanity will embrace Islam soon" (*Muhammad, the Messenger of God*, 186); his observation that only Muslims know real tolerance (*Questions and Answers about Islam, 1*, 242); that every religion except Islam has suffered distortions (*Questions and Answers about Islam, 1*, 246) and the identification of Jews and Christians as the people referred to in *surah al-fātiha* 1:7 (*Muhammad, the Messenger of God*, 320–21). Further-

suggest that we can only have a right opinion about Jesus thanks to the Qur'ān, an observation that is in line with the Islamic tradition but of course unacceptable to Christians.[115] I do not hold this against Gülen; quite the contrary, I think that it is a normal phenomenon in what I will describe as a form of discourse that is mainly directed to insiders.

The same style, and the same "esoteric" discourse is also discernible in Gülen's *Reflections on the Qur'ān* that has only recently been translated into English.[116] As the subtitle says, the book contains short commentaries on selected isolated verses, which makes it probable that articles in *Sızıntı* and *The Fountain* form the original sources for this publication. However, some of the *sohbetler* given by Gülen to his students could also be sources since he explicitly mentions that he wants to discuss those places in the Qur'ān that often give rise to questions. As is the case with the other books with an internal or "esoteric" discourse, the reflections obviously take Islamic interpretations as their frame of reference, as can be seen in the many references to *hadith* compilations, the traditional books of *tafsir bi'l ma'thūr,* or "interpretation based on transmitted sources,"[117] and other traditional sources. Yet he quotes Said Nursi, Ibn 'Arabi and the New Testament as well. I will give a more complete picture of the use of the Qur'ān in his work in the next chapter. There I will also discuss his general commendation of the Qur'ān and his more elaborate exegesis of its first chapter, *surah*

more, Gülen states in *Essentials of the Islamic Faith*, 194 that Christians identify the Holy Spirit with Archangel Gabriel, while this is part of the Islamic – not the Christian – tradition.

115. See Gülen, *Muhammad, the Messenger of God*, 128, and *Questions and Answers about Islam*, 120.

116. M. Fethullah Gülen, *Reflections on the Qur'ān: Commentaries on Selected Verses*, trans. Ayşenur Kaplan and Harun Gültekin (Clifton, N.J.: Tughra Books, 2012). The original Turkish books (two volumes) have been published as *Kur'an'dan İdrake Yansıyanlar* in 2000 (even though the English translation mentions 2011 as year of original publication – maybe that holds true for the one-volume version).

117. Jane Dammen McAuliffe, "The Tasks and Traditions of Interpretation," in *The Cambridge Companion to the Qur'ān*, ed. Jane Dammen McAuliffe (Cambridge: Cambridge University Press, 2006), 181–209.

al-fātiha. This book, originally published in 1998, has not yet been translated into English.[118]

The form of discourse is different in most of the other books that have recently been published in English translations since their style is more general, and references to Muslim sources are less frequent. These books are instances of a more general or "exoteric" discourse, in which Gülen aims at a broader public, without using the specific references to sources and terminology that are characteristic of the more particular or "esoteric" discourse of the *cemaat*. Sometimes, these books have been translated directly from the Turkish originals, but often editors compile them using Gülen's columns and articles in periodicals such as *Sızıntı*. As I showed before in this chapter, the stage between the Turkish column and the English book is often the English column in *The Fountain*.

One of the earliest books translated into English is *Towards the Lost Paradise.*[119] In their foreword "about the author," the anonymous editors say that "[t]he present book is composed of Fethullah Gülen's selected articles which have so far been published in different magazines." The articles in this book often concentrate on the ideals of a "new generation" and on the harmony of faith and sciences. There are no explicit references to Muslim sources in this volume. This English book has been published by Kaynak publishers in Izmir, but it is not included in the actual publisher's list.

Pearls of Wisdom is among Gülen's most often quoted books because it contains a number of short essays and aphorisms.[120] Members of the Hizmet Movement and of institutions associated with

118. M. Fethullah Gülen, *Fatiha Üzerine Mülâhazalar* (Istanbul: Nil Yayınları, 2007).

119. M. Fethullah Gülen, *Towards the Lost Paradise* (Izmir: Kaynak, 1998). The original edition was published in 1996. First editions of Gülen's Turkish books and some of his English books are listed under "Fethullah Gülen in Short" on http://fgulen.com/en/fethullah-gulens-life/about-fethullah-gulen/fethullah-gulen-in-short (accessed on June 18, 2014).

120. M. Fethullah Gülen, *Pearls of Wisdom,* trans. Ali Ünal (Fairfax, Va.: The Fountain, 2000).

the movement often quote some of these aphorisms or wise suggestions. A recent promotional video by Rumi Forum, for instance, begins with the well-known words: "Be so tolerant that your heart becomes wide like the ocean. Become inspired with faith and love for others. Offer a hand to those in trouble, and be concerned about everyone."[121] These aphorisms often contain references to the Qur'ān, Prophet Muhammad, or Sufi spirituality, but these references are of a general nature, and no specific sources are quoted. The essays compiled in this book, together with *Towards the Lost Paradise*, seem to represent a kind of discourse that lies between the "esoteric discourse" of the sermons and the religious conversations and the "exoteric discourse" of the essays for a more general public, since quite a few of these essays have a nationalist tone. As is the case in Said Nursi's works, in this specific strand of discourse Gülen tends to see the West as antagonistic to the Muslim world, so that he often sketches Western forms of philosophy and scholarship as negative and antireligious.[122] In contrast, the values of the Turkish nation are seen in a positive light. For instance, "Journalists and writers who do not write according to national sentiment and thought represent Babylonian enslavement."[123] Texts such as these would fit very well in the period between 1986 and 1996 when Gülen became a nationally acclaimed spiritual leader. Because of its popularity, *Pearls of Wisdom*, originally published in 1997, is still available with the publisher.

The exoteric discourse that is aimed at humanity in general,

121. Ibid., 61.

122. For Said Nursi, see Patrice Brodeur, "The Ethics of Bediüzzaman Said Nursi's Dialogue with the West in Light of his Concept of 'Europe,'" in *Globalization, Ethics and Islam: The Case of Bediuzzaman Said Nursi*, ed. Ian Markham and Ibrahim Ozdemir (Burlington, Vt.: Ashgate, 2005), 89–98; Sükran Vahide, "An Outline of Bediüzzaman Said Nursi's Views on Christianity and the West," in *Globalization, Ethics and Islam. The Case of Bediuzzaman Said Nursi*, ed. Ian Markham and Ibrahim Ozdemir (Burlington, Vt.: Ashgate, 2005), 109–18.

123. Gülen, *Pearls of Wisdom*, 60. This observation should be seen in its context: I do not mean to suggest that Gülen is a chauvinist, but I try to distinguish shades of difference in his discourse that are related to the changing political context in Turkey and internationally.

and that is predominant in Gülen's discourse from the second half of the 1990s onward, is clear in titles of books such as *Fethullah Gülen: Advocate of Dialogue, Love and the Essence of Being Human,* and *Toward a Global Civilization of Love and Tolerance.*[124] These books have been compiled by members of the Hizmet Movement specifically for an international public, without any comparable volumes being published in Turkish. Ali Ünal and Alphonse Williams are the compilers of the first book, which can only partially count as a book by Gülen since it also includes introductions and responses to his work by others. The Turkish sources in this book have been indicated in footnotes, and Ali Ünal translated most of the sources directly for the book. The second book has been published by the Journalists and Writers Foundation, and prepared for publication by Faruk Tuncer. The "Author's Biography" at the front of the book ends with a paragraph that says: "Some of Fethullah Gülen's books have been compiled from his articles, sermons, and the answers to the questions he has been asked over the years. The one in your hand is one of these."[125] M. Enes Ergene, the editor of the third volume, *Toward a Global Civilization of Love and Tolerance*, gives a similar general indication of the sources in his introduction: "The articles in this book are a collection from various writings of Gülen and speeches he has given at different times and on different occasions. Nevertheless, all the articles give a general picture of the world of his thought."[126] As far as I can see, this is the only one of the three books that is still in print.

Although it has a much more general title, the book *Essays, Perspectives, Opinion* has a similar structure.[127] It is a compilation of

124. *Fethullah Gülen: Advocate of Dialogue*, compiled by Ali Ünal and Alphonse Williams, trans. Ali Ünal (Fairfax, Va.: Fountain Publications, 2000); Fethullah Gülen, *Love and the Essence of Being Human*, prepared for publication by Faruk Tuncer, trans. Mehmet Ünal and Nilüfer Korkmaz (Istanbul: Journalists and Writers Foundation Publication, 2004); Fethullah Gülen, *Toward a Global Civilization of Love and Tolerance*, foreword by Thomas Michel (Somerset, N.J.: The Light, 2004).

125. Gülen, *Love and the Essence of Being Human*, 12.

126. Gülen, *Toward a Global Civilization of Love and Tolerance*, x.

127. M. Fethullah Gülen, *Essays, Perspectives, Opinions*, compiled by the Fountain (Rutherford, N.J: The Light, 2002).

articles from different sources, some in Turkish, some in English. This time, the sources are indicated in footnotes at the beginning of the articles themselves. It is a somewhat older book and no longer in print.

The final book with general essays by Gülen might be the only book of this kind that has been translated directly from a book in Turkish: *The Statue of our Souls* is a direct translation by Muhammed Çetin of *Ruhumuzun Heykelini Dikerken* published in 1998.[128] The central theme of the book echoes one of the central themes in *Towards the Lost Paradise*: the necessity for the younger generation to improve themselves and to become a "generation of hope." At the same time, it seems to be more optimistic about the chances for renewal than Gülen's earlier writings. The book contains a limited number of footnotes with references to Qur'ān and *hadīth* collections, but also explanatory footnotes for persons who do not know the meaning of some of the Arabic terms used in the book. In this respect, the book represents a mixed discourse since it is addressed to younger people in hopes of their renewing their souls. In principle, it addresses those who are sufficiently acquainted with the Islamic tradition to understand the notions discussed in the book: in this respect, it is not far away from the books on Sufi terminology – but at the same time it tries to attract younger people without such a religious background, yet who are willing to renew their souls for the service of humankind.

These are the most important of Gülen's books translated or compiled in English.[129] They give a fairly good picture of the two strands of his discourse: one strand is directed to insiders and presupposes a basic knowledge of the Islamic tradition – and sometimes a more specific knowledge in members of the *cemaat* – while

128. M. Fethullah Gülen, *The Statue of Our Souls. Revival in Islamic Thought and Activism*, trans. from the Turkish by Muhammed Çetin (Somerset, N.J.: The Light, 2005).

129. I have not mentioned one booklet about *The Necessity of Interfaith Dialogue* that I will use in the second half of this book. A few other titles, most of them recently translated into English, will be mentioned in the next paragraphs among the publications in Turkish.

the other strand aims at a wider public and tries to involve them in the movement for a renewal of faith-based service initiatives. The last book mentioned, *The Statue of Our Souls*, might be the book in which the transitions between the two strands of discourse are most clearly visible.

In summary, this survey of Gülen's books in English gives a reasonable idea of the different forms of discourse in his writing, but cannot be comprehensive since Gülen has written at least sixty books in Turkish, and only one quarter have been translated into English. The first form of discourse, "esoteric" or insider-oriented types of books on Sufi terminology, on Prophet Muhammad, and on Islam is fairly well represented by direct translations. The second, "exoteric" or outsider-oriented types of books with more general encouragements to renew oneself and to become a part of a future generation of service-oriented faithful and moral "golden generation," is much less represented in direct translations; yet many of Gülen's columns and articles in *Sızıntı* and other periodicals have been compiled in anthologies, either translated directly from the Turkish, or through publications in *The Fountain*. Nevertheless, some of Gülen's books in Turkish are not represented in English translations. The final paragraph of this chapter gives a short selection of these books.

Agai mentions one book that was published long before all other books by Gülen.[130] It is a collection of sermons published by *Yeni Asya*, one of the groups in the Nursi movement, in 1974. This shows once again that Gülen at that time had much in common with the followers of Said Nursi. The book, *Hitap Çiçekleri* ("Anthology of Sermons") is still in print.[131] Many of the short sermons in this book have been used again in later years.

Some of Gülen's books discuss matters of doctrine in some detail, for instance the Islamic teaching about destiny. As the title of this book, originally published in 1995, suggests, Gülen approaches the theological problem of God's power and human destiny from

130. Agai, *Zwischen Netzwerk und Diskurs*, 149.

131. M. Fethullah Gülen, *Hitap Çiçekleri* (Istanbul: Nesil Yayınları, 2009).

the perspectives of the Qur'ān and the *Sunna*.[132] The first three chapters go back to sermons on destiny, while the fourth chapter contains a number of question and answer sessions.

Another book that goes back to the sermons of the 1970s has recently been published as *Enginliğiyle Bizim Dünyamiz*.[133] It is a book on economics, a topic that Gülen discussed in some of his sermons on *iqtisad* (economics).

Kırık Testi ("Cracked Pitcher") is a series of books published not by Nil publishers, but by the Journalists and Writers Foundation, an organization that we will discuss in chapter six. The metaphor behind the title is the idea that knowledge is transmitted slowly just like drops from a cracked water bottle. The series contains *sohbetler*, some of them quite recent.[134] The title of the eighth volume in this series of publications, *Vuslat Muştusu,* refers to the person who brings good news concerning coming home with God.[135]

It is a tradition among Sufi masters to collect prayers and to publish them as a special guidance to prayer. Even though he is not a Sufi in the strict sense of the word, Gülen has followed this custom and collected several such prayer books, the first in 1988 (*Dua mecmuası*). The most recent (2014) catalogue of Tughra Books shows three books with prayers selected, compiled, and edited by Fethullah Gülen.[136]

132. M. Fethullah Gülen, *Kader. Kitap ve sünnet perspektifinde* (Istanbul: Nil Yayınları, 2009).

133. M. Fethulah Gülen, *Enginliğiyle Bizim Dünyamiz* (Istanbul: Nil Yayınları, 2009).

134. I assume that the publications sampled under the title "The Broken Jug" on http://fgulen.com/en/fethullah-gulens-works/thought/the-broken-jug (accessed June 18, 2014) contain quite a few of these *sohbetler* in English translation.

135. M. Fethullah Gülen, *Vuslat muştusu,* Kirik Testi, 8 (Istanbul: Gazeteciler ve Yazarlar Vakfı Yayınları, 2008). My translations of Turkish titles are based on conversations with Alper Alasağ in Izmir, August 2009. My dictionary gives "union" or "reunion" for *vuslat* but this might be problematic for orthodox Muslims. Alper suggested "arriving," but my translation is based on the Christian (and Sufi) idea that people are on their way to God; while we are wayfarers (*viatores* in Latin), we hope once to come home with God just like Christ and the saints who – Christians believe – are at home with God (*comprehensores* in Latin) already.

136. See http://www.tughrabooks.com/public/digital/publication2014/#24/z (accessed June 18, 2014).

Finally, Çelik points to a book that is very important for some of Gülen's admirers in the Hizmet Movement, since it contains a collection of his poetry. This book, *Kırık Mızrap* ("Broken Plectrum"), published in 2000, is important because it shows not only Gülen's creativity, but also the role of poetry in traditional Sufi teaching. Poems were important in the passing on of knowledge from master to student, but in many of his sermons Gülen quotes poems as well, and we have heard from Necdet İçel about the importance of learning poetry by heart in the tradition of oral culture. As far as I know, "Broken Plectrum" has not yet been published in English, but Gülen's website in English contains a reference to "Broken Plectrum" in which a number of poems are published online in translation.[137]

Even though the foregoing pages contain the most extensive survey so far of Gülen's publications in English, it is still far from doing justice to his immense oeuvre. Apart from the many books in Turkish that I have not been able to consult, there are some books published in English that I have not considered because they touch on subject matters outside of the field of my primary interest, subjects such as family life, education, and language.[138]

137. See http://fgulen.com/en/fethullah-gulens-works/thought/broken-plectrum (accessed June 18, 2014),

138. I found the following titles of books in English that I did not consider for this publication: *Islam and Democracy*; *From Seed to Cedar: Nurturing the Spiritual Needs in Children*; *Speech and Power of Expression: On Language, Esthetics, and Belief*. Gülen also wrote a few texts for two books with photos and pictures: a book about the two holy cities and a book about colors.

4

THE QUR'ĀN, RŪMĪ, NURSI, AND THE RENEWAL OF ANATOLIAN ISLAM

FETHULLAH GÜLEN is quite explicit about the fact that his ideas about contemporary forms of Islam are derived from the sources of the Islamic tradition. In the previous chapter, I have already pointed out that these sources are used differently in the several strands of Gülen's discourse. When Gülen tells about the family in which he grew up, he relates that his mother taught him the Qur'ān when he was four years old. Reading and reciting the Qur'ān was dangerous at that time, therefore much of the teaching had to be done during the night.[1] Gülen also describes how his father, who was a government-employed imam, taught him Persian and Arabic and constantly read books about Prophet Muhammad and his companions with his son.[2] So, the Qur'ān and the example of Prophet Muhammad were of paramount importance in the house in which he grew up. Therefore, it makes sense to consider the Qur'ān and the *sunna* (habitual practice) of Prophet Muhammad and his companions as the most important source of Gülen's theological thought, even though references to these sources are

1. Nevval Sevindi, *Contemporary Islamic Conversations: M. Fethullah Gülen on Turkey, Islam, and the West* (Albany, N.Y.: State University of New York Press, 2008), 16.

2. See the section "A Different Home," in M. Fethullah Gülen's biography on his English website: http://fgulen.com/en/biography/24650-a-different-home (accessed June 18, 2014).

not always explicit in Gülen's works. At least, this was the case in most of the books that were presented to me in my first contacts with the people inspired by Gülen: they gave me (and most other outsiders) books in which the external or "exoteric" discourse was prominent and references to the Islamic tradition were scarce. Only later did I become aware that Gülen had written other books – and had spoken in sermons and religious conversations – in which references to the Islamic tradition were much more common. Even though I think it is very understandable that members of the Hizmet Movement present outsiders with "exoteric" instead of "esoteric" communication, I still think this is one of the reasons why people suspect Gülen of a hidden – Islamist – agenda, as I explained at the end of chapters one and two. Therefore, it is important to understand that Gülen has an Islamic agenda although it is not an Islamist agenda: Islam functions as the source of a personal and socially active worldview but not as a blueprint to restructure society.

The same biographies tell about the importance of the Sufi tradition in Gülen's religious education. This influence is mostly connected with the name of Muhammad Lütfi Effendi, the honorary imam of Alvar where Gülen lived at the time. A few years later, Gülen became acquainted with the *Risale-i Nur*, an immense commentary on the Qur'ān by Said Nursi that, in the early days of the secular republic, taught many Turkish Muslims to engage in a rational and contemporary form of Islam. Although Gülen never met Nursi, and although he does not want to be called a follower of Nursi in the strict sense of the word – in a similar way, he denies being a Sufi in the strict sense of that word – it is clear that Nursi's writings have influenced Gülen and his followers to such an extent that the Gülen Movement is sometimes called the neo-Nur movement.[3] In the formative period of the Hizmet Movement in Izmir, Gülen and his first students shared the worldview, the lifestyle, and the educational format of the Nur movement, for instance

3. M. Hakan Yavuz, *Islamic Political Identity in Turkey* (New York: Oxford University Press, 2003).

when Gülen took over the methodology of reading the *Risale-i Nur* and other Scriptures together in Nursi's *dershanes* but at the same time gave a personal interpretation of these writings in the *ışık evleri* (houses of light).

THE QUR'ĀN AS THE PRIMARY SOURCE OF GÜLEN'S THOUGHT

When one surveys what scholars have written about the sources of Gülen's thought, one will come across a sizeable number of articles that explain the relation between Fethullah Gülen and either Jalāl al-dīn Rūmī or Said Nursi as important sources, but it would be quite difficult, especially if one limits oneself to English, to find more than one or two authors paying attention to the Qur'ān and *Sunna* as sources for Gülen's thought. In fact, to my knowledge, there is only one book that explicitly pays attention to Gülen and the Islamic sources of his thought, and that book was only recently published.[4] Yet no Muslim would endorse the idea that Rūmī or Nursi could be more important than the Qur'ān or the *hadith* as sources of Gülen's thought. Quite the contrary is true: Rūmī and especially Nursi would stress that their work is just an interpretation of the Qur'ān; and, although I have not come across an explicit statement, I think that Fethullah Gülen would certainly not disagree if one were to characterize his thought as a contemporary interpretation of the Qur'ān, or as an imitation of the example of the Prophet and his companions, focused on service to the entire world. He would probably add, though, that his work would not be worthy to be named in one breath with the Prophet and his early followers.

One of the reasons why there is a scarcity of literature concerning the relationship between Gülen's thought and the basic sources of Islam is that this relationship seems to be a matter of fact for Muslims who are inspired by Gülen's thought. They do not need

4. İsmail Albayrak, ed., *Mastering Knowledge in Modern Times: Fethullah Gülen as an Islamic Scholar* (New York: Blue Dome Press, 2011).

to dwell on the subject, as they see this relationship in all facets of Gülen's life. Some of the theologians who are close to Hocaefendi's thinking have paid attention to the relationship between his thought and the basic sources of Islam in their publications in Turkish, for instance Ali Ünal in his portrait of Fethullah Gülen's thought.[5] The Turkish contributors to the only book about Gülen as an Islamic scholar have also noted this relationship. Yet, as far as I know, Western scholars have not paid attention to this aspect of Gülen's work thus far. Therefore it makes sense to add a paragraph on the specific role of the Qur'ān in Gülen's writings here.

In the previous chapter, when discussing Fethullah Gülen's works, I have suggested that there might be a difference between an "esoteric" or insider-oriented form of Gülen's discourse in which he mainly addresses the members of the *cemaat* or the wider Islamic community on the one hand, and an "exoteric" or outsider-oriented form of discourse in which he addresses the wider public. It seems obvious that Gülen would use references to the Qur'ān and other sources of Islamic theology mainly in his esoteric discourse. Also, one might be inclined to look for references to the Qur'ān mainly in the earlier phase of Gülen's life, when he became famous among Muslims in Turkey because of his widely disseminated sermons (*vaazlar*) and religious conversations in the form of questions and answers (*sohbetler*), with the understanding that these sermons and instructions mainly functioned as contemporary explanations and interpretations of the Qur'ān and the *Sunna* of Prophet Muhammad. However, this would wrongly imply that references to the Qur'ān would be less prominent or visible in Gülen's later writings or in the writings he addressed to a larger public. As I wrote in chapter three, I was – following Bekim Agai's analysis – inclined to see a development from an esoteric toward a more exoteric discourse in Gülen's works, but contacts with some of Hocaefendi's supporters in Izmir, and a closer analysis of Gülen's recent articles as posted on

5. Ali Ünal, *M. Fethullah Gülen: Bir Portre Denemesi* [Essay of a portrait] (Izmir: Nil yayınları, 2002); summary in Ali Ünal, *Geçmişten Geleceğe Köprü Fethullah Gülen* (Istanbul: Işık yayınları, 2006).

the English version of his website, taught me that there have been esoteric and exoteric strands in Gülen's discourse all along.

The role of the Qur'ān as primary source of M. Fethullah Gülen's thought can be seen in two ways: in theoretical reflections on the Qur'ān at places in his works where Gülen explicitly discusses the Qur'ān, and at a more practical level in references to the Qur'ān throughout his works. At the theoretical level, the importance of the Qur'ān is highlighted in Gülen's most explicitly theological works, for instance in his book *Essentials of the Islamic Faith*.[6] The two volumes of *Questions and Answers about Islam* go back to a series of *sohbetler*, and they contain a few chapters on the Qur'ān as well.[7] The most recent theoretical reflection by Gülen on the Qur'ān is the article "On the Holy Qur'ān and Its Interpretation" that he wrote as an introduction to Ali Ünal's English interpretation of the Qur'ān.[8] In this introduction, which is included among the recent articles on Gülen's website in English as well,[9] Gülen expresses an attitude of religious awe when confronted with the Qur'ān; he confesses that he is not able to elaborate on the depth of meaning and the richness of expression and style of the Qur'ān, and that it is impossible to give a sufficient interpretation of it. As the Word of God, it is unique and untranslatable in human words. Nevertheless, it is necessary to render the contents of the Qur'ān in other languages, and to do so in a way that does justice both to the tradition of Qur'ānic exposition (*tafsīr*) and to the light of the mind and the rays of the heart. Gülen describes Ünal's interpretation of the Qur'ān – in which one often can find quotations from both Said Nursi and from Gülen himself – as an interpretation that is imbued with love for the truth

6. M. Fethullah Gülen, *Essentials of the Islamic Faith* (Fairfax, Va: The Fountain, 2000), 257–94.

7. M. Fethullah Gülen, *Questions and Answers about Islam, 1* (Somerset, N.J.: The Light, 2006), 79–109; *Questions and Answers about Islam,* 2 (Somerset, N.J: The Light, 2005), 3–32.

8. M. Fethullah Gülen, "On the Holy Qur'ān and Its Interpretation," in *The Qur'ān with Annotated Interpretation in Modern English by Ali Ünal* (Somerset, N.J.: The Light, 2006), xxxv–xlvi.

9. See http://www.fgulen.org/recent-articles/2266-on-the-holy-quran-and-its-interpretation.html, accessed July 26, 2010.

and a desire for learning, while at the same time having recourse to contemporary interpretations and commentaries, and articulating important things in today's language.[10]

At the more practical level, the Qur'ān is used by Gülen as a point of departure for some of his reflections. In earlier publications, I have tried to show how this is the case in Gülen's publications about the necessity of interreligious dialogue,[11] and about peace as the hermeneutical key to the Qur'ān.[12] At this place, it is important to mention that some of Gülen's works are built around themes that have their origin in the Qur'ān although they have been developed further in the Islamic tradition. This is certainly the case in the books that many would consider the most important of Gülen's writings, namely his discussion of basic Sufi terminology in the four volumes of *Emerald Hills of the Heart*.[13] According to Gülen, Sufism is immediately connected with the "Muhammadan Truth," and is "nothing more than the spirit of the Shari'a."[14] In Gülen's view, the key concepts of Sufism have their origin in the Qur'ān and the life of Prophet Muhammad and his companions. Therefore, Gülen takes great care to examine the connection between these Sufi notions and the Qur'ān as their origin. The same connection is one of the central topics in many of the spiritual meditations, for instance those assembled in the book *Vuslat Muştusu* ("The Good News of Meeting with God"), but it is also one of the

10. Gülen, "On the Holy Qur'ān and Its Interpretation," xlii-iii.

11. Pim Valkenberg, "Fethullah Gülen's Contribution to Muslim-Christian Dialogue in the Context of Abrahamic Cooperation," in *Islam in the Contemporary World 1: The Fethullah Gülen Movement in Thought and Practice* (Somerset, N.J.: Tughra Books, 2009), 1–10.

12. Gürkan Çelik and Pim Valkenberg, "Gülen's Approach to Dialogue and Peace: Its Theoretical Background and Some Practical Perspectives," *International Journal of Diversity in Organisations, Communities and Nations* 7, no.1 (2007): 29–37; Pim Valkenberg, "Fethullah Gülen and Peace as Horizon of Tolerance and Dialogue," in *Preventing Violence and Achieving World Peace*, ed. Ori Z. Soltes and Margaret A. Johnson (New York: Peter Lang, 2013), 41–53.

13. English translations published by The Light and later Tughra Books in New Jersey between 2004 and 2010.

14. M. Fethullah Gülen, *Emerald Hills of the Heart: Key Concepts in the Practice of Sufism, 1*, trans. Ali Ünal (Rutherford, N.J.: The Light, 2004), xviii.

main concerns in books of a more theological nature, for instance in a book on the intricate concept of *qadr or qudra*, which can be translated as fate, destiny, a decree of God, or the power of God.[15]

The theoretical and practical levels come together in a few publications in which Gülen explicitly engages in interpreting selected texts from the Qur'ān. When I started the research for this book, I could only find a small sample of such texts on Gülen's English website: four meditations published in 2008 under the heading "Reflections on the Quran."[16] Meanwhile, a book with the same title was published in 2012, containing more than one hundred short reflections on selected versions of the Qur'ān.[17] In his foreword to the 2012 book, Professor Suat Yıldırım says that it is immediately clear that Gülen has a thorough knowledge of the classical commentary tradition, and that he pairs this knowledge with original insights while still "remaining within the boundaries of the science of qur'anic exegesis."[18] Yet the most important aspect of Gülen's contribution to the interpretation of the Qur'ān is that he creates guidelines for contemporary Muslims in their daily lives and actions. In this aspect, his exegesis functions like the famous contemporary interpretations by Sayyid Qutb and Mawdūdī.[19] I think that Yıldırım is right in pointing out the parallel with the famous interpretations by Qutb and Mawdūdī, even though their interpretation of the relation between Islam and politics is very different from Gülen's. Yet in all cases the success of a particular interpretation of the Qur'ān is connected to its influence in the daily lives of Muslims, and in that sense

15. See M. Fethullah Gülen, *Vuslat muştusu* (Istanbul: Gazeteciler ve Yazarlar Vakfı Yayınları, 2008); M. Fethullah Gülen, *Kader. Kitap ve sünnet perspektifinde* (Istanbul: Nil Yayınları, 2009).

16. www.fethullahgulen.org/reflections-on-the-quran, accessed July 7, 2009. This website is no longer available; the new website (accessed June 19, 2014) now contains materials from the book "Reflections on the Qur'ān" (see next footnote).

17. M. Fethullah Gülen, *Reflections on the Qur'ān: Commentaries on Selected Verses,* trans. Ayşenur Kaplan and Harun Gültekin (Clifton, N.J.: Tughra Books, 2012).

18. Suat Yıldırım, "Foreword," in Gülen, *Reflections on the Qur'ān*, vii. Yıldırım's foreword is also included in the original Turkish version, *Kur'ân'dan İdrake Yansıyanlar* (Istanbul: Nil Yayınları, 2009).

19. Yıldırım, "Foreword," xvi.

Gülen's interpretations for those belonging to the Hizmet Movement function similarly to the interpretations of Qutb or Mawdūdī for Muslims belonging to Islamist movements. Gülen interprets the Qur'ān as a scholar in a specific tradition, but he provides guidance to Muslims who are looking for an interpretation of the Qur'ān that helps them in their *hizmet* activities. Yıldırım makes quite clear that Gülen specifically addresses Muslims in his interpretation, even though he does not specifically exclude others; yet, such an interpretation makes sense only for those who are willing to take the Qur'ān for what it claims to be: God's guidance for our lives. While many Muslims would probably emphasize the "liberal" or "democratic" nature of Gülen's interpretations, and contrast these with Qutb's and Mawdūdī's interpretations, non-Muslims like me will rather emphasize how obviously this "esoteric" strand in Gülen's discourse functions among Muslims only. Non-Muslims might find some of the interpretations interesting or stimulating, but they will not easily accept them as guidelines for their lives.

As I said before, I do not mention this difference between how Muslims and non-Muslims will read these works in order to distance myself from Gülen; quite the contrary, as a theologian studying a theologian from another tradition, I expect him to be true to the sources of his tradition. My point is that this is a type of discourse that functions well within the *cemaat* and the broader circle of those who belong to the Hizmet Movement, but causes ambiguity when the "esoteric" strand in Gülen's discourse is allowed to stand unmediated next to the "exoteric" strand in his discourse. Outsiders may think that the movement has a hidden agenda since the two types of discourse stand in tension to each other.

Let me give an example of what I mean. It is a well-known fact that the Qur'ān in some of its first surahs engages in a sometimes polemical discussion with the so-called "People of the Book," mainly Jews and Christians.[20] While Qutb's and Mawdūdī's inter-

20. I hope to be able to publish more about this topic in the near future. Meanwhile, see Mun'im Sirry, *Scriptural Polemics: The Qur'ān and Other Religions* (Oxford: Oxford University Press, 2014).

pretations of these verses apply the polemics to the contemporary political situation in which they write, Gülen seems to do something very similar. A first example comes from his interpretation of the second surah of the Qur'ān, *al-baqara* (2:78), "Among them are the unlettered folk who do not know anything about the Book except from hearsay, and they merely follow their conjectures."[21] Gülen starts his commentary as follows:

> This verse describes those who set their hearts on fantasies and utopias instead of the true religion throughout history. In fact, Marxism, communism, and capitalism are based on such conjectures, fantasies, and utopias that have their source in escape from the religion. Unfortunately, such history has repeated itself around these fancies; Jews were followed by Christians in wandering blindly on in such fancies and fantasies, and so were Christians followed by some Muslims.[22]

Gülen seems to make an association between those who are given to such "fancies from hearsay" in the present, namely communists and capitalists, and those who have been given to them historically: Christians following Jews, and some Muslims following Christians. The source for this association is a *hadith* in which Muhammad identifies Jews and Christians as the people who lead Muslims astray. Gülen also gives a short commentary on the famous "Common Word" verse that has often been quoted by Muslims as a source for better Muslim-Christian relations. The verse has given its name to a famous initiative by Jordanian prince Ghazi bin Muhammad.[23] It invites the People of the Book to come to a common word between us and you. Gülen interprets this verse as a reminder to Christians and Jews to go back to the things they knew but had forgotten or remembered incorrectly. This is the method of dialogue, according to Gülen, but the People of the Book need purification in order

21. Qur'ān 2:78 according to the interpretation by Ali Ünal, *The Qur'ān with Annotated Interpretation in Modern English*.

22. Gülen, *Reflections on the Qur'ān*, 26.

23. See www.acommonword.com; and *A Common Word: Muslims and Christians on Loving God and Neigbor*, ed. Miroslav Volf, Ghazi bin Muhammad, and Melissa Yarrington (Grand Rapids, Mich.: William B. Eerdmans, 2010).

to arrive at this common word. Why? Because they associated partners with God, began attributing sons or daughters to God, fell into errors such as the Trinity, and gave their rabbis and priests divine functions.[24] As far as I can tell from my studies of the *tafsīr* tradition on this verse, Gülen's interpretation is absolutely correct according to the mainstream Muslim tradition, and his invitation to Christians to purify themselves in order to collaborate with Muslims sounds very much like Said Nursi. Yet it does not seem that he talks to his dialogue partners in texts such as this; here he is clearly addressing a Muslim public, and texts addressed to his dialogue partners are of a different nature. "The People of the Book are offered bridges and entrances."[25] That is correct, but they will have to move, not the Muslims, according to the metaphor applied here. I do not criticize this metaphor as being not oriented enough toward dialogue, as some of my colleagues might do; quite the contrary, I think that Gülen is more correct in his interpretation than those who want to make the "Common word verse" a pluralist manifesto. But the point I want to make is that in his "Reflections on the Qur'ān" he clearly speaks to his Muslim friends and supporters about divine guidance for their engagement in dialogue. Yet when he directly addresses the topic of dialogue, or when he wants to address his partners in dialogue, he speaks in a different, much more general mode of discourse. I will give more examples of this in chapter six when explicitly discussing the topic of interreligious dialogue.

Another book with reflections on the Qur'ān has not yet been translated. In it, Gülen gives a general introduction to the Qur'ān and proceeds with an interpretation of *surat al-fātiha*, the first "chapter" of the Qur'ān that is of special importance in the daily prayer of Muslims.[26] This book is a good example of the way in which Gülen pairs traditional Islamic scholarship with contemporary insights. Just like Said Nursi in his book on the inimitability

24. Gülen, *Reflections on the Qur'ān*, 69.

25. Ibid., 1.

26. M. Fethullah Gülen, *Fatiha Üzerine Mülâhazalar* (Istanbul: Nil Yayınları, 2007).

(*iʿjāz*) of the Qur'ān, Gülen draws attention to the grammatical analysis of the root meanings and the order of the words in the Qur'ān.[27] He does not forget to mention the classical interpretations through collections of *hadīth* (stories about the example of Prophet Muhammad and his companions) and the works of *tafsīr* (qur'ānic exegesis). Someone who is more well-versed than I am in Turkish will better be able to appreciate the poetical style of many of Gülen's texts, with many metaphors and ornate descriptions. At the same time – as with every good sermon – his style is not too difficult, and the structure of his thoughts is very clear, so that anyone with a moderate mastery of language and religion should be able to follow his thoughts. Most scholars would agree that Gülen is not very original in his interpretations of the Qur'ān, but he is able to convey its spiritual significance to a larger public.

One of the reasons for paying so much attention to the qur'ānic background of Gülen's thought – apart from my own theological bias, of course – is that this background is not always visible for those who read his works without being familiar with the religion of Islam. As I argued before, many of Gülen's works can be read at a more general level without much knowledge of Islam. This is even one of the reasons why he is so successful in addressing non-Muslims and inspiring a general public with his words. However, this may often lead to the problem that I addressed at the end of the first chapter: people who are critical of Gülen assume that he has a so-called "hidden agenda" or that he even deliberately misleads the larger public by posing as a democrat while he secretly wants to introduce *shariʿah*. At the end of chapter two, I referred to a few anti-Gülen websites in the United States; the following quotation may be representative of what many people who are suspicious of Gülen may think: "in his public statements, Gulen espouses a liberal version of Sunni/Hanafi Islam and promotes the Muslim notion of hizmet – altruistic service to the common good.... In private,

27. Said Nursi, *Signs of Miraculousness: The Inimitability of the Qur'ān's Conciseness*, trans. Şükran Vahide (Istanbul: Sözler Neşriyat, 2004). (In the original Arabic: *Ishārāt al-Iʿjāz fi mazann al-Ijāz*, 1918.)

Gulen has stated that 'in order to reach the ideal Muslim society, every method and path is acceptable, [including] lying to people.'"[28] The author does not give a source of this quotation, but it sounds as though it comes from one of Gülen's sermons that has been manipulated to suggest a secret plot.[29] Such allegations misjudge the role of religion in general and of references to the Qur'ān in particular in Gülen's work: both are very important at the personal level for Gülen and those he inspired, but they are not meant as a blueprint to restructure society. In this sense, Gülen and his Hizmet Movement are unmistakably modern, since they accept the separation of religion from politics. Religion is important for private life and personal ethics, but one will not find any "Gülenist" mosque, let alone a "Gülenist" political party. In order to understand this, it is important to pay more attention to the way in which Gülen interprets the Qur'ān in his works.

GÜLEN'S METHODOLOGY IN INTERPRETING THE QUR'ĀN

It is important to state right away that Gülen's methodology in interpreting the Qur'ān can only be truly understood when it is compared to Said Nursi's interpretation in his *Risale-i Nur*. In that sense, much of the exposition on Nursi later in this chapter is relevant for this section as well.

To my knowledge, Faruk Tuncer is the first theologian to give an interpretation of Gülen's methodology of interpreting the Qur'ān, in his presentation on the "Gülen Movement" at a conference in Dallas in 2006.[30] Tuncer draws attention to two significant

28. Quotation from an entry by Paul Williams on www.familysecuritymatters.org, article dated April 7, 2010 (accessed May 7, 2010).

29. Muhammed Çetin, *The Gülen Movement: Civic Service without Borders* (New York: Blue Dome Press, 2009), 73.

30. An unedited version has been published as Faruk Tuncer, "Fethullah Gülen's Methodology of Interpreting Quran," in *Islam in the Contemporary World 2. The Fethullah Gülen Movement in Thought and Practice*, Conference Proceedings, Southern Methodist University, Dallas, Tex., March 4–5, 2006 (Somerset, N.J.: Tughra Books,

quotations in which Gülen shows how the Qur'ān functions in his thinking. The first quotation is from Gülen's considerations on *surat al-fatiha* and is translated by Tuncer as follows:[31]

> Quran is a translation of this universe as a book. Yes, the universe is a book. It is needed for a reader to read this book, which is well-organized with all of its verses and pages. The reader is human and the interpretation of this book is Quran. Allah has sent Quran as a translation of the universe to the human beings who cannot grasp the universe's immense, deep meaning and its huge vision. This meaning that we cannot easily understand by looking at the big pages and phrases of the universe, we can see at a first glance in the Quran, the Miraculous. This is a favor for the human beings. Allah is the one to make the universe book speak. As the others' thoughts upon the universe would be wrong, it is also the same with humans. The Universe is the universe of Allah, Quran is the speech of Allah and humans are the slaves of Allah. Allah is the one to establish the interrelation between these three.

In this quotation, Gülen refers to a tradition that can be found in both Islam and Christianity: the idea of the "two books" that display the Creator of heaven and earth: the book of the universe and the book of the revelation. In Islam, this tradition is particularly associated with the word *āya,* which can have the meaning of a verse in the Qur'ān, and of a sign of God's presence and of God's works in nature. The Qur'ān regularly refers to such signs of God in nature, for instance: "Surely in the creation of the heavens and the earth, and the alternation of night and day (with their periods shortening and lengthening), and the vessels sailing in the sea with profit to people, and the water that God sends down from the sky, therewith reviving the earth after its death and dispersing therein all kinds of living creatures, and His disposal of the winds, and the clouds subservient between the sky and earth – surely there are

---

2009), 89–103. It can also be found on Gülen's website in English: http://fgulen.com/en/gulen-movement/conference-papers/the-fethullah-gulen-movement-ii/25610-fethullah-gulens-methodology-of-interpreting-quran.

31. Originally: Gülen, *Fatiha Üzerine Mülâhazalar*, 46; Tuncer, "Fethullah Gülen's Methodology of Interpreting Quran," 89–90.

signs (demonstrating that He is the One God deserving worship, and the sole Refuge and Helper) for a people who reason and understand."[32] The idea that a rational observation of nature leads us to consider God as its origin is one of the main themes in the *Risale-i Nur* by Said Nursi, as I will show later in this chapter. For Gülen (as for Nursi) the rational observation of nature leads to the conclusion that there is a harmony of religion and science in Islam. Just like the tradition of "natural theology" in Christianity, this tradition states that it is possible to find signs of God's existence in the whole of creation. But at the same time – again, there is an analogy in Christianity – the consideration of nature is not enough; since we are weak and our knowledge is deficient, we need more guidance, a more conspicuous sign of God, and that has been given to us in God's Word through revelation. While Islam points to the Qur'ān as God's Word revealed to Prophet Muhammad, Christianity sees the Word of God embodied in the person of Jesus Christ. It is quite significant that the two "heavenly religions" here both display an analogous structure – God can be known through nature and more clearly through revelation – and an essential difference – God's Word is to be found in the Qur'ān or in Christ. A second difference is that Christians would see the Word of God in Christ not only as revealing but as saving as well, while Muslims do not see the Qur'ān as a saving word but as a guiding word. The idea of humanity's sinful character and the need for revelation that is essential to some forms of Christianity, is absent in Islam.

In the quotation given above, Gülen adds a third element to this tradition of the "two books" of nature and Qur'ān: the human being itself is also related to God as its Creator. And it is God as the universal Creator who constitutes the relationship between the three: universe, book, and human beings. The same idea returns in the second significant quotation given by Tuncer in his article, this time from Gülen's treatment of the Qur'ān in *Essentials of the Islamic Faith*.[33]

32. Qur'ān, *al-baqara* (2:164), in the interpretation by Ünal, *The Qur'ān with Annotated Interpretation in Modern English.*

33. Gülen, *Essentials of the Islamic Faith*, 262.

The Qur'an also unveils the mystery of humanity, creation, and the universe. The Qur'an, humanity and the universe are the three "books" that make the Creator known to us, and are three expressions of the same truth. Therefore, the One Who created humanity and the universe also revealed the Qur'an.

Gülen uses this image of the universe, human beings, and the Qur'ān as three books to make clear that Islam teaches the harmony of the sciences and the humanities on the one hand, and revelation on the other hand. Yet there is a difference, since faith in God's revelation is the only knowledge that will lead to the afterlife. Again, this concept of revelation as necessary for human beings to reach their ultimate goal has a clear parallel in Christianity, where Thomas Aquinas, for instance, says that we can gain some knowledge of God by using the insights of the philosophers, but we need the knowledge of God's revelation to reach our ultimate goal with God. This basic insight, gained in the very first article of Aquinas's *Summa Theologiae,* is unfolded in the structure of this theological masterpiece as follows: the first book discusses God as Creator of the universe; the second book discusses human beings and their moral lives as a way toward God, and the third book discusses Christ and the sacraments as guidance that God gave us to help us on our way to God.[34] Although Gülen would not agree with all the phrases used by Aquinas, he might see an interesting parallel with his concept of the three books – universe, human beings, Qur'ān – that guide us to knowledge not only of the world here and now but also to knowledge of the afterlife.

In this respect, it is significant that the Qur'ān in the first *āya,* after the opening prayer and the *basmala,* introduces itself as a book of guidance; "This is the (most honored, matchless) Book: there is no doubt about it (its Divine authorship and that it is a collection of pure truths throughout); a perfect guidance for the

34. Wilhelmus G. B. M. Valkenberg, *Words of the Living God: Place and Function of Holy Scripture in the Theology of St. Thomas Aquinas*, Publications of the Thomas Instituut te Utrecht 6 (Leuven: Peeters, 2000).

God-revering, pious, who keep their duty to God."[35] This is the second verse that Gülen explains in his collection of *Reflections on the Qur'an.* This explanation of the verse is quite technical since it discusses the indefinite form of the Arabic word *hudan* (a guidance) that, according to Arabic grammar, indicates perfect meaning. It indicates that God has given us a perfect guidance, however, we will not be able to attain perfection without making an effort. Gülen uses this insight to say that the Qur'ān is a perfect and transcending divine guide for the pious who "are ready to comply with both the commandments of the Religion ... and the principles that are in effect in nature."[36] However, he points to a different use of the concept of "guidance" a bit later in the same *sura,* "those (illustrious ones) stand on true guidance (originating in the Qur'ān) from their Lord; and they are those who are the prosperous."[37] Gülen explains that the word *hudan* here is in the form of a verbal noun, implying God's creation, while the indefinite form implies human responsibility. As Gülen himself indicates, this detailed analysis can be found in the works of Said Nursi, for instance in his *Signs of Miraculousness* where Nursi discusses the inimitability *(i'jāz)* of the Qur'ān's conciseness, and where he refers to the two different constructions of the word "guidance" as well.[38] Gülen, however, uses this difference to make a theological point, namely that God bestows God's guidance on all human beings, but it is the responsibility of God-fearing people to use this guidance on their way to God. I quote the conclusion from the meditation on "perfect guidance."[39]

As far as we can deduce from the expression of "*for the God-revering, pious,*" how one attains such guidance is by attaining a true level of piety. Faith

35. Qur'ān, *al-baqara* (2:2), in the interpretation by Ünal, *The Qur'ān with Annotated Interpretation in Modern English.*

36. Gülen, *Reflections on the Qur'ān*, 3.

37. Qur'ān, *al-baqara* (2:5), in the interpretation by Ünal, *The Qur'ān with Annotated Interpretation in Modern English.*

38. Nursi, *Signs of Miraculousness,* 46 and 69 respectively.

39. Gülen, *Reflections on the Qur'ān*, 3–4.

and knowledge of God are the first steps of progress on this path, the last being the good pleasure of God Almighty. Finally, as clearly expressed in the verse, only those who can live up to such guidance will attain salvation. It can be derived from the context of this last verse that "*guidance*" is dependent upon God's having created it. However, the behavior and preferences adopted through the exercise of free will on the part of the human beings are necessary if such guidance is to ensure safety and comfort in this world and if it is to become a means of salvation in the Hereafter. To conclude, the first "*guidance*" is a cause and the second one is a blissfully granted result. Both are an answer to the prayer of "*ihdinā*" or "*Guide us* to the straight path" found in the previous chapter al-Fātihah (1:6), while serving as guidelines for those on the road."

This quotation shows some of the major characteristics of Gülen's methodology in interpreting the Qur'ān. His interpretation is entirely in line with the mainstream Islamic tradition in both its intellectual aspects — the problem of God's omnipotence and human free will — and its spiritual aspects — the role of faith and knowledge as steps of progress on the path (*tarīqa*) with God's good pleasure as the goal.[40] While Said Nursi is a representative source for the intellectual interpretation of the Qur'ān in Gülen's works, Jalāl al-dīn Rūmī is a representative source for its spiritual interpretation. But the entire explanation of the word "guidance" in Gülen matches with the other Abrahamic traditions as well, since it wonderfully interprets what David Burrell has pointed out as a basic idea in the three Abrahamic religions: the notion of "created freedom."[41]

As Tuncer points out in his article, Gülen is aware that every human interpretation of the Qur'ān is an imperfect interpretation.[42] He says that, although you may be convinced that your interpretation of the Qur'ān is the truth, it is always better to leave open the possibilities for other interpretations and thus to say "this is the

40. The notion of "God's pleasure" (*rıza-i İlahi* in Turkish, *ridwan Ilahi* in Arabic) will be an important key to our analysis of the formation of the Hizmet Movement in chapter five of this book.

41. David B. Burrell, CSC, *Faith and Freedom. An Interfaith Perspective* (Malden, Mass.: Blackwell Publishing, 2004).

42. Tuncer, "Fethullah Gülen's Methodology of Interpreting Quran," 91.

truth but it may be interpreted differently." Again, this is no innovation since it is the meaning of the traditional phrase with which most Muslim interpreters ended their commentaries in the tradition of *tafsīr,* namely *Allahu a'lam*: God knows better. Yet Gülen seems to be more aware than traditional *mufassirun* (commentators) that this principle of "God knows better" leads to an openness toward the future and toward nontraditional interpretations. Gülen shows this awareness when discussing the relation between the Qur'ān and science.[43] Since the Qur'ān is the Word of God, some pious Muslims believe that it contains all the scientific truths as well, and they search for indications that the Qur'ān has foreseen all technological developments. At this point, Gülen warns that we should keep a "balanced interpretation": "Everything is contained in the Qur'an, but at different levels. Therefore, not everything is readily apparent. The Qur'an's main duty is to teach about God's perfection, essential qualities, and acts, as well as our duties, status, and how to serve Him."[44]

So we should keep in mind the main purpose for which God has revealed the Qur'ān, and we should refrain from interpretations that narrow down the meanings of the Qur'ān to a specific interpretation that might hinder us from seeing the larger context. For instance, if we want to see a reference to AIDS in Qur'ān 27:82,[45] we make the mistake of jumping to conclusions without envisaging the broader context of possible meanings of the Qur'ān. "So, we must not show haste in trying to find some type of correspondence between a Qur'anic verse and every new development in science and technology."[46] The "balanced," meditative reading of the Qur'ān that Gülen embodies in his own life and commends to his

43. Gülen, *Essentials of the Islamic Faith*, 271–91.

44. Ibid., 268.

45. Qur'ān, *an-naml* (27:82), in the interpretation by Ünal, *The Qur'ān with Annotated Interpretation in Modern English*: "When the time for the fulfillment of the word (of punishment) about them comes, We will bring forth for them a living creature from the earth who will speak to them – that people have no certainty of faith in Our signs and Revelations," Ünal, 2006: 601

46. Gülen, *Essentials of the Islamic Faith*, 276.

followers, forms a stark contrast to the overhasty and narrowing interpretations of some literalist and fundamentalist Muslims. Again, the same tension is visible in Christianity where the belief in the Bible as God's word also may lead to the idea that "the Bible contains all truths" and "the Bible is always right." Of course, Gülen would agree that the Qur'ān contains all truth and that – being the Word of God – it is always right. But he would also say that in our interpretation of the Qur'ān we would have to make a distinction between the main reason for which the Qur'ān has been revealed – to function as our guidance on our way to God – and everything else that might be interesting but of secondary importance. As Gülen says at the end of his *Essentials of the Islamic Faith*: what ultimately counts is our faith (*iman*), not the amount of our knowledge.

> After we have understood as much as we can about the objective and subjective evidence we have gathered, we must break our dependence on the outer circumstances, qualities, and conditions of such evidence. Only by doing this will we be able to make any spiritual progress. When we abandon this dependence and follow our heart and conscience within the Qur'ān's light and guidance, then, if God wills, we will find the enlightenment for which we are looking. As the German philosopher Immanuel Kant once said: "I felt the need to leave behind all the books I have read in order to believe in God."
>
> Undoubtedly, the grand Book of the Universe and the book of humanity's true nature, as well as their commentaries, have their proper place and significance. But after we use them, we should put them aside and live with our iman, as it were, face to face. This might sound rather abstract to those who have not gone deep into the experience of faith and conscience. But for those whose nights are bright with devotion, and who acquire wings through their longing to aspire to their Lord, the meaning is clear.[47]

This quotation may serve as the conclusion to stress the core value of personal faith in God in Gülen's interpretation of the Qur'ān, but it may just as well serve as the introduction to the influence of Sufism in general and of Jalāl al-dīn Rūmī in particular

47. Gülen, *Essentials of the Islamic Faith*, 290–91.

on his theology. But first I want to compare Tuncer's analysis—and my interpretation of that analysis—with the more comprehensive view of Fethullah Gülen as interpreter of the Qur'ān, given by Professor İsmail Albayrak in the first chapter of his book devoted to *Fethullah Gülen as an Islamic Scholar*.[48] One of the main points for Gülen in his approach to the Qur'ān, according to Albayrak, is not to narrow down God's guidance to something that only appeals to the intellectual or the esthetical or the ethical dimensions of humanity. If the Qur'ān is a book of guidance, it should guide our entire life as human beings, specifically our actions.[49] He also emphasizes the fact that the Qur'ān, because of its inimitability, can never be adequately explained or translated; Albayrak concludes from this that Gülen probably has a better understanding of the limits of any human interpretation of God's Word than most classical or modern commentators. Yet we should study the Qur'ān meticulously because every word and every sentence is part of a harmonious order of its own kind.[50] But maybe the most important contribution that Albayrak makes in his article is to show how Gülen tries to give a balanced interpretation in which he does justice to a number of different approaches to the Qur'ān (mystical, theological, legal, scientific approaches), however without letting one approach become dominant over the others. He comes to the conclusion that Gülen is a fine representative of a somewhat overlooked Ottoman exegetical school that tries to do justice to both classical and modern approaches. On the one hand, he is clearly rooted in the classical tradition; on the other hand the stress on interfaith dialogue in his life and work causes him to engage a number of nonclassical and even non-Islamic sources.[51]

In the last chapter of the book *Fethullah Gülen as an Islamic Scholar*, Ergün Çapan allows those of us who are outsiders to the

48. İsmail Albayrak, "Fethullah Gülen's Approach to Qur'anic Exegesis," in *Mastering Knowledge in Modern Times: Fethullah Gülen as an Islamic Scholar*, ed. İsmail Albayrak (New York: Blue Dome Press, 2011), 1–37.

49. Albayrak, "Fethullah Gülen's Approach to Qur'anic Exegesis," 6–7.

50. Ibid., 11.

51. Ibid., 37.

cemaat a very interesting look into Gülen's teaching methodology.[52] In a detailed sketch he gives an impressive list of books that Gülen read when he was a student himself, but, more importantly, also a list of books that he reads together with his own students in his own private teaching. Such a list, for instance of books of qur'ānic exegesis (*tafsīr*), gives a good idea of the type of sources that Gülen uses in conversation with his students on a daily basis.[53] Even more interesting are the notes that Çapan gives about Gülen's actual teaching, including matters such as choice of books, teaching hours, methods of preparation, and teaching style. In the next chapters I will follow many others in stating that, according to Gülen, education is the most important task for a Muslim. If this is so — and the Hizmet Movement gives abundant evidence in this regard — one cannot imagine anything other than education being the main task that Gülen has set for himself. Consequently, Çapan's article gives a much better insight into how Gülen spends most hours of his day than do the fantasies spread by his many adversaries. The retreat center where Gülen lives in the Pocono Mountains of Pennsylvania is not an "Islamic armed fortress" as Paul Williams imagines, but a place of prayer and teaching. These characteristics bring us to Jalāl al-dīn Rūmī and Said Nursi, and their influence on Fethullah Gülen's works.

JALĀL AL-DĪN RŪMĪ AS A SOURCE OF GÜLEN'S THOUGHT

In a certain sense, it is easy to observe how Jalāl al-dīn Rūmī and Said Nursi still influence not only Gülen's discourse but also the movement that he inspired, and — in the case of Rūmī — even more the type of external discourse that the movement wants to

52. Ergün Çapan, "Gülen's Teaching Methodology in His Private Circle," in *Mastering Knowledge in Modern Times: Fethullah Gülen as an Islamic Scholar,* ed. İsmail Albayrak (New York: Blue Dome Press, 2011), 127–56.

53. Çapan, "Gülen's Teaching Methodology in His Private Circle," 130–32, gives a list of exegetical works. But the works of *hadith* (132–35), jurisprudence (135–37), mysticism (137–38), *kalām* (141–42), and grammar (138–40) are relevant as well.

communicate to outsiders. Therefore, some of the works by Rūmī and Nursi are sold – and sometimes donated – by publishers and organizations connected with the Hizmet Movement. At several conferences on the Gülen Movement in Europe (Turkey, Germany, and the Netherlands) and the United States, I saw Rūmī's and Nursi's books being displayed side by side with the books published by Gülen. The only other books that I saw during these conferences were books produced by influential Turkish scholars whose thought largely coincides with the general opinion of the volunteers inspired by Gülen, such as Ali Bulaç, Mehmet Ergene and Ali Ünal (in Germany I saw copies of Ali Ünal's translation of the Qur'ān in German). Since Jalāl al-dīn Rūmī, who lived from 1207 to 1273, wrote in a form that is not easy to understand without sufficient prior knowledge, many of the books displayed are not texts by Rūmī himself, but studies about his thought and practice, such as Şefik Can's masterful survey of Rūmī's life and thought, written from the perspective of a Mevlevi Sufi himself, and the volume edited by Fatih Çitlak and Hüseyin Bingül about Rūmī's path of love.[54] In the Netherlands, the Islam en Dialoog Foundation did not only publish an adapted version of the volume just mentioned, but it published a Dutch translation of the first book of Rūmī's *Masnevi* as well.[55] In the United States, in Washington, D.C., the Rumi Forum, one of the most important dialogue organizations to be discussed in chapter six, often uses the poems and the spirituality of Rūmī in its public statements. Both in the Netherlands and in the United States I had on several occasions the privilege to be invited to a dance of the whirling dervishes, sometimes in the form of a cultural event, but often in its real context: the liturgical *sema* in which the mystical dance

54. Şefik Can, *Fundamentals of Rumi's Thought: A Mevlevi Perspective,* Foreword by M. Fethullah Gülen, trans. Zeki Saritoprak and Cüneyt Eroğlu (Somerset, N.J.: The Light, 2004); M. Fatih Çitlak and Hüseyin Bingül, eds., *Rumi and His Sufi Path of Love* (Somerset, N.J.: The Light, 2007).

55. Emrullah Erdem, ed., *Mewlana Djalaladdin Rumi en zijn "mystieke pad van de liefde."* (Rotterdam: Stichting Islam en Dialoog, 2007); Abdulwahid van Bommel, *Het Lied van het Riet: Djalâluddîn Rûmî Masnawî.* Vertaald door Abdulwahid van Bommel (Amsterdam: Türkevi Productions, 2008).

finds its proper setting. Finally, the visit to Konya and the Mevlâna Müzesi (another religious place turned into a museum) with the Sufi lodge, the mosque and the dance floor, but also the tombs of Jalāl al-dīn Rūmī and his family and companions, is certainly one of the most popular sites in Turkey, not only for tourists, but for religious people in particular. It is therefore not surprising that many institutions – in particular the dialogue organizations – of the Hizmet Movement like to use the connection between Hocaefendi Gülen and Mevlana Rūmī in their external communication.

It is not so difficult to find traces of this relationship in Gülen's works. One of his main works and, according to several scholars certainly the most systematic fruit of his authorship, is the four-volume text of *Emerald Hills of the Heart: Key Concepts in the Practice of Sufism*, which is translated from the Turkish *Kalbin Zümrüt Tepeleri*. In these volumes, Gülen discusses a number of key terms in the teachings and practice of the Sufi *tariqa* (way or brotherhood). Although Rūmī is certainly not the only author quoted in these volumes, he is – probably together with Yunus Emre – the Sufi poet quoted most often throughout Gülen's works.

I think there are basically two reasons for the spiritual bond between Gülen and his supporters and Rūmī and his specific interpretation of the Sufi path. In the first place, Rūmī is just as centered on the relationship with God as the basis of the faith for Muslims as Gülen is. The quotation from *Essentials of the Islamic Faith* given in the previous section of this chapter clearly shows that *iman* or personal faith in God is the core of Islam for Gülen, and in fact the only thing that ultimately matters. The same is the case for Rūmī: the core of the *Mevlana* movement that is named after "Our Master" (*maulana*) Jalāl al-dīn Rūmī is the liturgy of the *sema* in which the dancers perform a *dhikr* (continuous remembrance of God). The second characteristic that unites both spiritual masters is the central place of the notion of love. Rūmī is known as the founder of the "Sufi Path of Love."[56] "Love" is also one of the central no-

56. See William Chittick, *The Sufi Path of Love: The Spiritual Teachings of Rumi* (Albany, N.Y.: State University of New York Press, 1983).

tions in Gülen's writings. In his introduction to Can's book about Rūmī, Gülen defends this notion as follows:

> Some people do not consider it proper to use the phrase "love of God" in the Islamic tradition. Like many of God's lovers, Rumi, in a way that is appropriate to the holiness and exaltedness of God, courageously defended that the concept of love of God should be above all human concepts of love and relationships. He left a legacy of ambiguous divine love which was open for interpretation to the generations that followed him.[57]

Earlier in the same introduction, Gülen adds something that is of paramount importance to a proper understanding of both Rūmī and Gülen: the "love of God" is deeply shaped by the Islamic tradition and therefore it goes together with a deep love for God's messenger, Prophet Muhammad. The same is the case with Gülen, as his eloquent book on Prophet Muhammad shows.[58] It is important to notice this, since Rūmī's popularity in the Western world leads many people to disregard the close connection between Sufism and Islam; while there are obviously non-Sufi ways to be a Muslim – Muslims in the tradition of Hanbalism and Wahhabism do not like Sufism – one has to stretch the historical meaning of the word "Sufism" to accommodate for non-Muslim Sufis.[59] In a similar way, many people do not see how Gülen's thinking is deeply rooted in the Muslim tradition. Being a non-Muslim myself, it might be easier for me to say this than for Muslims whose words might be taken as defensive by outsiders.

While the notion of "love" is central in the writings of both Rūmī and Gülen, there is another obvious difference in that Gülen concentrates more on "love" as an all-encompassing dimension of

57. Fethullah Gülen, "Introduction," in Can, *Fundamentals of Rumi's Thought*, xvii.

58. M. Fethullah Gülen, *Muhammad, the Messenger of God: Aspects of His Life* (Somerset, N.J: The Light, 2005).

59. This is not to deny the seriousness of those who claim to be Sufis without being Muslims, mainly in the United States, but to point to the historical fact that Sufism originated within the Muslim tradition. For a comprehensive survey of contemporary (Muslim and non-Muslim) interpretations of Rūmī, see Franklin D. Lewis, *Rumi: Past and Present, East and West: The Life, Teachings and Poetry of Jalāl al-Din Rumi* (Oxford: Oneworld, 2003).

human beings, and he tries to find ways to let this love be operative not only in religious and interpersonal relations, but in social and political relations as well. This is of course one of the major themes in Gülen's books on intercultural and interfaith dialogues, such as *Love and the Essence of Being Human* – my edition has a "whirling dervish" on its frontispiece – and *Toward a Global Civilization of Love and Tolerance*.[60]

Gülen describes the stress on love, tolerance, and openness that he shares with Mevlana Jalaluddin Rūmī as a specific kind of Islam. Sometimes, he refers to it as "Turkish Islam" or "Anatolian Islam" in contrast with Iranian or Arabian Islam. Sufism is certainly one of the most important dimensions of this form of Islam, as Gülen says in an interview with Nevval Sevindi.[61]

> Islam is one, but interpretations and practices are different. There is something called the Turkish Islamic conception. This is a conception that was formed by the thousand-year old Turkish culture and understanding, and reached its highest point with Yunus Emre and Mawlāna Jalāl al-Dīn Rūmī. Mawlana describes Sufism by saying: "They asked a divine what Sufism is; he said, finding space in the age of hardships." The Turkish Islamic conception is entwined with Sufism.

A bit later, Gülen says: "Arab Islam is based on fear of Allah, Turkish Islam is an Islamic understanding based on love of Allah."[62] At other places, Gülen connects this idea of an "Anatolian Islam" with greater openness to modernity, to democracy, to the equal place of women, and, last but not least, openness to other cultures and religions.[63]

60. M. Fethullah Gülen, *Love and the Essence of Being Human* (Istanbul: Journalists and Writers Foundation Publication, 2004); M. Fethullah Gülen, *Toward a Global Civilization of Love and Tolerance* (Somerset, N.J., 2004).

61. Nevval Sevindi, *Contemporary Islamic Conversations. M. Fethullah Gülen on Turkey, Islam, and the West* (Albany, N.Y.: State University of New York Press, 2008), 68.

62. Sevindi, *Contemporary Islamic Conversations*, 73.

63. These claims were discussed at the beginning of chapter two.

SAID NURSI AS A SOURCE OF GÜLEN'S THOUGHT

When Fethullah Gülen introduces Jalāl al-dīn Rūmī, he does so in terms that could be taken to refer to Said Nursi as well – and many of Gülen's followers would add that he might give a self-portrait here, although Gülen himself, in his humility, would deny this:

In addition to his ascetic life, his fear of God, his chastity, his divine protection from sinfulness, his self-sufficiency, and his pure life that was directed toward the world of the unseen, Rumi's knowledge of God, his love of God, and his utmost longing for God kept him, throughout his life, rising as one of the moons that illuminate the sky of sainthood. His love for God was one that surpassed the normal bounds of love – it was a transcendental love.[64]

It is also not difficult to show the influence of Bediüzzaman Said Nursi (1877–1960) and his *Risale-i Nur* collection on Fethullah Gülen and his followers. First of all, in many of his works Gülen follows Nursi's style of reasoning, so much so that one does not immediately notice that he adopts a number of arguments for God's unity from Nursi's *Words* at the beginning of his *Essentials of the Islamic Faith*.[65] The careful observation of nature leads both Nursi and Gülen to conclude that there is but one Creator of the universe. While Rūmī is the greatest poet of love in the Islamic tradition, Nursi is for Gülen the greatest interpreter of the signs of God in the universe and the Qur'ān. And yet the two approaches – love and knowledge – can go together very well as I hope to show.

Although Gülen could have met Nursi somewhere in Anatolia during his studies, in fact he did not meet him in person but became acquainted with the *Risale-i Nur* when he began to preach and teach in the years between 1955 and 1964. As several of Gülen's early com-

64. Gülen, "Introducion," in Can, *Fundamentals of Rumi's Thought*, xv.

65. Compare Gülen, *Essentials of the Islamic Faith*, 9–18, with Said Nursi, *The Words: From the Risale-i Nur Collection*, trans. from the Turkish by Şükran Vahide (Istanbul: Sözler Neşriyat, 1992), 299–317.

panions in Izmir told me, many people were reading works by Said Nursi at that time although it was illegal to study his works openly, and therefore many circles of readers of Said Nursi's works formed in private houses. Gülen soon noticed that Nursi's approach to religion and science had much in common with his own approach, and he began to join communities of readers of the *Risale-i Nur* during the early period of his preaching career. Being a member of the Nurcu community helped Gülen to gain some fame although it sometimes made relations with other Muslim communities more difficult. Gülen's ideas about religious education, and his first practical steps toward establishing summer camps, student dorms, and—a bit later—schools were obviously inspired by ideas in the Nurcu Movement.[66] Although Gülen has always denied his belonging to the Nurcu Movement in the strict sense of the word, some scholars see so many similarities that they write about Gülen's followers as the neo-Nur movement.[67] Indeed, I have often noticed that supporters of the Hizmet Movement refer not only to Gülen's thoughts but to Nursi's works as well. In the first years of its existence, the community gathered around Gülen read Nursi's works together, and it is still fairly common to do so in present-day *sohbetler* (religious lessons or conversations).[68]

Of course, there are differences between Gülen and Nursi; in this context, I want to point out two important differences. In the first place, Nursi is more straightforwardly an intellectual who—at least in the second period of his life, the so-called "New Said" in contrast with the "Old Said"—wants to concentrate on a life of study devoted to the Qur'ān.[69] Gülen is an intellectual as well, but

66. Bekim Agai, *Zwischen Netzwerk und Diskurs: Das Bildungsnetzwerk um Fethullah Gülen (geb. 1938): Die flexible Umsetzung modernen islamischen Gedankenguts* (Schenefeld: EB-Verlag, 2004), 140–45.

67. M. Hakan Yavuz, *Islamic Political Identity in Turkey* (New York: Oxford University Press, 2003), 179.

68. Joshua Hendrick, *Gülen: The Ambiguous Politics of Market Islam in Turkey and the World* (New York: New York University Press, 2013), 116.

69. Sükran Vahide, "Bediüzzaman Said Nursi and the *Risale-i Nur*," in *Globalization, Ethics and Islam. The Case of Bediuzzaman Said Nursi*, ed. Ian Markham and Ibrahim Ozdemir (Burlington, Vt.: Ashgate, 2005), 15.

he is much more interested in exploring the possibilities of translating intellectual ideas into practice, even though that aspect was not lacking in Nursi. Yavuz describes Gülen's ideas as a "theology of action," characterized by three traditional Islamic principles: "*hizmet* (rendering service to religion and state), *himmet* (giving donations and protecting good work), and *ihlas* (seeking God's appreciation for every action)."[70] The Jesuit theologian Thomas Michel compares Nursi and Gülen in terms of "thinker" and "activist" in a common project to further education among Muslims; while Nursi laid the foundation in his Risale-i Nur, Gülen put many of Nursi's ideas into practice and built a bridge to the Western world.[71] This comparison reminds me of the fruitful interaction between Ramakrishna (1836–86) and Vivekananda (1863–1902) in exporting neo-Hinduism to the Western world. Ramakrishna was a deep thinker and a devoted lover of the deity, who inspired many while his own frame of reference remained confined to the Indian subcontinent; Vivekananda popularized Ramakrishna's thinking and was able to translate neo-Hinduism to the Western world, for instance at the first Parliament of World Religions in Chicago.[72] In a similar way—and this is the second main difference between Nursi and Gülen—Said Nursi had the tendency to approach the West and its philosophers negatively, seeing them as antireligious. While the "Old Said" was interested in philosophy and sciences and involved in politics, the "New Said" decided to concentrate on the religious sciences of the Qur'ān only.[73] Although he sometimes wrote about the possibility for collaboration

70. Yavuz, *Islamic Political Identity in Turkey*, 186.

71. Thomas Michel, "Turkish Experience for Muslim-Christian Dialogue. A Thinker: B. S. Nursi; An Activist: M. F. Gülen," in *Travelling Together beyond Dialogue: Peace and Dialogue in a Plural Society: Common Values and Responsibilities* (Melbourne: Australian Intercultural Society, 2002), 33–40.

72. See Pim Valkenberg, *Sharing Lights on the Way to God: Muslim-Christian Dialogue and Theology in the Context of Abrahamic Partnership* (New York: Editions Rodopi, 2006), 309. For a similar exploration of the relationship between Said Nursi and Fethullah Gülen, see ibid., 313–17.

73. Vahide, "An Outline of Bediüzzaman Said Nursi's Views on Christianity and the West," 112.

between Muslims and Christians, this collaboration was mainly a defense against the powers of atheism. Consequently, although they are interested in the West, most followers of Said Nursi begin with other Islamic countries when they want to spread his writings. In the case of Gülen, it is quite clear that he and his network are interested in spreading their ideas primarily to Asian countries with Turkic roots in Asia and the former Soviet Union, secondarily to the Western world, and only thirdly to the Arabic-speaking Islamic nations.

Before ending this chapter by comparing the three authors discussed in the chapter as interpreters of God's Word in the Qur'ān, I want to mention a proposal that shows both the great similarity between Nursi and Gülen and the difference between them. It is the proposal for a university in Anatolia that was to combine traditional and modern teaching methods. Nursi, who was born in Nurs, a small village in the province of Bitlis in eastern Anatolia, wanted to establish a university in the nearby city of Van, in which the teaching of the religious sciences would be combined with the modern sciences.[74] Nursi proposed this idea for a university that would give new opportunities to this impoverished Anatolian – and largely Kurdish – region of Turkey, and he even secured some funding for a university (the Medresetü z-Zehrā) on the shores of Lake Van, but the World War I prevented its construction.[75] Gülen is said to have proposed a similar idea for a university where scholars and students from the three Abrahamic religions would come together, in Urfa or in Harran, two places in Anatolia associated with prophet Abraham.[76] Significantly, Gülen proposed the idea for this new university not to an Islamic leader, but to Pope John Paul II, the leader of another Abrahamic religion, when he visited him in 1998. As we have seen in the third chapter of this book,

74. Vahide, "Bediüzzaman Said Nursi and the *Risale-i Nur,*" 8.

75. Ibid., 19; also, Fred Reed, *Anatolia Junction* (Burnaby, Canada: Talon, 1999).

76. See texts and documents in *Fethullah Gülen: Advocate of Dialogue*, compiled by Ali Ünal and Alphonse Williams, trans, Ali Ünal (Fairfax, Va.: Fountain Publications, 2000), 284 and 294.

Gülen was one of the first Muslim leaders to visit the Vatican; this openness to equal dialogue marks a difference between him and Nursi, but once again this difference is not without similarity since, long before, Nursi had sent the pope a complimentary copy of his *Risale-i Nur*.

LOVE, YEARNING, AND AUSTERITY

In concluding this chapter I want to focus once more on the similarities between Jalaluddin Rūmī, Said Nursi, and Fethullah Gülen, repeating and deepening some of the elements that have been named already. First of all, the three authors may count as representatives of what Gülen in his interviews with Nevval Sevindi calls an "Anatolian style of Islam": an open, tolerant style of Islam with the love of God as its central focus. Even though Rūmī was born in present-day Afghanistan, he settled in Konya and is therefore considered a representative of the Anatolian Sufi tradition just like Nursi or Gülen, although neither has been a Sufi teacher or master *(shaykh)* in the traditional sense of the word. His name "Rūmī" refers to the land of the east Romans of Byzantium, whose capital was Constantinople (present-day Istanbul).

In his writings on love, tolerance, and dialogue, Gülen frequently refers to the models of Rūmī and Nursi who lived their lives with these concepts as central values. He likes to quote Nursi's words "love is the essence of creation."[77] The words "tolerance" and "dialogue" appear on almost every page of Gülen's writings, and he explains that a Muslim should by nature be inclined to dialogue and peace, since the very name *muslim* refers to someone with whom others may feel secure. He quotes the Prophet, saying that true Muslims are "those who harm no one with their words and actions, and who are the most trustworthy representatives of universal peace."[78]

Another aspect that Gülen mentions in referring to Rūmī that

77. *Fethullah Gülen: Advocate of Dialogue*, 195.
78. Ibid., 248.

may be just as true of Nursi—or Gülen himself—is the insight that love grows through hardships and suffering. For Rūmī, this yearning that grows out of suffering is a yearning for the lost participation in God, as expressed in the famous "Song of the Reed" at the beginning of his *Mathnawi,* in which the characteristic wailing sound of the *ney* (reed flute) is interpreted as its lamentation over being severed from its living roots on the river bank. Rūmī suffered in his own life, since he was forcefully separated from two of his best spiritual friends, Shams al-dīn Tabrizi and Husām al-dīn Chalabi. Nursi suffered in a different way, since he spent a number of years in prison or in isolation because of his resistance to the political changes during the transition from the Ottoman Empire to the secular Republic of Turkey. At least, Nursi's adversaries thought he was resisting; Nursi himself said he was not interested in politics anymore and only wanted to spread the message of the Qur'ān. Nursi interpreted his long imprisonment as a lesson that God wanted to give him in the "school of Joseph," referring to the prophet Joseph who "languished in prison for a number of years."[79] But for Nursi, the situation of loneliness and alienation caused him to find a new sense of community through faith in God, trust in God, and endurance.[80] Gülen was imprisoned in 1971 following accusations that were very similar to the accusations used against Said Nursi, and he describes his experiences as a "school of Joseph" as well.[81] Although Gülen was not imprisoned as long as Nursi, he has also lived a life of hardships, partially because of his poor health, but also because he chose the way of frugality and asceticism for himself. In his *Emerald Hills of the Heart,* he suggests that the notion of *taqwa* (piety; fearing God) on the way of the Sufi does not only imply a strict observance of *shari'ah* by avoiding what is forbidden, but also a cautious use of what is permitted. Gülen refers to a *hadith* that says: "A servant

79. Qur'ān, Yusuf (12:42), in the interpretation by Ünal, *The Qur'ān with Annotated Interpretation in Modern English.*

80. Valkenberg, *Sharing Lights on the Way to God,* 287.

81. Agai, *Zwischen Netzwerk und Diskurs,* 144.

cannot be truly pious unless he refrains from certain permissible things lest he should commit risky things."[82] Gülen sees his commitment to live a life of *hizmet, himmet,* and *ihlas* (service, charity, and sincere devotion) as implying a farewell to other human commitments, including marriage and family life. Apart from his personal sacrifices, Gülen has had to endure suspicion from those who did not appreciate his "middle way" between secularism and Islamism, or who were simply jealous of the number and the power of his supporters. One of the consequences of this jealousy has been that they present an image of Gülen as a political leader who reigns over a well-organized army of followers. As I said before, this picture is highly misleading since there is no central authority in the network of people inspired by Gülen; he is not their political leader or their spiritual master (*shaykh*); he is their source of inspiration. And as Ergün Çapan makes abundantly clear in his article about Gülen's own teaching activities, he was and still is first and foremost a teacher, *hoca*, even though he is the esteemed teacher, Hocaefendi. Yet the best teacher is one who knows that he is still a student.[83]

Therefore, it is important to understand the relationship between Fethullah Gülen and the community that is inspired by his thinking and his teaching. We will consider this relationship in the next chapter, first looking at the nature of the community, and, through examining the nature of the community, describing the community's most important internal and external functions.

82. M. Fethullah Gülen, *Emerald Hills of the Heart: Key Concepts in the Practice of Sufism, 1* (Rutherford, N.J.: The Light, 2004), 47.

83. Çapan, "Gülen's Teaching Methodology in His Private Circle," 156.

5

THE FORMATION OF FAITH-BASED SERVICE NETWORKS

THE FOCUS IN THE second part of this book will switch from Fethullah Gülen to the movement that is associated with his name.[1] One may say that this movement has been the subject of a rapidly growing number of studies that are to a large extent the results of conferences organized by the so-called Gülen Movement itself. In the first part of the chapter, I will explain why I have serious reservations about the term "Gülen Movement." These reservations are partly based on a significant number of sociological studies on the nature of this movement.[2] They are also based

1. In this chapter and elsewhere in the book I use the words "network" and "movement" interchangeably. I am aware that there is a sociological difference, but sociologists studying the Hizmet community have argued in favor of both terms. While generally preferring "network," I sometimes comply with the more general use of the word "movement," since my real interest is not in the sociological description but in its theological basis.

2. Bekim Agai, *Zwischen Netzwerk und Diskurs: Das Bildungsnetzwerk um Fethullah Gülen (geb. 1938): Die flexible Umsetzung modernen islamischen Gedankenguts*, Bonner Islamstudien 2 (Schenefeld: EB-Verlag, 2004); Mehmet Enes Ergene, *Tradition Witnessing the Modern Age: An Analysis of the Gülen Movement* (Somerset, N.J.: Tughra Books, 2008); Muhammed Çetin, *The Gülen Movement: Civic Service without Borders* (New York: Blue Dome Press, 2009); Gürkan Çelik, *The Gülen Movement: Building Social Cohesion through Dialogue and Education* (Delft: Eburon, 2010); Helen Rose Ebaugh, *The Gülen Movement: A Sociological Analysis of a Civic Movement Rooted in Moderate Islam* (Dordrecht: Springer, 2010).

partly on theological convictions. I will discuss these theological convictions by characterizing the goal of the movement as "renewal by conduct."[3] However, following what I argue is Gülen's core motivation, I prefer to call it: pleasing God by serving humankind. I will also show how this renewal is enacted in the religious conversations (*sohbetler*) that form a very important form of communication within the Hizmet Movement. After having discussed these theological notions that are in my opinion essential for a right understanding of the Hizmet as a faith-based movement, I will discuss the forms of the internal and external communication of the movement. In chapter six, I will discuss the three most important fields of faith-based service in the Hizmet Movement.

RENEWAL BY CONDUCT: THE HIZMET (SERVICE) MOVEMENT

The different sociological studies of the so-called Gülen Movement clearly show that the relationship between Fethullah Gülen and the movement associated with his name cannot be framed in terms of "leader" and "followers." Gülen does not lead a hierarchical organization nor does he give his followers instructions on what they are to do. Even a superficial acquaintance with Gülen's thought makes clear that he is not interested in leadership or in political power at all. He leads a life of study and prayer quite far away from any religious center in the Islamic world. However, sometimes he gives reflections on political developments that can be interpreted as guidelines; yet, the tenor of these remarks is diametrically opposed to the forms of political use of Islam labeled as "Islamism" by political scientists. For instance, in an interview about the so-called flotilla incident, Gülen did not endorse the sending of a convoy from Turkey to help the beleaguered Palestinians of the Gaza Strip without Israel's permission in May 2010. The fact that Gülen grant-

3. Ihsan Yilmaz, "*Ijtihad* and *Tajdid* by Conduct: The Gülen Movement," in *Turkish Islam and the Secular State: The Gülen Movement*, ed. M. Hakan Yavuz and John L. Esposito (Syracuse, N.Y.: Syracuse University Press, 2003), 208–37.

ed an exceptional interview to a journalist of the *Wall Street Journal* shows that he is very keen to distance himself from anything that can be perceived as political agitation.[4] In that interview, he repeated time and again: "I do not consider myself someone who has followers" and "I am not the leader of a faction or someone who would cause some state officials to follow me despite their official duties."[5] When Gülen gives instruction to his individual students, it is about the religious sciences or about the way in which they can put their faith and their loyalty into practice. In the few cases in which he gives political advice, it is to distance himself from radical political movements with an Islamist flavor rather than to endorse them. For instance, when Fatih University – a private university in Istanbul that is connected to the Hizmet network – wanted to apply for a development grant from an Islamic bank located in Saudi Arabia, Gülen strongly advised against pursuing a grant from a Saudi bank.[6]

The second reason for my reservations about the term "Gülen Movement" has been mentioned already in the introduction to this book: it is related to the danger that human beings become the focus of our attention while Gülen would be the first to agree that he does not deserve to be the focus of our attention. Therefore, he prefers to talk about the "volunteer movement."[7] In another recent interview he said to a journalist from the *New York Times*: "I believe that calling this movement the 'Fethullah Gulen movement' is not right, and doing so is disrespectful to many people dedicated to carrying out

4. The same can be said about interviews that Gülen gave on the occasion of the mounting tensions between the AKP government and Prime Minister Erdoğan on the one hand, and the Gülen Movement on the other, in the spring of 2014. It is, however, somewhat contradictory that Gülen gives interviews in order to deny political engagement, since giving an interview itself can be considered an act of political engagement. I have written more about these tensions and about the ambiguity of Gülen's public statements at the end of the second chapter.

5. Joe Lauria, "Reclusive Turkish Imam Criticizes Gaza Flotilla," *Wall Street Journal*, June 4, 2010; online.wsj.com/article, accessed July 30, 2010.

6. Ebaugh, *The Gülen Movement*, 91.

7. Gürkan Çelik and I used that term in the title of our recent volume in Dutch: *Fethullah Gülen & de Vrijwilligersbeweging* (Budel: Damon, 2010).

its activities. My role in the movement is very limited, and there is no leadership, no center, no loyalty to a center, and no hierarchy."[8] Gülen does not mention the theological argument here ("all honor and glory is due to God") but only the sociological argument ("I am not the leader of a hierarchical organization"). So I had to ask myself whether my theological problem with mentioning his name so prominently in describing the organization he inspired might be a theological bias of mine or not. Since I have not been able to interview Gülen himself about this issue, I asked some of his students in Turkey about it when I interviewed them in Izmir. In the next paragraph I will discuss their answers, and try to connect them with my own observations about the nature of the movement, about its goals, and about the role of religion in the movement. These considerations lead me to talk about the Hizmet Movement as a faith-based service network inspired by Gülen.[9]

I decided to use part of the time that I was able to spend with some of Gülen's closest supporters in Izmir in August 2009 to discuss their reactions to the term "Gülen Movement," which at that time was universally used in English literature about the movement. They all said that Hocaefendi would certainly not be happy with the fact that the movement that is called *hizmet*, "service," in Turkey is usually called the Gülen Movement abroad. One of them, who introduced me to the Kestanepazarı Mosque and Qur'ān-school where Gülen began his longtime engagement in Izmir, used rather strong words in describing this protest.

Hocaefendi would rather have someone cursing his mother—an awful insult—than having Hizmet named after him. Some opponents intentionally call Gülen's supporters *Fethullahçılar* (Fethullahists), but this is

8. Brian Knowlton, "Turk Who Leads a Movement Has Advocates and Critics," *New York Times*, June 11, 2010; www.nytimes.com, accessed July 30, 2010.

9. The following sections have been published before as the first part of my article "The Hizmet Movement in the Dialogue between Muslim and Christian Religious Traditions," in *The Gülen Hizmet Movement and Its Transnational Activities: Case Studies of Altruistic Activism in Contemporary Islam*, ed. Sophia Pandya and Nancy Gallagher (Boca Raton, Fla..: BrownWalker Press, 2012), 35–54. I thank the publisher and the editors for their permission to use most of the article here.

perceived as an insult. The reason is that it would misjudge the movement as a political movement or – even worse – as a fanclub of a famous personality. Yet Gülen does not want to be a political leader or a famous personality. The cult of a personality would be a form of *shirk* in which we ascribe to human beings what belongs to God alone. It would also run contrary to Gülen's characteristic humility. He says that all glory and honor belongs to God; he has done nothing but make visible God as source of all good things that happen."[10]

The old friends of Fethullah Gülen whom I interviewed in Izmir said that they liked the Turkish name Hizmet much better than the English designation Gülen Movement, since the name "service movement" or "volunteer movement" better expresses the goal and the character of the movement. Only one of them added that he could imagine people talking about the Gülen Movement, since it is Hocaefendi who has shown this particular way or reviving true Islam by *tajdīd* (renewal). "He has been a *rehber*, a true guide who lives an exemplary life, and whose deeds are in accordance with his words. Therefore his name is important. But if Hocaefendi is an outstanding guide, praise is due to God, since he got everything from God."[11]

On this issue, Mehmet Küçük referred to Khalid ibn al-Walid (592–642), one of the companions of the Prophet, who was nicknamed *Sayf Ullah*, "the sword of God."

> He was a very successful warrior for the sake of God after his conversion to Islam, but caliph Umar gave the supreme command to someone else, a slave, and said: "You have become a cause of *fitna* (discord) since many believe that we are successful because of you. But I want the people to know that it is Allah who grants victory." In a similar way, it is Allah who inspires Hocaefendi, and if mentioning the name Gülen causes discord, it is better not to use his name.

Muhammed Çetin, one of three sociologists to write a book with the title *The Gülen Movement,* agrees that "Gülen himself neither

10. Reconstructed from interview with Mehmet Küçük, Izmir, August 7, 2009.
11. Interview with Gürbüz Dönmez, Izmir, August 5, 2009.

approves nor ever uses the terms 'Gülen Movement' or 'Gülen Community.' He prefers the action to be called 'volunteers service.'"[12] Yet, the name "Gülen Movement" is still used by the editors of a series of proceedings from the conferences on *Islam in the Contemporary World: The Fethullah Gülen Movement in Thought and Practice* in Houston, Dallas, Oklahoma, and San Antonio, mainly "for the sake of brevity and convenience."[13] I can understand these considerations but I do not agree with them, since I think that there is more at stake here than just convenience. In my view, what is at stake here is the very religious identity of the movement.[14]

So if we stop using the convenient but theologically problematic term "Gülen Movement," how should we refer to the supporters of Fethullah Gülen? In some question and answer sessions with American news media in 2010, Gülen time and again rejects the term "Gülen Movement" and at the same time proposes to talk about "volunteers' movement."[15] In my opinion, this reaction is characteristic of Gülen's humility: he does not want all attention to be focused on him, but rather on the persons who are in fact performing the activities that create the image of the movement. Yet my problem is that the term "volunteers' movement" only gives a formal characterization and does not refer to any content. In this chapter, I will explain why I prefer the term Hizmet Movement, derived from the Turkish word *hizmet*, as the best description of the basic characteristic of this movement. Whereas social scien-

12. Çetin, *The Gülen Movement*, 119.

13. "Publisher's Note," in *Islam in the Contemporary World, 2: the Fethullah Gülen Movement in Thought and Practice* (Somerset, N.J.: Tughra Books, 2009), vii.

14. I remember that this remark and similar remarks by other speakers caused some debates during the conference "East and West Encounters: The Gülen Movement" at the University of Southern California in Los Angeles, December 4–6, 2009. Some of the speakers wanted to retain the term "Gülen Movement" while others rejected it. See the article by Muhammed Çetin in *Sunday's Zaman* of December 14, 2009. As a compromise, the volume that was published with some of the papers of this conference bore the title *The Gülen Hizmet Movement*. See also note 9 in this chapter.

15. An interview with *USA Today* on his connections to a number of charter schools in the U.S.: http://www.usatoday.com/news/education/2010-08-17-turkish final17_CV_N.html, accessed August 24, 2010.

tists seem to agree on using the word "movement" to describe the organization of the supporters of Fethullah Gülen, this term may give a wrong impression if it suggests an organization with a central authority. Although Gülen certainly functions as an authority for those who follow him, this is a spiritual and not a political authority. Also, it is very important to notice that Gülen does not want to exert any power and he lives an austere life far away from all centers of power. He does not act like the type of leader who decides what is to be done, nor does he own the movement or any of its parts. Bekim Agai suggests that we should speak about a network of closely related small organizations in which personal relationships determine the coherence of the network.[16] These personal relationships also determine the position that different persons have in the network. Those who have been Gülen's own students, especially in the first period of the network, function as secondary instances of authority. They are the *ağabeyler* (short: *abis* or *abiler,* "elder brothers") whose stories about the beginning of Gülen's ideas and activities form important frames of reference for the discourse of the community.[17] These "elder brothers" often have access to Hocaefendi and visit him in Pennsylvania to ask specific questions about the service in which they want to engage. Several of his students in Izmir told me that they visit Hocaefendi from time to time, in order to receive advice. Many of them try to go and visit Gülen every year for a few weeks. Even though Gülen's health does not allow him to talk with them for an extended period of time, he is always very glad when he sees his old friends, since they share an important spiritual heritage together. They sometimes have the feeling that the distance between them and Hocaefendi is growing, because of

16. Agai, *Zwischen Netzwerk und Diskurs.*

17. Marcia Hermansen, "The Cultivation of Memory in the Gülen Community," in *Muslim World in Transition: Contributions of the Gülen Movement*, Conference Proceedings, London, 25–27 October 2007 (London: Leeds Metropolitan University Press, 2007), 60–76; Bekim Agai, "Discursive and Organizational Strategies of the Gülen Movement," in *Islam in the Contemporary World 1: the Fethullah Gülen Movement in Thought and Practice,* Conference Proceedings, November 12–13, 2005, Rice University, Houston, Tex. (Somerset, N.J.: Tughra Books, 2009), 47–59.

his God-centeredness that grows stronger and stronger.[18] When they visit Gülen, they always ask him: "What can we do? Can we do more?" and Gülen sometimes gives them specific suggestions, for instance, to go to Uzbekistan or to open a school in Uganda.

This example shows once again that the idea of *hizmet* or service is at the center of the communication within the network. If there is a form of leadership, it is a spiritual leadership that can be summarized in the apt phrase coined by İhsan Yilmaz: "*tajdid* by conduct."[19] Gülen does not seek leadership, but he is perceived to be a spiritual leader because he renews Islam by embodying spiritual principles in his own personality and lifestyle; the "elder brothers" participate in this form of leadership because they share the stories, the lessons and the virtues that are connected with the idea of "*tajdid* by conduct." Another way to express this form of leadership is the notion of "servant-leadership."[20]

Since the Hizmet network does not have formal positions of authority, it is not correct to speak about Gülen as its leader or its president. Some of the organizations, such as the Rumi Forum in Washington, D.C., for instance, call Fethullah Gülen their "honorary president," but this is indeed only an honorary title. Gülen does not govern any of these organizations, nor does he have any financial interest in them. The same holds true for the schools founded by the Hizmet Movement, nowadays often called "Gülen Inspired Schools." In the next chapter I will argue that one will not find any reference to Gülen's name in these schools, apart from the stories that some of the older educators might tell. As Agai noted in his research, only some of the teachers in the schools that are connected to the Hizmet are aware of the role that Gülen's ideas played in the foundation of these schools.

18. Interview with Mehmet Eldem, Özbek/Urla, August 5, 2009.

19. Ihsan Yilmaz, "*Ijtihad* and *Tajdid* by Conduct"; see also Mehmet Kalyoncu, "Understanding the Hizmet Discourse of the Gülen Movement," in *Islam in the Contemporary World 4: The Fethullah Gülen Movement in Thought and Practice*, Conference Proceedings, San Antonio, November 3, 2007 (Somerset, N.J.: Tughra Books, 2009), 25–37.

20. Çelik, *The Gülen Movement*, 68–78.

Maybe the most important issue for debate is the character of the Hizmet Movement. Some speak of a volunteer organization or a civil society movement.[21] Yet this does not express the goals or character of this network: is it based on religion or only inspired by religion? Some sociologists tend to define the Gülen Movement as a faith-inspired movement, which means that religion may be an inspiration for Gülen himself and for the prominent people in the network at the personal level, but it does not determine the public character of the movement.[22] When I interviewed Hüseyin Bingül, one of the editors of Gülen's works in English, at the Akademi in Istanbul, he emphatically stated that it is a faith-inspired social movement but not a religious movement.[23] I agree with him that Hizmet does not form a separate religious tradition within Islam, nor a public or political formation based on religion. Even in Izmir, where Hizmet was active more than anywhere else, one will look for a "Gülen mosque" in vain. In the brochure that was given to me at the religious foundation that administers the Kestanepazarı Qur'ān-school where Gülen was the director during a very important period, I have not found his name.[24] Yet I think that faith is more than just the personal inspiration of some in the network. I do not exclude the possibility that the network may develop in a direction in which faith is indeed not more than a personal option for some in the movement, but at this moment I think that faith is more than just a personal motivation. Of course I realize that

21. Loye Ashton and Tamer Balci, "A Contextual Analysis of the Supporters and Critics of the Gülen/Hizmet Movement," in *Islam in the Age of Global Challenges: Alternative Perspectives of the Gülen Movement* (Washington, D.C.: Rumi Forum, 2008), 73–113.

22. This is the opinion of Ergene, *Tradition Witnessing the Modern Age*, and Çetin, *The Gülen Movement*, xvi.

23. Interview with Hüseyin Bingül at the Akademi, Istanbul, August 11, 2009.

24. The title of the brochure is *Izmir Millî Kültür ve Ahlâka Hizmet Vakfi* (Religious foundation for the service of national culture and ethics in Izmir), and the brochure was published in 1992. This religious foundation (*waqf* in Arabic) administers a number of *imam-hatip* schools, dormitories, and has relations with the Department of Theology (İlâhiyat Fakültesi) of the September 9 University. As far as I can see, there is no connection with similar institutes inspired by Fethullah Gülen.

I am speaking as a (Christian) theologian for whom the religious dimension may be more important than for researchers in the social sciences. But I think I can provide two strong indications for arguing that faith is at the basis, not just an inspiration for some of the participants in the network. The first indication is what I consider to be the core of Fethullah Gülen's own inspiration: the idea of *rıza-i İlahi*, "seeking God's approval." The second is the role of the *sohbet* or "religious conversation" in the community. In the next section, I will try to explain both aspects, because they will lead to a better insight into the core of this network of faith-based service communities.

RIZA AND SOHBET AS CHARACTERISTICS OF SPIRITUAL RENEWAL

If one wants to determine the character of a movement, it often helps to trace the driving force behind the founder's activity. This was one of the reasons for me to study Fethullah Gülen, not only by reading his books but also by listening – though I needed assistance with Turkish – to some of his sermons and to the stories of a dozen of his earliest supporters whom I interviewed in Izmir and Istanbul in August 2009. Some of the people who met Fethullah Gülen when he came to Izmir in 1966 told me that he not only stayed on the grounds of the mosque and its school but also went to the coffee houses to talk with all people, even those who did not believe – Izmir at that time was known as the most secular city in Turkey – and that he began his talks by asking people what their problems were and what they wanted to talk about. The people told him that students in Izmir needed help and so he and his friends began to raise funds to establish dormitories, organize summer camps, and build schools.[25]

In my very first interview, Gürbüz Dönmez, who met Fethullah Gülen when he was the new imam of the Kestanepazarı Mosque in Izmir in 1966, gave me an important hint to understand

25. Interview with Yusuf Pekmezci, Izmir, August 6, 2009.

the driving force behind Gülen's activism by referring to his humility: he does not seek any fame. Any popularity only bothers Gülen since it may distract people from God as the only source of goodness, and therefore may lead them to *shirk* (attributing partners to God). Gülen only seeks God's pleasure.[26] The next day, Yusuf Pekmezci confirmed this, saying: "He was someone who tried to love anyone, not only his friends, but also the strangers and the enemies. He did not care for money or possessions; he only cared about *rıza-i İlahi*."[27] Two somewhat younger people in the Hizmet Movement echoed these words in describing their own activities: "We try to help wherever we can, in Izmir or Africa. We do not expect to get anything back; we do it for God's pleasure."[28] Indeed, if one reads in Gülen's books about the principles of the Islamic faith, Prophet Muhammad, and Sufism, one comes across many references to the idea of "God's pleasure" as the basic motivation for a Muslim to act. When describing the future generation of Muslims who may help us toward the lost paradise, Gülen says: "They should never be given over to carnal appetites and temporary aspirations. They should aim purely at gaining God's approval and strictly preserve the purity of their intention."[29] In his book about Muhammad, Gülen explains that Muslims always should seek God's pleasure in what they do: "Intention is the spirit of our actions. For example, if we fulfill our religious duties without making a specific intention to do so, they are unacceptable to God. If we do not seek God's pleasure, what we do is not rewarded by God."[30] In a discussion on Islam and science, he says that we should not try to impress others or silence their arguments; "our primary aim must be to win the pleasure of God."[31] Speaking once

26. Interview with Gürbüz Dönmez, Izmir, August 5, 2009.

27. Interview with Yusuf Pekmezci, Izmir, August 6, 2009.

28. Interview with Cemal Yavuzer and İhsan Taşpınar, Izmir, August 7, 2009.

29. M. Fethullah Gülen, *Towards the Lost Paradise* (Izmir: Kaynak, 1998), 88.

30. M. Fethullah Gülen, *Muhammad, the Messenger of God: Aspects of His Life* (Somerset, N.J: The Light, 2005), 103.

31. M. Fethullah Gülen, *Questions and Answers about Islam, 1* (Somerset, N.J.: The Light, 2006), 108.

more about his ideal of a "golden generation" of human beings devoted to God, he makes perfectly clear why he cannot agree with the term "the Gülen Movement": he says that "[t]hese devotees never desire to boast about themselves or to advertise or spread propaganda about themselves, nor are they ambitious to be well-known or appreciated. Instead, they endeavor, with all their might and strength, to reach the spiritual life and they depend all their acts in this regard on sincerity, intending merely to please God."[32]

In his books on *Key Concepts in the Practice of Sufism*, Gülen shows the dimensions of this notion of "seeking God's pleasure" on almost every page: it is an element of asceticism that seeks no worldly pleasure or fame, but prefers to serve God and seek to attain God's pleasure over anything else.[33] It is an element of *taqwa* or piety to not pursue anything other than God and God's pleasure, and the same can be said of sincerity or *ikhlas*.[34] These are among the most important notions in Islamic spiritual life, but it is significant that Gülen spends the longest entry in the first volume of his book about Sufism on the very notion of *ridwan* or *rida* (Turkish *rıza*) that we are discussing here.[35] At first sight, it might seem strange that the English translation of this word is "content(ment)," but in the Sufi context the word refers to a spiritual level where God is pleased with you and your actions. In this sense, *rida* refers to a very sophisticated state of spiritual life in which there is contentment and mutual pleasure between God and those seeking God. For this reason, Al-Ghazālī talks about *rida* together with love and desire as the highest of the mystical stages in his *Ihyā' 'ulūm ad-dīn*.[36] The qur'ānic background for this high rank can be found

32. M. Fethullah Gülen, *Toward a Global Civilization of Love and Tolerance* (Somerset N.J.: The Light, 2004), 101.

33. M. Fethullah Gülen, *Emerald Hills of the Heart: Key Concepts in the Practice of Sufism, 1.* (Rutherford, N.J.: The Light, 2004), 42–43.

34. Gülen, *Emerald Hills of the Heart, 1*, 48, 62.

35. Ibid., 104–14.

36. See Abu Hamid Muhammad al-Ghazālī, *Love, Longing, Intimacy and Contentment: Kitāb al-mahabba wa'l shawq wa'l uns wa'l ridā*, Book 36 of *The Revival of the Religious Sciences, Ihyā' 'ulūm al-dīn,* trans. with an introduction and notes by Eric Ormsby

in *surat al-bayyinah* where this mutual pleasure is part of paradise: "And those who believe and do good, righteous deeds – they are the best of creatures. Their reward is with their Lord: Gardens of perpetual bliss through which rivers flow, abiding therein forever. God is well-pleased with them, and they are well-pleased with Him. That is for him who stands in awe of his Lord."[37] *Surat at-tawbah* even suggests that God's pleasure is greater than paradise: "God has promised the believers, both men and women, Gardens through which rivers flow, therein to abide, and blessed dwellings in Gardens of perpetual bliss; and greater (than those) is God's being pleased with them. That indeed is the supreme triumph."[38]

Gülen explains:

> One can have no greater reward or higher rank than God's being pleased with him or her, which is only attainable by personal resignation to what He has decreed.... As the greatest rank in God's sight, resignation or God's pleasure is a final target that has been sought by the greatest members of humanity, from the glory of creation, upon him be peace and blessings, to all the other Prophets, saints, and purified scholars who have passed the final test through sincerity, certainty, reliance, surrender, and confidence.[39]

If this goal of seeking God's pleasure is the driving force, not only for Fethullah Gülen's personal engagement, but also for the people involved in the Hizmet Movement, this should imply that the movement is based on faith (or faiths) and not just inspired by faith. However, it should be noted that "faith" here refers to actions rather than to words; it is, as İhsan Yilmaz has written, a form of renewal by conduct, but of course the conduct is based on certain religious convictions.[40] Taking this into account, Marcia

(Cambridge: Islamic Texts Society, 2011). Background in Richard Gramlich, *Muhammad al-Gazzālī's Lehre von den Stufen zur Gottesliebe* (Wiesbaden: Franz Steiner Verlag, 1984).

37. Qur'ān, *al-bayyinah* 98:7–8 in the interpretation by Ünal, *The Qur'ān.*

38. Qur'ān, *at-tawba* 9:72 in the interpretation by Ünal, *The Qur'ān.*

39. Gülen, *Emerald Hills of the Heart, 1*, 113–14.

40. Yilmaz, "*Ijtihad* and *Tajdid* by Conduct."

Hermansen points out that the idea of renewal (*tajdīd*) and the renewer (*mujaddid*) for Gülen refers to the "collective personality" (*shakhs-i manevi*) of the community rather than to the individual leader.[41] This is why Gülen stresses the idea of a "golden generation" (*altın nesil*) and the importance of education over the importance of one person.[42] Although I do not wish to exclude the possibility that some people may please God by doing good without being explicitly religious, the persons who told me that they are inspired by Fethullah Gülen are practicing Muslims for whom the intention and the sincerity of their engagement is most important. I can understand why some social scientists argue that the movement is faith-inspired rather than faith-based, since they argue that it is possible to participate in the Hizmet without any personal faith, and, moreover, they want to keep open the possibility that the religious character of the Hizmet Movement may fade away in the future, so that it may develop into an aid-oriented NGO without an explicit religious background.[43] I agree with them that this could be a future possibility, but in the present the Hizmet Movement still presupposes a personal faith engagement, and it is therefore faith-based rather than faith-inspired.

My second argument for the faith-based character of the Hizmet Movement takes as its point of departure the important place of the *sohbet* in the movement. The Turkish word *sohbet* may refer to any form of talk or conversation, but among the supporters of Fethullah Gülen it specifically refers to a conversation

41. Marcia Hermansen, "Understandings of 'Community' within the Gülen Movement," in *Islam in the Contemporary World 1: The Fethullah Gülen Movement in Thought and Practice*, Conference Proceedings, November 12–13, 2005, Rice University, Houston, Tex. (Somerset, N.J.: Tughra Books, 2009), 280–96.

42. In his interview with me on August 5, 2009, Mehmet Eldem said: "Hocaefendi does not like it if attention is focused on his person. The focus of the *cemaat* is *hizmet,* not his person. We do not work for a person, we work for God and for the realization of *hizmet.* Because of *hizmet*, we are one person, we are a *shakhs-i manevi*, a spiritual person."

43. This was — if I understood him correctly — Hüseyin Bingül's argument in my interview with him in Istanbul, August 11, 2009.

among friends. In the second volume of *Key Concepts in the Practice of Sufism*, Gülen discusses the Arabic concept *sohba* or "conversation." He defines it as follows: "*sohba* (conversation) means making effective speeches to direct people to the Almighty, enlightening others with words and thoughts, using other's good opinions of oneself to guide hearts to eternity, and always wishing well for others."[44] This description starts from the point of view of the one who guides the conversation, and Hendrick points out that in Sufi circles *sohbet* refers to the communication between a *shaykh* and his disciple.[45] Yet, at the same time, service is the central notion from the point of view of the disciples who are guided in conversation: "Service denotes seeking God's good pleasure and approval with sincerity and purity of intention, and putting oneself in the hands of one with whom God is pleased for teaching and guidance."[46] Accordingly, Hendrick points out that *sohbetler* are not only theological lessons but have very practical dimensions as well: "Sohbetler are also used for fund-raising, organizational planning, and social networking."[47] Yet the most important aspect of the *sohbet* is that it functions as an entrance ticket to the inner circle of the Hizmet Movement; in Hendrick's interviews with students in the "light houses" of the movement, the invitation to join a *sohbet* means that the *ağabey* (older brother) considers the student as good enough – both intellectually and morally – to contribute to the goals of the Hizmet Movement in the future.[48]

According to Alper Alasağ, my friend and interpreter in Izmir, *sohbet* is the style of teaching associated with the prophets in Islam: they like to teach by answering questions.[49] It is the style that

44. M. Fethullah Gülen, *Emerald Hills of the Heart: Key Concepts in the Practice of Sufism,* 2 (Somerset, N.J.: The Light, 2004), 238.

45. Joshua Hendrick, *Gülen. The Ambiguous Politics of Market Islam in Turkey and the World* (New York: New York University Press, 2013), 116.

46. Gülen, *Emerald Hills of the Heart,* 2, 239.

47. Hendrick, *Gülen*, 116.

48. Ibid., 106–8.

49. Conversation with Alper Alasağ, Izmir, August 5, 2009. See also Agai, *Zwischen Netzwerk und Diskurs* 30, note 59.

Fethullah Gülen adopted as a teacher as well: several of the persons that I interviewed in Izmir told me that Hocaefendi distinguished himself from others in that he took every question seriously, even if it came from children.[50] But, Yusuf Pekmezci added, he went to the coffee houses as well to answer questions from non-believers. Gülen has never stopped giving such question and answer sessions; even in the United States he continues giving *sohbetler* that are broadcast on the Internet and taped on CDs.[51] Some of these form the basis of books such as *Questions and Answers about Islam*.

Historically speaking, the *sohbet* functioned as a means to strengthen the communication between Gülen and his first pupils. In his discussion of the Sufi concept of *sohba,* Gülen points out that disciples used to live together in the Sufi lodge where the spiritual guide used to teach; they lived together because they wanted to be enlightened with the knowledge of God. "In those buildings of light, which they saw as being similar to the hall adjacent to the Prophet's Mosque in Madina, where those of the Companions stayed who had dedicated themselves, during his lifetime, to studying the Qur'ān and the Sunna."[52] The term "houses of light" indicated the main function of these communities: study for the sake of knowing God. Among followers of Said Nursi, reading his *Risale-i Nur* was an important means of forming the community or *cemaat*. Nursi's followers founded *dershanes* where students could live together and receive inspiration by reading Nursi's works together. These "reading circles" formed, in the words of Hakan Yavuz, new textual communities.[53] Fethullah Gülen did something

50. Interviews with Mehmet Yıldız, Izmir (Bornova), August 7, 2009 and Necdet İcel, Izmir (Şadırvan) Mosque, August 9, 2009.

51. Many of these *sohbets* (in Turkish) can be found on the Internet at www.herkul.org. Some of the American *sohbetler* can be found on CDs in the collection *Gurbet Solukları: Amerika Notları,* published by Nil in 2004. The most extensive collection is M. Fethullah Gülen, *Vaaz Külliyatı*: eleven DVDs and twenty-two CDs with many sermons and *sohbets* from different periods (1975–ca. 2005). I discussed these in some detail in the last section of chapter three.

52. Gülen, *Emerald Hills of the Heart,* 2, 240–41.

53. M. Hakan Yavuz, "Islam in the Public Sphere: the Case of the Nur Move-

very similar when he began to form his "houses of light" or *ışık evleri* in Izmir. The spiritual communication in these dormitories, both between the students who lived there and the wider circle of adherents who took care for financial support and spiritual lessons, was evident in these *sohbetler*.

When I stayed in Burç, a private boarding school for higher education in the neighborhood of Buca in Izmir, in August 2009, the guests (students, teachers, parents) shared the top floor of the building with two rooms that were specifically dedicated to *sohbet* meetings, and the rooms were used frequently. The reason is, as Ali Yurtsever told me, that most people in the Hizmet Movement try to participate in a *sohbet* at least once a week.[54] Bekim Agai points out that these "houses of light" and the "conversational readings" are not frequently mentioned in the publications of and about Fethullah Gülen, although there are some exceptions.[55] Since these *sohbetler* are related to the spiritual development of the individual, they are not advertised but they are well attended by quite a few members of the service communities. Margaret Rausch, for instance, gives some insight into the motives of women participating in *sohbet* in the Kansas City area, stressing the idea of the renewal of spirituality and interaction between the private and public realms.[56]

When questioned about his activities related to the Hizmet in an average week, Mustafa Duğral, a prominent member of the Izmir Employer's Organization IZIAD, who owns a company pro-

ment," in *Turkish Islam and the Secular State: The Gülen Movement*, ed. M. Hakan Yavuz and John L. Esposito (Syracuse, N.Y.: Syracuse University Press, 2003), 13.

54. Interview with Ali Yurtsever, Akif Topal, Bahadır Tantay, and Mustafa Akçay, Izmir, August 8, 2009, and with Ali Yurtsever and Zeki Sakman, Izmir, August 9, 2009.

55. Agai, *Zwischen Netzwerk und Diskurs*, 142. Marcia Hermansen, "The Cultivation of Memory in the Gülen Community" is such an exception.

56. Margaret Rausch, "Gender and Leadership in the Gülen Movement: Women Affiliates' Contributions to East-West Encounters," in *The Gülen Hizmet Movement and Its Transnational Activities: Case Studies of Altruistic Activism in Contemporary Islam*, eds. Sophia Pandya and Nancy Gallagher (Boca Raton, Fla.: Brown Walker Press, 2012), 133–59.

ducing and selling office furniture, told me that he has a *sohbet* and meeting on Monday evening with local employers about Hizmet programs, a *sohbet* breakfast on Tuesday morning in his company with some neighbors, a smaller *sohbet* with fellow neighbors on Tuesday evening, another *sohbet* breakfast on Wednesday morning in the neighborhood of one of his colleagues, and a more meditative *sohbet* on Thursday night, which is a holy night in preparation for Friday. Friday morning, some of the employers come together in an industrial building to do *sohbet* and study religious books, and finally on Saturday morning there is another *sohbet* at his office building in a more relaxed atmosphere. Almost all of these *sohbetler* are followed by business meetings. Two of the other participants in the interview, Mehmet Yıldız and Sinan Koyun, work as teachers, and they frequently give *sohbetler* so that they usually see one another three to four times every week, but they have individual *sohbetler* as well.[57] I was able to observe some of these "religious conversations" in the boarding school where I stayed in Izmir, and in a warehouse in an industrial neighborhood. They usually begin with a lecture, either on the Qur'ān or on another important religious text—for instance Said Nursi's interpretations of the Qur'ān in his *Risale-i Nur*—and continue with some exchange of ideas, first on the contents of the text, but gradually shifting toward the practical implications of the texts. The *sohbet* usually ends with a business meeting in which the participants discuss their plans for the next weeks. One of the *sohbetler* in August 2009 ended with a discussion of some of the political problems involved in the plan to put up tents during the upcoming month of Ramadan in order to give *iftar* dinners to the poor and hungry. The *sohbet* ended with a call for prayer since the "leftist" (meaning: secularist) city government did not like this plan, so we were all asked to pray for its success. This shows, once again, how the faith that is at the basis of the Hizmet Movement encompasses words and deeds together.

57. Interview with Mehmet Yıldız, Mehmet Bafalı, Mustafa Duğral, and Sinan Koyun in Mustafa's summer residence near Izmir, August 10, 2009.

The reason I pay so much attention to the *sohbet* is that I think it not only gives an indication of the faith basis of the service communities in Turkey, but it also shows how these communities are able to build bridges between religious and action-oriented discourse. While the *sohbetler* are the main form of internal communication, the Hizmet network has a number of external forms of communication at its disposal as well. I will discuss some of these in the remainder of this chapter, and some others in the next chapter.

FORMS OF COMMUNICATION IN THE HIZMET NETWORK

In the previous paragraphs, I have elaborated on the importance of the ritualized religious conversation (*sohbet*) as an internal form of communication, but the Hizmet network uses more forms of internal and external communication. It comes as no surprise that these forms of communication in the Hizmet Movement form an extension of the strands of discourse in the works of Fethullah Gülen that I discussed in the third chapter. I will look at some of these forms of discourse once again, but now with a focus not on Gülen as author but on the internal and external channels of communication in the Hizmet Movement.

It is difficult to draw a neat separation between means of internal and means of external communication, since some media of communication may be primarily directed toward insiders but have a more general outreach as well. For instance, the oldest means of communication between Fethullah Gülen and his supporters were two oral forms of communication that are part of Islamic prayer and teaching: the sermon (*vaaz* and *hutpe*) on the one hand, and the religious conversation (*sohbet*) on the other. In the beginning, some of Gülen's students recorded these oral communications privately, but after some time they became merchandise that could be bought in shops and other venues.

While the recordings are, of course, in Turkish – sometimes an Ottoman form of Turkish with many Arabic phrases that is often used for traditional *khutba* sermons in mosques – many of them have been transliterated into text format by Gülen's supporters, and some of them have later been translated into English as well.

Another form of communication that began mainly as internal communication, but rapidly widened to include people outside of the *cemaat* as well, was the periodical *Sızıntı.* The first issue of this monthly scientific-cultural magazine was published in 1979; its aim was to tell a future generation of students about the harmony between science and religion. This agenda is quite obvious for someone who leafs through one of the issues of this periodical. The magazine aims at students in colleges and universities and tries to guide them in their lives by pointing to the possibility of reconciling their faith as Muslims with their professional interests as scholars and scientists. Such harmony between faith and reason not only continues one of the major traditions in the writings of Said Nursi and his followers, but it also has a clear parallel in a very similar development among Catholics, as exemplified by popes John Paul II and Benedict XVI, in a tradition that goes back to Albert the Great and Thomas Aquinas in the Middle Ages.

Through the years, a number of more specialized magazines were added to *Sızıntı*, but another development that would have important consequences for the spreading of the ideas outside of the core of the Hizmet Movement was the start of similar magazines in other languages, such as German, Spanish, French, Arabic, and Russian.[58] The process of translation is an important contribution to the spreading of Gülen's works throughout the world. As a collection of colorful nameplates on the wall of the Akademi on Camlica Hill in Üsküdar in the Asian part of Istanbul shows, Kaynak has many imprints in Turkish and other languages.[59] Apart from the English, German, Russian, and Arabic versions of *Sızıntı,* Kaynak carries

58. The English index page of the Kaynak Publishing Group mentions foreign editions and imprints, but also foreign language editions of *Sızıntı*: http://www.kaynakpublishing.com/en/index/ (accessed June 21, 2014).

59. A similar collection of imprints may be found on Kaynak's website in Turkish: http://www.kitapkaynagi.com/yayinevlerimiz.php (accessed August 13, 2010).

sixteen Turkish imprints, among which Nil is the major publisher of Gülen's works. Tughra Books is the most important imprint in English, while Édition du Nil serves the French market, Fontäne Verlag the German, Editorial La Fuente the Spanish, Novi Svet the Russian, and Dār al-Nīl the Arabic public.[60] Although the Akademi may be considered to be the "intellectual center of the movement," it is seldom visited by groups who come to Turkey as part of the intercultural exchanges organized by the Hizmet.[61] Therefore, I visited the Akademi in order to interview Hüseyin Bingül, one of the main translators, just before I began my trip with members and guests of the Maryland branch of the Rumi Forum organization in August 2009. I asked him about the process of translating Gülen's articles and books into English. He explained that Hocaefendi in some cases takes the initiative to publish a book, for instance the books on Sufism. In other cases, some of the people who know his works well compile a number of chapters and edit the materials into a book which is then presented to Hocaefendi. If he agrees, it is usually published under a somewhat poetic title suggested by Gülen himself, while the more prosaic subtitles are given by the editors. The English books generally go back to Turkish books that originate from articles in one of the magazines, or from conversations with questions and answers (*sohbetler*), or sermons. Sometimes Gülen makes the selection himself because he thinks that this is what people need, sometimes it is suggested by editors who are among the older students of Hocaefendi, for instance Reşit Haylamaz who is the editor in chief of Kaynak publishing company. Publishing Gülen's books started with Nil Publishing in Izmir between ten and twenty years ago; since that time many books have been published, also in English. The first publishing company was Fountain, later it changed to Light, and now we have Tughra and Blue Dome books.[62]

60. See http://www.kaynakpublishing.com/en/publishing-groups (accessed August 13, 2010).

61. The quotation is from Hermansen, "The Cultivation of Memory in the Gülen Community," 68.

62. Interview with Hüseyin Bingül, Akademi, Üsküdar (Istanbul), August 11, 2009.

The clever use of publication media brings about a dramatic widening of the circle of possible readers, but it changes the form of discourse as well. In the form of discourse that I have labeled "exoteric," the writer can no longer assume a basic knowledge of the Islamic tradition on the part of the reader, and therefore he has either to explain the tradition or let it be tacitly present, so that only those readers who know the tradition well are able to grasp the implied references to the tradition. As Yasin Aktay observes, the use of new communication media in the Hizmet Movement creates new and different circles of audiences.[63] The transition from a mainly esoteric discourse based on religion as the common denominator to a mainly exoteric discourse aimed at larger segments of Turkish society took place in the 1980s and 1990s through the creation of the Journalist and Writers Foundation, the Abant Platform, and a number of periodicals and mass media.[64] I will discuss the Journalists and Writers Foundation and the Abant Platform in the next chapter since they are an important part of the intercultural and interreligious dialogue activities of the Hizmet Movement, but the role of the *Zaman* newspaper will be discussed in this chapter.

Zaman (the word means "time" or "period" in Arabic and Turkish) was founded in 1986 as a newspaper in the Turkish market. Agai tells that in the beginning different Islamic groups participated in the newspaper, and that it voiced Islamist opinions from time to time.[65] After a short time, however, the businessmen inspired by Fethullah Gülen became the most important group and it was their idea that the newspaper "would be inclusive in terms of reporting various ideological perspectives and opinions, would report the most current news in an objective fashion, would emphasize dia-

63. Yasin Aktay, "New Media Figures and Instruments of Religious Authority in Turkey: Understanding Gülen and his Religious Leadership," in *Islam in the Contemporary World 1: The Fethullah Gülen Movement in Thought and Practice,* Conference Proceedings, November 12–13, 2005, Rice University, Houston, Tex. (Somerset, N.J.: Tughra Books, 2009), 303.

64. Agai, *Zwischen Netzwerk und Diskurs*, 167–72; Hakan Yavuz, "The Gülen Movement: The Turkish Puritans," 35–42.

65. Agai, *Zwischen Netzwerk und Diskurs*, 168.

log and tolerance rather than hatred among groups, and … would deemphasize alcohol and nudity in its advertising."[66] The only connection between Fethullah Gülen and the newspaper is that he functions as a source of inspiration for many managers and journalists, and that he regularly contributes to the Turkish edition. The newspaper turned out to be a huge success and it now has the largest circulation of any newspaper in Turkey with some 700,000 daily subscriptions. When I visited the Zaman headquarters in Istanbul, together with my fellow travelers from the Rumi Forum Maryland, on August 15, 2009, one of the journalists told us that Zaman is different from other newspapers in that it does not concentrate on the world of showbiz and starlets and other ephemeral phenomena, but tries to promote collaboration and political civility. The newspaper avoids pictures and gossip that are not in line with the standards of Islam, and tries to reach out to intellectuals and religious people. As the journalist declared, "we try to give not only the facts but some backgrounds as well, for instance concerning the relations between the Turkish and the Kurdish people." *Zaman* does not specialize in religion; even though it sometimes includes articles by or about Gülen, it does not specifically cover news items from a religious point of view. It tries to be more reliable and to give more quality than the papers that are written from a specifically religious point of view. On the other hand, it does not cover many of the things in which the secular people are most interested, such as sports and stardom. The newspaper is somewhat profitable, although the number of subscriptions is decreasing because of the Internet. The profits go to a foundation that gives the money to local schools and other initiatives of the Hizmet Movement.[67]

Zaman does not publish newspapers only in Turkey, but has special editions in countries where many Turkish immigrants live as well. During my encounters with people from the Hizmet Movement in the Netherlands, described in the first chapter of

66. Ebaugh, *The Gülen Movement*, 87.

67. Interview with a journalist from *Today's Zaman*, Istanbul, August 15, 2009.

this book, I encountered a number of journalists from *Zaman*. I still remember being present at the opening by the Dutch Prime Minister of the media center of Time Media Group in Rotterdam in December 2005, and I also remember returning to the same building a number of times for interviews with Allaattin Erdal, director of the media group. At that time, *Zaman Hollanda* was published in Turkish, but it had a Dutch supplement every month.[68]

The English newspaper *Today's Zaman* started in 2007 for tourists and foreigners in Turkey. It quickly developed a wide circulation; more importantly it is very accessible on the Internet, where it offers a good source of news concerning Turkey and the world for those who are not able to read Turkish.[69]

Establishing an English edition of *Zaman* was one of the consequences of the fact that in the 1990s the Hizmet Movement widened its horizon to include a global audience. Something similar happened with the television network inspired by Gülen that was founded in 1989. Samanyolu TV (the name refers to the Milky Way) started to broadcast in 1993 and after a few difficult years it is now financially independent. The TV stations apply the same principles as the *Zaman* newspaper: quality and objectivity in the gathering of news, and family-friendly programming that excludes nudity and violence.[70] With the group of visitors from Rumi Forum Maryland, we talked with Hasan Bozaslan, who works in international sales and acquisitions with Samanyolu Broadcasting Group on August 17, 2009. He told us that the success of the TV programs was mainly based on a few simple rules: do not lie, and treat others well. He also told us that the organization is now rapidly expanding to include six channels: in 2007 a second channel was added, Mehtap [Moonlight] TV, which is a special channel for cultural

68. Even though *Zaman Hollanda* now has merged with its Belgian sister to become *Zaman Benelux,* it still has its own website, http://www.zamanhollanda.nl (accessed June 21, 2014).

69. See the self-presentation at http://www.todayszaman.com/about-us (accessed June 21, 2014).

70. Ebaugh, *The Gülen Movement*, 86.

and religious programs.[71] The third channel, Samanyolu Haber, is a news channel, while the fourth channel, Yumurcak TV is aimed at children. It is the first channel aimed solely at children in Turkey, and it does not show any violence or "magic," since this stimulates bad behavior. The fifth channel, Ebru TV, is aimed at the Turkish public in America and has its headquarters in New Jersey. Hasan Bozaslan told us that Ebru TV is now available on cable television in certain parts of that state, and it will be available soon in other parts of the United States as well. The sixth and final channel is Xazar TV which is aired in Azerbaijan. Bozaslan also talked about the future launching of Ebru TV Europe, but Samanyolu TV's website shows that this channel has become reality.[72] While Samanyolu Avrupa broadcasts mainly in Turkish, and sometimes in English or German, Ebru TV broadcasts entirely in English, so we see here a similar process as with *Zaman* and *Today's Zaman*. First, the original "esoteric" communication is broadened to include more and more forms of "exoteric" communication so that it is accessible to a wider public in Turkey, for instance through periodicals such as *Sızıntı*. Second, in the 1980s, in preparation for the years leading up to the new millennium, external forms of communication were opened that aim at a wider Turkish public and include an international dimension. In this way, the Hizmet network has been able to build bridges between the faith-based forms of internal communication and the more general forms of external communication that include not only the larger public in Turkey but in the Western world as well.

A final form of communication that should be mentioned here is the communication of the Hizmet network about itself. Again,

71. When I visited the channel's website (http://www.mehtap.tv/) during Ramadan 2010, it had photos of the Qur'ān and the Ka'ba, but also of Fethullah Gülen (accessed August 16, 2010).

72. Samanyolu Publishing Group's website now shows eight TV and three radio channels at the bottom of its website, see http://www.samanyolu.com.tr (accessed August 16, 2010). Since then, the broadcasting group has added Dünya TV which broadcasts in Kurdish. See http://www.samanyolu.tv/kurumsal/about-us (accessed June 21, 2014).

a mixture of internal and external communication is noticeable here. On the one hand, members of the network, in a number of scholarly articles and Ph.D. theses, increasingly describe the characteristics of this network, and of Fethullah Gülen's thinking as source of inspiration. On the other hand, members of the network are increasingly inviting scholars from outside to study these characteristics and to give their academic feedback about the characteristics. Being one of these scholars myself, I have attended a number of conferences on Fethullah Gülen and the so-called Gülen Movement in which "insiders" and "outsiders" collaborated to give a balanced approach that could pass critical tests. Because of these collaborations, the growing number of scholarly approaches of both insiders and outsiders is of great importance for the movement's self-image. At times such as ours in which many unfriendly outsiders try to discredit Fethullah Gülen and the people he inspired as Islamists with a hidden agenda, it is of the utmost importance to be able to show that they are open to research by everyone who is willing to take them seriously for what they are: a faith-based service movement consisting of volunteers inspired by the life and works of Fethullah Gülen.

Since I began writing this book, many new books and conference proceedings have been published; therefore, the survey that follows reproduces the "state of the art" in August 2010 with some updates for the years 2010–14; it might be quite different when this book is published and adds its voice to all the others. It is my impression that in the years between 2005–9, the main energy of the movement went into organizing the conferences and publishing all the conference papers in sometimes thick volumes and on websites; in the years after 2009 fewer conferences are being organized and more energy is being used to get some of the conference papers published in an academically sound environment. This development can be summarized as: fewer, but better publications.

The oldest of these conference volumes, and certainly among the best edited of the volumes, is a book edited by M. Hakan Yavuz and John L. Esposito, *Turkish Islam and the Secular State: The Gülen*

Movement. The book, published in 2003, contains contributions to a conference organized by the Center for Muslim-Christian Understanding at Georgetown University and Rumi Forum, both in Washington, D.C. Other conferences followed a few years later. At the moment of this writing, most of the contributions to these conferences are available on a number of websites devoted to Fethullah Gülen in English.

A first website contains the programs from and links to nine conferences organized by members of the Gülen Movement in cooperation with different universities. First, there is a series of five conferences organized in the southern United States with the title *Islam in the Contemporary World: the Fethullah Gülen Movement in Thought and Practice*, in Houston, Texas (Rice University, November 12–13, 2005); Dallas, Texas (Southern Methodist University, March 4–5, 2006); Norman, Oklahoma (University of Oklahoma, November 4–5, 2006); San Antonio, Texas (University of Texas at San Antonio, November 3, 2007) and Baton Rouge, Louisiana (Louisiana State University, 2009). Other conferences accessible through this website have been organized in Melbourne, Australia ("From Dialogue to Collaboration: the Vision of Fethullah Gülen and Muslim-Christian Relations," Australian Catholic University, July 15–16, 2009); London ("Muslim World in Transition: Contributions of the Gülen Movement," SOAS University of London, House of Lords, and London School of Economics, October 25–27, 2007); Rotterdam, the Netherlands ("Peaceful Coexistence: Fethullah Gülen's Initiatives in the Contemporary World," Erasmus University, November 22–23, 2007), and Los Angeles, California ("East and West Encounters: The Gülen Movement, December 4–6, 2009).[73]

Another website with Fethullah Gülen's name contains the papers of seven conferences on Gülen and the movement named for him: the conferences in Houston, Dallas, Norman, Melbourne, London, and Rotterdam, but also a conference in Washington, D.C.

73. http://fethullahgulenconference.org (accessed June 21, 2014).

("Islam in the Age of Global Challenges: Alternative Perspectives of the Gülen Movement," Georgetown University, November 14–15, 2008).[74] Still another website that bears Gülen's name refers to academic papers and conference proceedings without a clear order but containing the papers of a conference on "Preventing Violence and Achieving World Peace: the Contributions of the Gülen Movement to World Peace," organized by the Rumi Forum at the University of Maryland College Park on October 29, 2009.[75] A more extended search on the website will give a broader range of papers but such papers are not academic publications, as I have discussed in the introduction to this book, referring to the negative evaluations of such nonacademic approaches by a number of scholars.[76]

Meanwhile, Tughra Books has recently republished these proceedings in a series that could become an encyclopedia for research on Gülen and the Hizmet Movement. The series contains the proceedings of the conferences in Houston, Dallas, Oklahoma, San Antonio, London, Rotterdam, and Washington D.C. I bought the first four volumes in the Kaynak International Bookstore in Cağaloğlu (Istanbul), and saw the others in the offices of the president of the Rumi Forum in Washington, D.C, but the books are not included in the official publisher's list, probably because they have not been reedited for publication.[77]

As I said before, in recent years there have been fewer publi-

74. See http://www.fgulen.org/conference-papers.html (accessed August 17, 2010, and June 21, 2014).

75. See http://www.fethullah-gulen.org/conference-proceedings/ (accessed August 26, 2010, and June 21, 2014).

76. In the introduction, I referred to the recent publication by David Tittensor, *The House of Service* (Oxford: Oxford University Press, 2014), x.

77. The volumes edited by Tughra Books and the proceedings of the London and Rotterdam conferences have International Standard Book Numbers (ISBNs) and therefore are available to the public. The proceedings from the conferences in Washington and Los Angeles do not have an ISBN. From an author's point of view, it is frustrating that sometimes the "best" contributions to a conference are selected for a scholarly publication but the unedited proceedings may be on the market for a number of years before the scholarly edited publication finally reaches the market. Therefore, I sometimes follow the growing custom of quoting from the contributions to these conferences as official publications.

cations but those have been of better quality. Apart from the early volume by Yavuz and Esposito,[78] five volumes were published between 2007 and 2013. Contributions to the conferences in Houston and Dallas were published in-house in 2007, and an academic volume still awaits publication.[79] Similarly, some of the papers for the conferences in London, Rotterdam, and Washington, D.C. were published in-house in 2010, but the academic publication was not published until 2012.[80] Papers from the conferences in Los Angeles and College Park (Maryland) were published in 2012 and 2013 with different academic publishers.[81] I might have missed one or two publications, but it certainly looks as though the organizers of these conferences gradually aim for a more academically visible result of their work. Meanwhile, some publishing projects are still under way, and the conference "Mapping the Gülen Movement" in Amsterdam (October 2010) included a book-signing session with five authors of recent books about the movement.

These conferences might be the most important scholarly venue promoting knowledge about the Hizmet Movement to outsiders,

78. *Turkish Islam and the Secular State: The Gülen Movement,* ed. Hakan Yavuz and John Esposito (Syracuse, N.Y.: Syracuse University Press, 2003).

79. See Robert A. Hunt and Yüksel A. Aslandoğan, eds., *Muslim Citizens of the Globalized World: Contributions of the Gülen Movement* (Somerset, N.J.: The Light, 2007). After the conference in Houston, I was invited to edit my paper on "Fethullah Gülen's Contribution to Muslim-Christian Dialogue in the Context of Abrahamic Cooperation" for an academic publication edited by one of America's foremost scholars on Islam who chaired our panel at the conference in Houston. Unfortunately, plans for publication have not made any progress since. Very recently, I have been invited to submit my paper to the *Hizmet Studies Review*, a new scholarly peer-reviewed international journal on the Hizmet Movement, edited by Erkan Erkan Toğuşlu and Johan Leman at the Catholic University of Leuven, Belgium. See www.hizmetreview.com (accessed October 13, 2014).

80. John L. Esposito and İhsan Yilmaz, eds., *Islam and Peacebuilding: Gülen Movement Initiatives* (New York: Blue Dome Press, 2010); Paul Weller and Ihsan Yilmaz, eds., *European Muslims, Civility and Public Life: Perspectives on and from the Gülen Movement* (New York: Continuum, 2012).

81. Sophia Pandya and Nancy Gallagher, eds., *The Gülen Hizmet Movement and Its Transnational Activities: Case Studies of Altruistic Activism in Contemporary Islam* (Boca Raton, Fla.: BrownWalker Press, 2012); Ori Z. Soltes and Margaret A. Johnson, eds., *Preventing Violence and Achieving World Peace: The Contributions of the Gülen Movement* (New York: Peter Lang, 2013).

but there are other venues as well. Zeki Saritoprak, the first president of the Rumi Forum and one of the first members of the Gülen Movement to be appointed as a Muslim theologian in a Catholic university in the United States, edited a special edition of *The Muslim World* in 2005. Finally, there is a growing number of scholars from countries with a Muslim background who recently published their Ph.D. theses on Gülen and his movement, even though almost all of these theses have a social-scientific nature. Some others, such as Rainer Hermann, Mehmet Enes Ergene, and Nevval Sevindi contribute to our knowledge of the life and works of Fethullah Gülen from the perspective of a (well-informed) journalist.[82] Jill Carroll and Helen Rose Ebaugh have written the most mature scholarly contributions thus far, from a philosophical and a sociological point of view respectively.[83] Walter Wagner's book, that I saw just before writing these lines, looks like an interesting Christian theological contribution even though it is quite different from mine.[84] These scholarly approaches are necessary to balance the more numerous occasions in which the names of Fethullah Gülen and of the Hizmet Movement are mentioned in the public media. Some of this media attention is positive, such as reports about Gülen's election as the top public intellectual in a contest organized by Foreign Policy and Prospect in 2008. Some of the media attention is less positive, such as the suspicions about Gülen's hidden agenda concerning a political Islam, brought up by several political commentators in both the United States and the Netherlands (and in Turkey, of course, as described in the second chapter of this book).

82. Rainer Hermann, *Wohin geht die türkische Gesellschaft? Kulturkampf in der Türkei.* (München: Deutscher Taschenbuch Verlag, 2009); Ergene, *Tradition Witnessing the Modern Age*; Nevval Sevindi, *Contemporary Islamic Conversations. M. Fethullah Gülen on Turkey, Islam, and the West* (Albany, N.Y.: State University of New York Press, 2008).

83. B. Jill Carroll, *A Dialogue of Civilizations. Gülen's Islamic Ideals and Humanistic Discourse* (Somerset, N.J.: The Light, Inc, 2007); Helen Rose Ebaugh, *The Gülen Movement: A Sociological Analysis of a Civic Movement Rooted in Moderate Islam* (Dordrecht: Springer, 2010).

84. Walter Wagner, *Beginnings and Endings: Fethullah Gülen's Vision for Today's World* (New York: Blue Dome Press, 2013).

However ambiguous the attention to Gülen by journalists, politicians, and other opinion leaders sometimes may be, it shows that favorable conditions have developed during the last couple of years for a truly scholarly study of the person and the thought of Fethullah Gülen, and of the network of faith-based service that he inspired. This book focuses on the theological dimension of the person and the network, and in that sense it is one-sided and can only contribute a preliminary understanding for a more encompassing study to be written in the future. But it is guided by the conviction that the theological dimension is the decisive dimension of Gülen's life and works, since he constantly repeats the assertion that he dedicates his whole life to the aim of fulfilling God's pleasure. Yet the study of Gülen, and in particular of the faith-based service network, cannot limit itself to these theological dimensions, since the notion of faith in Islam has an eminently practical connotation as we saw at the beginning of this chapter. We turn to this practical side in the next chapter, to discuss the three forms of service that are suggested by Gülen and organized by the institutions he inspired: education, dialogue, and charity. Since many contributions to the conferences mentioned above have focused on both Gülen's ideas and the institutions that enact these forms of *hizmet*, the next chapter will concentrate on a few concrete examples that I have encountered in my work with and research on the people in the Hizmet Movement.

6

THREE ELEMENTS OF FAITH-BASED SERVICE

In chapter five I tried to explain a characteristic of the faith-based service movement inspired by Fethullah Gülen, or in short the Hizmet Movement, by describing the basis of the motivation for renewal of faith by *hizmet,* or service, that can be detected in Gülen's writings. After reading a number of Gülen's works and consulting a number of his first followers, I have come to the conclusion that this basic motivation is *rıza-i İlahi*, seeking God's pleasure. This theological motivation is discussed and put into practice through a specific form of religious communication in the Hizmet Movement: the *sohbet.* This does not only include a religious conversation about basic texts from the Qur'ān or important interpretations by Said Nursi or Fethullah Gülen, but it includes a "business meeting" as well in which proposals for service activities are brought forward and discussed. In this way, there is a strong connection between the theological idea of "working for God's pleasure" and the practical implementation through forms of service for the benefit of humankind. In the next chapter, I will try to show that this strong connection has analogies in Christian forms of religious life, for instance in the Jesuit idea of working *ad maiorem Dei gloriam* (to the greater glory of God), which translates itself in educating young students to become "men and women for (and with) others."

In this chapter, however, I want to pay more attention to the several forms in which this faith-based *hizmet* or service is put into practice by persons from the network inspired by Gülen. Since this is the aspect of the Hizmet Movement that is studied most often in the contributions to the conferences on the so-called Gülen Movement mentioned at the end of the last chapter, I can limit myself largely to discussing my own experiences with the movement, and to referring to the most important studies in the fields in which the movement has become active. As is now recognized by most scholars, there are three fields in which the Hizmet network develops its activities: education, dialogue, and charity.[1] These fields are not chosen by coincidence but are connected with developments in Fethullah Gülen's thinking. While one gets the impression, looking back at the beginnings of the activities of the Hizmet Movement, that Gülen did not have a fixed plan but answered the need for education expressed by the people at the Kestanepazarı religious foundation in Izmir, yet education has always been a primary field of interest for Gülen. This is because, as I mentioned in the introduction, he saw ignorance, together with poverty and disunity, as the basic diseases that tormented the Muslim world at the time and that continue to torment it in the twenty first century. Gülen is quite consistent in his analysis of these root causes, since in a recent interview he states: "the foundation of terrorism has always been poverty, ignorance, and lack of education in the Islamic world."[2] This analysis goes back to Gülen's teacher Bediüzzaman Said Nursi, who, in his programmatic Damascus sermon back in 1911, mentioned these three among the sicknesses that caused the backwardness of the Islamic world.[3] In his article on Kimse Yok Mu, the central organization for the charity activi-

1. These are not the only fields in which activities have been developed. Helen Ebaugh, *The Gülen Movement. A Sociological Analysis of a Civic Movement Rooted in Moderate Islam* (Dordrecht: Springer, 2010), for instance, discusses activities in the world of banking and finance as well.

2. See Nevval Sevindi, *Contemporary Islamic Conversations: M. Fethullah Gülen on Turkey, Islam, and the West* (Albany, N.Y.: State University of New York Press, 2008), 57.

3. Said Nursi, *The Damascus Sermon*, trans. Şükran Vahide (Istanbul: Sözler Neşriyat, 1996).

ties of the Hizmet Movement, Jesuit theologian Thomas Michel shows how Gülen took the initiative to overcome these evils by developing initiatives in the three fields.[4] First, in the 1980s, the battle against ignorance was central in building a great number of schools and other educational institutions; therefore, I will discuss my experiences with some of these schools and institutions in the first section of this chapter. Next, in the 1990s, in order to combat disunity between believers and other human beings, a number of dialogue activities were developed both in Turkey and around the world. Therefore, the intercultural and interreligious dialogue initiatives will be the subject of the second section of this chapter. Finally, the beginning of the twenty-first century saw the start of the fight against poverty through Kimse Yok Mu, a more central organization with a name that can be translated as "Isn't there anybody who cares?" In this way, those who are inspired by the thoughts and initiatives of Fethullah Gülen put his analysis into practice by developing activities that can be summarized as *hizmet*, the Turkish word for service: opening schools to overcome ignorance, opening dialogue institutions to overcome disunity, and organizing charity to overcome poverty.

EDUCATION AS FAITH-BASED SERVICE

The Hizmet Movement found its origins in initiatives in the field of education because of Gülen's pragmatic approach. Since he did not want to limit his function to teaching at the Qur'ān-school at the Kestanepazarı Mosque in Izmir and to preaching in the city, he tried to reach out to all people, including nonreligious Turkish workers and students in the coffee houses. He also told the members of the board of directors of the religious foundation that they should do more than just care for preaching and religious educa-

4. Thomas Michel, SJ, "Fighting Poverty with Kimse Yok Mu," in *Islam in the Age of Global Challenges: Alternative Perspectives of the Gülen Movement*, Conference Proceedings, Georgetown University, Washington, D.C., November 14–15, 2008 (Washington, D.C.: Rumi Forum, 2008), 523–33.

tion. He wanted to spend his energy – and the persons that I interviewed in Izmir agreed that he was full of energy – to mend the situation at those places where the need was greatest. So, when Yusuf Pekmezci and his friends suggested that education was the field where the need was greatest, Gülen decided to spend his energy and his religious devotion to please God by serving those in need of better education. Even though he was a teacher and a preacher in a religious context himself, Gülen did not aim for explicitly religious education but for better educational standards and for circumstances that made this better education possible. This is a very important difference from the Islamist models in which religious education was the central focus. Even more significantly, Gülen is reported to have said: "We do not need mosques, but we need schools."

Even beyond this pragmatic approach, education has always been a very important focus for Fethullah Gülen. His autobiographical interviews deal with the topic of education at great length, and over the years it would remain the most visible characteristic of the Hizmet Movement. From *Towards the Lost Paradise* to *The Statue of Our Souls*, a large part of Gülen's intellectual discourse focuses on education as probably the most important task that this generation faces.[5] He has a saying, "most people can be teachers, but the number of educators is very limited."[6] This expresses his sense of urgency well, just like Gülen's wish that many of the students in the Hizmet Movement not choose professions that might pay well or give prestige, but rather choose to educate others. "Gülen advised his students to become teachers so that the most intelligent would no longer strive to be engineers or doctors, but educators."[7] Consequently, the status of educators within the Hizmet Movement is high.[8] Therefore, the stress on education in Gülen and the Hizmet

5. See M. Fethullah Gülen, *Towards the Lost Paradise* (Izmir: Kaynak, 1998); *The Statue of Our Souls: Revival in Islamic Thought and Activism* (Somerset, N.J.: The Light, 2005).

6. M. Fethullah Gülen, *Pearls of Wisdom* (Fairfax, Va.: The Fountain, 2000), 34.

7. Interview with Ali Yurtsever, Izmir, August 8, 2009.

8. Ian Williams, "'A Station Above That of Angels': The Vision of Islamic Education within Pluralistic Societies in the Thought of Fethullah Gülen – A Study of

Movement is more than just a pragmatic solution to a problem that occurred by coincidence. As Gürbüz Dönmez indicated when I interviewed him, Said Nursi had already taught Gülen that ignorance is one of the basic vices of the Muslim world, and that education is therefore one of the basic medications needed to mend the situation of the Islamic world. Moreover, as several authors have indicated, Gülen's thoughts on education link up with a long and deep tradition in the history of Islam.[9] Nor is he the only one to identify ignorance as the basic problem of the Muslim world today.[10] Finally, as discussed in chapter four, Ergün Çapan's precious insight into Gülen's own teaching activities shows that his life is in accordance with his message.[11]

All of this is enough of an indication that education, rightly, is the most important institutional aspect of the Hizmet Movement, both in theory and in practice, and many authors have studied this aspect from different points of view. Even a selective choice from the recent contributions to conferences and other publications gives a rich harvest. Some authors concentrate on an analysis of Gülen's philosophy of education, both from outsider (Christian) perspectives (Michel, Williams) and from insider perspectives (Aslandoğan).[12]

Contrasts between Turkey and the UK," in *Muslim World in Transition: Contributions of the Gülen Movement*, Conference Proceedings, London , 25–27 October 2007 (London: Leeds Metropolitan University Press), 585–96.

9. See Williams, "'A Station Above That of Angels,'" and Asma Afsarrudin, "Education: Classical Views and M. Fethullah Gülen's Perspectives," in *Islam in the Contemporary World 1: The Fethullah Gülen Movement in Thought and Practice*, Conference Proceedings, November 12–13, 2005, Rice University Houston, Tex. (Somerset, N.J.: Tughra books, 2009), 78–94.

10. See Joseph Lumbard, "The Decline of Knowledge and the Rise of Ideology in the Modern Islamic World," in *Islam, Fundamentalism, and the Betrayal of Tradition*, ed. Joseph E. B. Lumbard (Bloomington, Ind.: World Wisdom, 2009), 39–77.

11. Ergün Çapan, "Gülen's Teaching Methodology in His Private Circle," in *Mastering Knowledge in Modern Times: Fethullah Gülen as an Islamic Scholar*, ed. İsmail Albayrak (New York: Blue Dome Press, 2011), 127–56.

12. Michel, Thomas, SJ, "Fethullah Gülen as Educator," in *Turkish Islam and the Secular State: the Gülen Movement*, ed. M. Hakan Yavuz and John L. Esposito (Syracuse, N.Y.: Syracuse University Press, 2003), 69–84; Bekim Agai, *Zwischen Netzwerk und Diskurs: Das Bildungsnetzwerk um Fethullah Gülen (geb. 1938): Die flexible Umset-*

Some others have interviewed teachers from the Hizmet Movement, and the interviews with female teachers by Özdalga and Turam are often quoted.[13] In his recent monograph, David Tittensor takes a somewhat more critical approach by comparing the views of teachers with the views of students in schools operated by the Hizmet Movement.[14]

Still others have described the situation and the contribution of these schools in different parts of the world. Many of the contributions to several conferences on the Hizmet Movement have been devoted to the description of what is nowadays often called, in different parts of the world, "Gülen-inspired schools."[15]A selection of these conference papers gives a fair idea of the different

zung modernen islamischen Gedankenguts, Bonner Islamstudien 2 (Schenefeld: EB-Verlag, 2004), 191–260; Yüksel Aslandoğan and Muhammed Çetin, "Gülen's Educational Paradigm in Thought and Practice," in *Muslim Citizens of the Globalized World*, ed. Robert A. Hunt and Yüksel A. Aslandoğan (Somerset, N.J.: The Light, 2007), 34–61; Y. Alp Aslandoğan, "Pedagogical Model of Gülen and Modern Theories of Learning," in *Islam in the Contemporary World 2: The Fethullah Gülen Movement in Thought and Practice* (Somerset, N.J.: Tughra Books, 2009), 115–23.See also Ruth Woodhall, "An Examination of Fethullah Gülen's Philosophy of Education and the Educational Activities of His Movement," in *Islam in the Contemporary World 1*, 60–77; Gürkan Çelik, *The Gülen Movement: Building Social Cohesion through Dialogue and Education* (Delft: Eburon, 2010), 97–116; Hakan Yavuz, *Toward an Islamic Enlightenment: The Gülen Movement* (New York: Oxford University Press, 2013), 92–116.

13. Elizabeth Özdalga, "Following in the Footsteps of Fethullah Gülen," in *Turkish Islam and the Secular State*, ed. Yavuz and Esposito, 85–114; Berna Turam, *Between Islam and the State: The Politics of Engagement* (Stanford, Calif.: Stanford University Press, 2007), 67–88; Jill Irvine, "The Gülen Movement and Turkish Integration in Germany," in *Muslim Citizens of the Globalized World. Contributions of the Gülen Movement*, ed. Robert A. Hunt and Yüksel A. Aslandoğan (Somerset, N.J.: The Light, 2007), 62–84.

14. David Tittensor, *The House of Service: The Gülen Movement and Islam's Third Way* (New York: Oxford University Press, 2014), 95–133.

15. A website named "Gulen Inspired Schools" (http://gulenschools.org/home.html, accessed June 22, 2014) gives information about Fethullah Gülen and the so-called Gülen Movement, and also explains the difference between Gülen (Inspired) Schools and Public Charter Schools. However, the website does not contain a list of such schools. Later in this chapter we will see that anti-Gülen websites in the United States carry such lists. A link to a blogger's website (http://www.guleneducation.com, accessed June 22, 2014) provides positive stories about these schools from all around the world.

places where the schools are located.[16] Historically speaking, the first schools were of course founded in Turkey.[17] From there, the schools expanded in the 1990s to the some of the Turkic nations that were parts of the former Soviet Union.[18] Around the turn of the millennium, schools began to spread to different nations in Europe: among the countries that have been studied are the United Kingdom,[19] Germany and France,[20] the Netherlands,[21] and Russia.[22] Other articles describe the situation of the schools in Asia,[23]

16. The symposium "The Hizmet Movement and Peacebuilding: Global Cases" in Washington, D.C. (October 24–26, 2013), emphasized local initiatives, so many papers at this conference could be added to the literature in this section. However, the website of the conference only gives abstracts of the papers; see http://www.peacebuilding2013.org/synopses (accessed June 22, 2014).

17. Agai (*Zwischen Netzwerk und Diskurs,* 268–98) gives information about the schools in Turkey, compared to those in Albania and Germany.

18. See Turam, *Between Islam and the State*, for Kazakhstan; Victoria Levinskaya, "Resemblance of Fethullah Gülen's Ideas and Current Political Developments in Uzbekistan," in *Peaceful Coexistence: Fethullah Gülen's Initiatives in the Contemporary World* (London: Leeds Metropolitan University Press), 331–43, for Uzbekistan.

19. See Williams, "A Station above that of Angels," and Ian Williams, "The Vision of Education within Pluralistic Societies in the Thought of Fethullah Gülen: The Contribution of Non-Denominational Education towards Inter-Religious and Communal Understanding, Peace and Identity. A Study of Contrasts in the UK, Turkey and the USA," in *Peaceful Coexistence: Fethullah Gülen's Initiatives in the Contemporary World* (London: Leeds Metropolitan University Press, 2007), 407–15.

20. Emre Demir, "The Emergence of a Neo-Communitarian Discourse in the Turkish Diaspora in Europe: The Implantation Strategies and Competition Logics of the Gülen Movement in France and in Germany," in *European Muslims, Civility and Public Life: Perspectives on and from the Gülen Movement*, ed. Paul Weller and Ihsan Yilmaz (New York: Continuum, 2012), 101–12. For the situation in Germany, see Walter Homolka et al., eds., *Muslime zwischen Tradition und Moderne. Die Gülen-Bewegung als Brücke zwischen den Kulturen* (Freiburg: Herder, 2010).

21. Tineke Peppinck, "From 'New Man' to 'World Citizen': The Replication of Fethullah Gülen's Renovation Vision in the Dutch Context," in *European Muslims, Civility and Public Life: Perspectives on and from the Gülen Movement*, ed. Paul Weller and Ihsan Yilmaz (New York: Continuum, 2012), 91–100.

22. Farhod Alimuhamedov, "Peaceful Muslim – Non-Muslim Coexistence in a Secular Context," in *Peaceful Coexistence: Fethullah Gülen's Initiatives in the Contemporary World* (London: Leeds Metropolitan University Press, 2007), 373–81.

23. See Michel, "Fethullah Gülen as Educator" for the Philippines (Mindanao); Philipp Bruckmayr, "Pnom Penh's Fethullah Gülen School as an Alternative to Prevalent Forms of Education for Cambodia's Muslim Minority," in *Islam and Peacebuild-*

Africa,[24] and Australia.[25] Of special interest are some articles that describe the role of schools in conflict-ridden areas such as the Kurdish region of southeast Turkey and northern Iraq, or the Mindanao Islands in the Philippines, or Kosovo in southeast Europe.[26] The survey of countries gives a fairly good idea of the distribution of the Gülen-inspired schools over the world.[27] It is, however, remarkable that there is no survey of the situation of these schools in the United States.[28]

---

ing: Gülen Movement Initiatives, ed. John L. Esposito and İhsan Yilmaz (New York: Blue Dome Press), 225–48.

24. Yasien Mohamed, "The Educational Theory of Fethullah Gülen and its Practice in South Africa," in *Muslim World in Transition: Contributions of the Gülen Movement* (London: Leeds Metropolitan University Press, 2007), 552–71; Mehmet Kalyoncu, "Gülen Inspired Schools in East Africa: Secular Alternative in Kenya and Pragmatist Approach to Development in Uganda," in *Islam in the Age of Global Challenges*, 350–73; Hasan Aydin and Stephen K. Lafer, "Promoting Multicultural Harmony in Nigeria: the Gülen-Inspired Schools," in *The Gülen Hizmet Movement and Its Transnational Activities. Case Studies of Altruistic Activism in Contemporary Islam*, ed. Sophia Pandya and Nancy Gallagher (Boca Raton, Fla.: BrownWalker Press, 2012), 195–211.

25. Greg Barton, "How the Hizmet Works: Islam, Dialogue and the Gülen Movement in Australia," in *Islam in the Age of Global Challenges*, 114–43; Çemen Polat, "Gülen-Inspired Schools in Australia and Their Funding," in *The Gülen Hizmet Movement and Its Transnational Activities*, ed. Pandya and Gallagher, 171–93.

26. See Mehmet Kalyoncu, "Building Civil Society in Ethno-Religiously Fractured Communities: The Gülen Movement in Turkey and Abroad," in *Islam and Peacebuilding: Gülen Movement Initiatives*, ed. John L. Esposito and İhsan Yilmaz (New York: Blue Dome Press, 2010), 273–90; Harun Akyol, "The Role of Turkish Schools in Building Trusting Cross-Ethnic Relationships in Northern Iraq," in *Islam and Peacebuilding: Gülen Movement Initiatives*, 311–39. For Mindanao, see Michel, "Fethullah Gülen as Educator." For Kosovo, see Jeton Mehmeti, "The Role of Education in Kosovo and the Contribution of the Gülen Movement," in *The Gülen Hizmet Movement and its Transnational Activities*, ed. Pandya and Gallagher, 213–21.

27. Apart from these articles, it is noteworthy that the *New York Times* published an article, "Turkish Schools Offer Pakistan a Gentler Vision of Islam" in its issue of May 4, 2008 (written by Sabrina Tavernise), and *Time Magazine* published an article titled "Muslim Missionary: The Preacher and His Teachers" about Gülen-inspired teachers in Kazakhstan (written by Pelin Turgut) in its issue of April 26, 2010. More such articles can be found on the website about Gülen-Inspired Schools.

28. The book *The Gülen Hizmet Movement and Its Transnational Activities*, ed. Pandya and Gallagher, contains a section on "Hizmet, Women, and Gender," 97–168, with articles by Sophia Pandya, Fran Hassencahl, Margaret Rausch, and April Naj-

In chapter three I discussed the beginning of the educational initiatives of Fethullah Gülen and his supporters in Izmir. The first house that would serve as a boarding school was rented in 1968, and the first dormitory, Güzelyali, was founded in 1971. The first preparatory courses for universities were organized in Manisa in 1974, and finally in 1982 the first high school, Yamanlar Koleji, was established in Izmir. In later years, the schools spread, first in Turkey in the 1980s, later in the central Asian countries in the 1990s after the dissolution of the Soviet Union, and in Europe, where these schools were founded by Turkish immigrants. Finally, schools were founded in Australia, Africa, and North America as well. It is difficult to give the precise number of these schools since there is no central administration or registration, but the most recent survey gives a number of more than 1,000 schools in some 100 countries over five continents.[29] In the United States, there might be almost 100 schools inspired by Gülen, concentrated mainly in Texas, Ohio, California, and Arizona, but this information comes from a website that is hostile toward Gülen's thinking and should therefore be taken with some caution.[30] I came across another website with the neutral title "A Guide to the Gulen Movement Activities in the US," and this website gives a list of 115 "Gülen schools" in the U.S., mainly publicly funded charter schools, but some private schools as well. The home page of the website, though, says the following:

> We're assuming you've arrived at this website because you are a parent or teacher at a Gulen charter school. You've somehow found out about allegations that your school is associated with a Muslim preacher and leader called Fethullah Gulen, or with the Gulen Movement. We assume you would like more facts about this. There is a large amount of conflict-

jaj that discuss the situation of female members of the Hizmet Movement and that touch on matters of teaching as well.

29. See Ebaugh, *The Gülen Movement*, 97.

30. Paul Williams, "Education Jihad Sweeps the Country – A Guide to the Gulen Schools in America" (www.familysecuritymatters.org, accessed July 5, 2010). On Williams's hostility towards Gülen, see the last section of chapter two.

ing information on the internet about Gulen and his schools. The Gulen Movement itself has many websites, and they will not give you accurate information. This is why we've put together this site as a place for you to get started in your research. We hope you find it helpful.[31]

The only two places where I could find information about "Gülen schools" in the United States are in fact websites that alert people to the dangers lurking behind these seemingly decent schools. They count and list schools, suggesting that a clandestine organization tries to extend its influence while the people who built and financed the schools do not seem to be aware of such a central organization.[32] Yet since people working in the Hizmet sometimes seem engaged in covering up connections that might suggest a many-branched network, their opponents see the shadows of such a secret organization. A more balanced recent article in *USA Today* still focuses on the question of why the people responsible for these charter schools deny "any organic connection" with Fethullah Gülen.[33]

One of the most common findings of the research on the schools inspired by Gülen is that they belong to the most successful schools in every nation where they are founded. Helen Rose Ebaugh makes the following general observation:

A major characteristic of the Gülen institutions is their recognized quality, regardless of the sector in which they are operating. The Gülen-inspired schools are recognized both in Turkey and in many other countries in which they now operate as first-rate schools. The fact that a very high per-

31. See http://turkishinvitations.weebly.com/index.html (accessed August 20, 2010). This website contains some very suggestive texts, but some objective information as well.

32. See, for instance, a suggestive article by Claire Berlinski in *City Journal*, Fall 2012 (http://www.city-journal.org/2012/22_4_fethullah-gulen.html, accessed October 31, 2012 and June 22, 2014). The subtitle characterizes Gülen as "Controversial Muslim preacher, feared Turkish intriguer — and 'inspirer' of the largest charter school network in America."

33. See Greg Toppo, "Objectives of Charter Schools with Turkish Ties Questioned," (http://www.usatoday.com/news/education/2010-08-17-turkishfinal17_CV_N.html, accessed August 25, 2010).

centage of their students pass the university entrance exam and go to colleges within Turkey and abroad and the extraordinary number of students from Gülen schools who win top prizes in the Turkish as well as national academic Olympiads is testimony to the excellence of the education provided in these schools.[34]

If one wonders what the reason is for this excellence, the research described above comes to a fairly unanimous conclusion: the curriculum of these schools is not very special, because the Gülen-inspired schools adapt to the requirements of the country or state where they operate; but the teachers are very special. They really care about the students and work with them day and night in order to provide them with the best education possible. Ebaugh reaches the following conclusion: "In addition to sharing a common culture of ideas and values, and as part of this culture, a major reason for the success of the Gülen institutions is the commitment and dedication of the personnel who run them."[35] Inspired by Gülen's model, they do more than necessary, or in Gülen's words: they are real educators who contribute to a new, "golden" generation. This motivation makes clear how education is more than just a job for those who are inspired by Gülen: it is indeed a faith-based form of service to the younger generation.

I want to finish this section on education as faith-based service in the Hizmet Movement by telling about my own experience, using impressions gained in visiting different types of schools in different countries, and in several interviews.

As I said in the first chapter, my first encounter with dialogue-oriented Turkish Muslims in the Netherlands was on the occasion of an *iftar* during Ramadan 2001. This *iftar* dinner took place at

34. Ebaugh, *The Gülen Movement*, 106–7.

35. Ibid., 105. Even though Hendrick (*Gülen*) and Tittensor (*House of Service*) agree with Ebaugh's conclusion concerning the academic excellence of the schools, they are more skeptical of the motives of the teachers and of the students: applying the rational choice theory, they argue that such education also serves them to gain a better position in society.

the boarding school where Turkish children lived and did their homework, supervised by elder brothers who were inspired by Fethullah Gülen. In the first couple of years I came to this boarding school a few times for interfaith meetings, and the impression that I got during these meetings was that the students were very nice and polite, that the place was neat and clean, but that it also reflected the poor conditions of the first and second generations of foreign Turkish "guest workers" (*gastarbeiders*) in the Netherlands. A few years later, I came into contact with the Cosmicus Foundation that supervises, among others, a limited number of schools by that name in the Netherlands. The word *cosmicus* refers to the idea of a world citizen, and this is the leading idea of the foundation and its schools. The website of the foundation (in its 2010 version) contained a very interesting statement on its vision and mission, prefaced by a motto from the University of Notre Dame's president Father Theodore Hesburgh: "The very essence of leadership is that you have to have a vision. You can't blow an uncertain trumpet."[36] The Cosmicus Foundation began as an association for students, alumni, and academics of Turkish origin, and at the time of our encounter, which is described in the first chapter of this book, Gürkan Çelik was its president. After years in which the foundation mainly organized homework tutoring courses and circles of entrepreneurs, Cosmicus succeeded in founding Cosmicus College which is now quite a famous school in Rotterdam, the second largest city in the Netherlands and also the city with the highest percentage of Muslims. All organizations inspired by Gülen have their base in Rotterdam, but it is also the city of Pim Fortuyn, the politician who was murdered in 2002 by an animal rights activist after he made a name with his protest against the "Islamization of Dutch culture." In February 2007, Cosmicus College was inaugurated by Maria van der Hoeven, the Dutch minis-

36. http://www.cosmicus.nl/site/index3.php?id=186&catid= (accessed August 20, 2010). This page was no longer active in 2014; the new mission statement of Cosmicus can be found at http://www.stichtingcosmicus.nl/stichting-cosmicus/over-cosmicus (accessed June 22, 2014).

ter of education, with a resoundingly positive speech.[37] But other politicians began to ask why the government would pay for such a school, and this led to a highly profiled news item in the summer of 2008 that spread imputations concerning the hidden agenda of Fethullah Gülen and his followers, as I described in chapter one.[38] Consequently, the school had to place an FAQ item on its website, denying that it was an Islamic school: "contrary to what many people think, the school is not an Islamic school. There is no religious education, and no distinction is being made between different faith backgrounds of the students. They get an introduction to world citizenship, but this course is of an anthropological, not of a religious nature."[39]

Some of the leading men in the media who discussed Fethullah Gülen and his schools in the Netherlands were Dutch scholars of Turkish history and of Islam. I knew some of them personally, and I saw how they were divided into camps either in favor of or against the "Gülenist institutions" in the Netherlands. It came as no surprise, therefore, that when one of them, Dr. Karel Steenbrink, gave a paper on the Cosmicus school at a conference on "Muslims between Tradition and Modernity: The Gülen Movement as a Bridge between Cultures" at the University of Potsdam, May 26–27, 2009, he began his speech by saying that some of his colleagues had told him not to go since his appearance would be misused as support for the movement.[40]

37. See *Today's Zaman* of February 3, 2007 (www.todayszaman.com, accessed August 20, 2010).

38. A news item concerning this political inquiry about the trustworthiness of the Gülen Movement was published in an article in the Dutch newspaper *Nederlands Dagblad* of May 1, 2010. The article ("De inclusieve islam," or Inclusive Islam) focuses on Cosmicus College and contains a number of interviews with insiders and outsiders related to Cosmicus and other organizations inspired by Gülen in the Netherlands, on the occasion of the publication of a book about Gülen in Dutch: *Fethullah Gülen & de Vrijwilligersbeweging*, ed. Gürkan Çelik and Pim Valkenberg (Budel: Damon, 2010).

39. My translation from http://www.cosmicuscollege.nl/index.php?option= com _content&view =article&id=242&Itemid=76 (accessed August 20, 2010).

40. Unfortunately, the conference proceedings have not been published yet, and the abstracts have only been distributed on paper. However, I recently found a link

In the context of this same conference, I was able to visit another school associated with the ideas of Fethullah Gülen in nearby Berlin-Spandau on May 28, 2009. While this school did not differ very much from other public or private schools that I would visit later in the Netherlands, Turkey, or the United States – in the latter case, looking for a suitable middle school or high school for my own children – I remember four things that I found remarkable, and that I would see in other Gülen-inspired schools as well. In the first place, the students are very courteous, polite, and proud of their schools; they seem to like to show them to visitors. In the second place, students and teachers alike are proud of qualitative innovations and state of the art equipment, specifically in the natural sciences. In the third place, multilingual education is the common standard, and in Germany this means that students do not only learn German and Turkish but English as well. The school building has an "English street" that looked like an exact copy of the English street in the school that I would visit three months later in Izmir. In the fourth place, the building and the place where we had lunch together could be described as clean but simple; the money that was available was being spent for education, not for luxury. This combination of cleanliness and austerity is characteristic of Hocaefendi's lifestyle as well.

The school in Berlin is part of TÜDESB, an organization of Turkish schools in Germany. In her interviews with teachers and parents at this school, Jill Irvine found out that, like the Cosmicus school in Rotterdam, they do not offer any course in religion but teach a general course in ethics.[41] Her interviews also confirmed my impression that the relations between the civil authorities and the private school are quite good. Apparently, the situation is less tense in Germany than it is in Rotterdam. Nevertheless, when Turkish Prime Minister Recep Tayyip Erdoğan suggested, in March 2010,

---

to the papers on the website of the Journalists and Writers Foundation; Steenbrink's paper may be viewed at http://gyv.org.tr/content/userfiles/pdf/makaleing_karel_steenbrink.pdf (accessed June 23, 2014).

41. Jill Irvine, "The Gülen Movement and Turkish Integration in Germany," 77.

building more Turkish schools in Germany, his colleague Angela Merkel did not agree as she insisted that Turkish children in Germany should attend schools where they have to speak German. Even though Erdoğan did not specifically refer to schools inspired by Gülen's ideals, he might very well have had the existing bilingual Turkish *gymnasia* in Berlin, Cologne, Mannheim, and Hannover in mind.[42] But the multicultural ideals that some see as promoting integration are considered to hinder real integration by others.[43]

I can give a brief impression of one of the first Turkish schools founded by Gülen and his supporters in Izmir as well. I visited this school, one of the many locations of Yamanlar Koleji, together with Ali Yurtsever on August 9, 2009. Since this was a Sunday in August, it was quiet in the school, but Ali and some of his friends told me some interesting stories about its history. Originally, in 1976, it was built as the first boarding school initiated by Fethullah Gülen in Izmir, and in 1982 it became the first school of the movement. Yurtsever remembers that Gülen expressed his expectations of the students as follows: "I want them to be disciplined like soldiers, knowledgeable like doctors, spiritual like members of a *tekke* (Sufi lodge), and healthy like athletes." Originally, the building housed all classes, but later it only retained grades six through eight, while other grades were transferred to other buildings. It is the oldest of nine Yamanlar schools in Izmir, and Dr. Yurtsever was its director between 1993 and 1997. He told me that Hocaefendi personally assisted in building the school and that he refused money from Saudi Arabia since he wanted the school to be an entirely local initiative. He even brought in the benefactors to guard the buildings during the night, so that they would remain connected to the project. This has since then always been characteristic of the schools inspired by

42. My Dutch newspaper, *NRC Handelsblad*, March 26, 2010, mentions these four schools in a news item. Erdoğan's proposal was mentioned by *Die Zeit*, March 24; see http://www.zeit.de/politik/ausland/2010-03/erdogan-eu-beitritt-gymnasium (accessed June 22, 2014).

43. *Die Zeit* published an article on Berlin's *TÜDESB-gymnasium* in its online edition of February 25, 2010: *Die Streber Allahs*, http://www.zeit.de/2010/08/Deutsch-Tuerkische-Privatschulen

Gülen: they were funded with money gathered by local businessmen. When the school no longer requires support, the local entrepreneurs often go on to find another educational project; originally these were in eastern Anatolia, but later more frequently on other continents as well.[44] Later in this chapter, I will give some examples of this process. Meanwhile, Ali Yurtsever explained that local support was essential for the institutions in the United States as well. When he was the president of Rumi Forum, until 2009, the principle was that the organization could only support projects insofar as they could be locally financed. Thanks to local money, Rumi Forum could hire a somewhat larger building and it could also start a school in Virginia, but they could not fund activities elsewhere in the United States.[45]

Regarding the present state of Yamanlar Koleji, I observed that the buildings were simple but clean, with much attention to languages and sciences. Also, there was a special corner devoted to Mustafa Kemal Atatürk, which one would not expect in an institution inspired by Gülen; but this is not so strange if one considers the identity of these schools as not explicitly Islamic but as adapting to local or national customs.[46] Moreover, as I said before, Gülen does not like to be in opposition to local or national government, but to work with them whenever possible. In the Burç boarding school where I stayed during the week, there was a statue of Atatürk and some attention to his educational ideas as well. Another specific thing that I noticed in Yamanlar College was the attention to the prizes that a number of students of the college won in school Olympiads. This was one of the themes that recurred in the public relations materials of the schools, and on the notice boards in the school itself.[47]

44. Ebaugh, *The Gülen Movement*, 106.

45. Interview with Ali Yurtsever, Izmir, August 9, 2009.

46. Tittensor (*The House of Service*, 45) explains that until 2008 every school was required to have an *Atatürk köşesi*, a corner devoted to the memory of Mustafa Kemal Atatürk. While many Islamists would object to such a custom, Gülen and the Hizmet Movement have always complied with the rules.

47. I consulted a few numbers of the *Okul Bülteni* (School Bulletin) from the first half of 2009.

The final school that I visited, together with my travel companions from Maryland, in August 2009 is one of the crown jewels of the educational institutions inspired by Gülen: Fatih University in Istanbul. I had heard of this institution a few years before when Dr. Şerif Ali Tekalan, head of the board of trustees of the university, visited my university in the Netherlands.[48] But we received a more complete survey during our visit at Fatih University's campus on August 17, 2009. First, we received some basic information from some of the administrators, and next we had a lively discussion with Mohamed Bakari and Cemal Karaata, chair and assistant professor in the Department of American Culture and Literature.

Fatih University is named after Mehmet II, the "Opener" or conquerer of Constantinople. The university opened in 1996 as a private university. It has five faculties (arts and sciences, engineering, economics and administrative sciences, law, and medicine) and four vocational schools (nursing, medical sciences, and vocational schools in Istanbul and Ankara). Fatih University is proud of its international character, with 70 international faculty from 25 countries, and students from 50 countries; 600 of the total number of 10,000 students are international students.[49] Most of the programs are taught in English, and international education is the university's focus, as symbolized in its motto: *Bir Dünya Universitesi*, "One World University." The school is a private institution in name only, since it is in fact controlled by the state's Council of Higher Education. Much of the funding comes from tuition, but some is funded by the board of trustees that collects money from, among others, a number of hospitals in Ankara.[50] The spokesper-

48. Professor Şerif Ali Tekalan is the rector or president of Fatih University (from 2010 onward) and also the secretary general of the Journalists and Writers Foundation (more about this organization in the next section of this chapter).

49. The information that we received reflects the situation in August 2009; meanwhile, most of the numbers have changed. For instance, Fatih University now has nine faculties and 1,560 foreign students. See the website of Fatih University: http://www.fatih.edu.tr/?genel (accessed June 22, 2014).

50. Ebaugh (*The Gülen Movement,* 90–92) gives more and somewhat different financial and historical details on the founding of Fatih University.

sons of the university stressed its fully secular character: religion does not play any part, and there is no religious education. Since a sizeable number of the American visitors from Rumi Forum Maryland work at private universities where the religious background very much influences the curriculum, they expressed their surprise at the lack of explicit attention to religion at Fatih University.[51] Professor Mohamed Bakari responded that all universities are constrained by the national ideology which is secularism, so they cannot teach religion directly, but they can teach moral values and virtues that are universal. While ethics are taught explicitly in philosophy courses, these subjects are also touched upon in courses of engineering and medicine. Fatih University just opened new departments of law and education, and a Department of Fine Arts is in the planning. They try to establish a balance between the natural sciences – which are the most popular in Turkey – and the humanities. When we asked about the possibility of a department in which religions would be studied from a comparative perspective – I referred to Gülen's ideas about an Abrahamic university – they responded that such a department might be a part of a faculty of education, but that they were bound by the requirements of the Council of Higher Education.[52] Besides, as long as the different religions train their own personnel, the idea of an Abrahamic University is doomed to remain a utopia.[53]

The previous paragraph makes clear that the representatives of Fatih University who received us in August 2009 saw the identi-

51. The institutions at which they worked are Gettysburg College (Charles Myers, Department of Religion), College of Notre Dame of Maryland (Eileen Eppig, Department of Religious Studies), Mount Saint Mary's College (Indrani Mitra, Department of Literature), Coppin State College (State Senator Delores Kelly, Department of Literature, Emerita), and Loyola University (Pim Valkenberg, Department of Theology).

52. These requirements have changed since 2009. Fatih University opened a Faculty of Theology in 2011, and in 2013 a mosque was built on the grounds of the campus.

53. Discussion with a number of representatives of Fatih University, including Mohamed Bakari and Cemal Karaata from the Department of American Culture and Literature, Fatih University campus, August 17, 2009.

ty of their university mainly in terms of international relations and academic excellence. This is probably true for most schools founded by members of the Hizmet Movement. For many teachers who work there, and for many parents who send their children there, academic excellence and international relations are major selling points. However, we were surprised that the name of Fethullah Gülen was mentioned neither in conversation nor in the public relation materials, and that the religious inspiration that is so important for the good results of the schools, as is evident in the research quoted above, is not mentioned either.[54] Ebaugh notes that Fatih University is well-known as inspired by Gülen, but there are no courses on Gülen or his ideas, and any initiative to study his thoughts is considered a private initiative. Again, "[t]here is a preference to hire administrators who are inspired by Mr. Gülen so that they can maintain the mission of the university in the spirit of Mr. Gülen. Among the faculty, however, less than 50% are from the movement."[55] Of course, the political situation in Turkey prevents religion from being part of the curriculum in most universities, but it may seem strange that it was not mentioned as a motivational factor. For teachers working at private universities in the United States, the situation is totally different, and that explains why both parties had difficulty understanding one another in the conversation that I reported in the previous paragraph—something similar had happened in our conversation with representatives of Şifa Hospital in Izmir, a few days before. But the main point that I want to make here is that the difference between esoteric and exoteric discourse that I discussed in chapters three and four contributes to such misunderstandings as well. However, our conversation led to a better understanding of the different contexts in which the different schools inspired by religious motivations have to work.

54. I consulted a CD-ROM and the brochure "Fatih University" that was given to us after the conversation. Basically the same information is to be found on the university's website: www.fatih.edu.tr

55. Ebaugh, *The Gülen Movement*, 91.

DIALOGUE AS FAITH-BASED SERVICE

In the first chapter of this book I wrote about the way in which I came to know the Hizmet Movement inspired by Fethullah Gülen through the activities of a foundation in the Netherlands that focused on interreligious dialogue. This second form of faith-based service, dialogue, will be the subject of this second section: dialogue between cultures and religions in order to remove the forms of disunity between believers and other human beings, and to promote better mutual understanding. As I wrote at the beginning of this chapter, Gülen's contributions to this field of service began in the 1990s with the Journalists and Writers Foundation and continued with many similar organizations abroad. Since most of them organize activities according to the same pattern – with some local variations, of course – I will limit myself once again to a selected number of institutions that I encountered personally in the last couple of years. But before I delve into these concrete examples, with the help of interviews and public relations materials, I want to refer to the most important studies about Gülen's thoughts on intercultural and interreligious dialogue, and the most important research into some of the organizations as well.

I began the section on education by saying that Gülen's decision to start Hizmet activities by helping out in the field of education was to a large extent a pragmatic decision: this was the field where help was most obviously and most urgently needed. In a similar way, the situation in Turkey in the 1990s made it possible for Gülen to develop initiatives in the public realm to overcome discord in the nation, but this does not imply that the initiative to reach out to those with another faith or with no faith at all was a totally new idea; quite the contrary, the interviews with Gülen's early supporters and students in Izmir have made clear that Gülen already took the initiative to reach out to the whole of humanity in 1965. In that sense, one can argue that the dialogue-oriented discourse is just as characteristic of Gülen and the Hizmet Movement as the education-oriented discourse. Yet, because of the particular conditions of the time, the dialogue activities started about a decade after the educational activities, and they became widely visible in the 1990s.

Because of the decentralized nature of the Hizmet Movement, it is hardly possible to give an idea of the number of institutions that specifically display their service in the fields of intercultural and interreligious dialogue, but a recent estimate mentions a number of some 400 dialogue organizations worldwide.[56] I will give a closer analysis of some of these organizations in a moment, but first I want to give a survey of the most important recent publications discussing the dialogue initiatives in the Hizmet Movement.

The most important articles and columns that Fethullah Gülen wrote about dialogue have conveniently been translated and collected by Ali Ünal and Alphonse Williams.[57] Of these texts, Gülen's contribution to the 1999 conference of the World Parliament of Religions in Cape Town, South Africa, is still the best introduction to Gülen's approach to interreligious dialogue.[58] A number of related notions such as love, peace, friendship, tolerance, and the unity of humanity, have been collected in two books with very similar titles: *Love and the Essence of Being Human* and *Toward a Global Civilization of Love and Tolerance*.[59] Since the field of interreligious dialogue is my special interest, I have analyzed Gülen's thinking on this point several times in the past.[60] I do not want to repeat that analysis here, but

56. This number was mentioned by Emre Çelik, president of Rumi Forum, at an intercultural and interreligious *iftar* dinner in Washington, D.C., on August 24, 2010.

57. *Fethullah Gülen: Advocate of Dialogue*, compiled by Ali Ünal and Alphonse Williams, trans. Ali Ünal (Fairfax, Va.: Fountain Publications, 2000).

58. M. Fethullah Gülen, *The Necessity of Interfaith Dialog: A Muslim Perspective* (Somerset, N.J.: The Light, 2004). For a more specific analysis of this text, see my "Fethullah Gülen's Contribution to Muslim-Christian Dialogue in the Context of Abrahamic Cooperation," in *Islam in the Contemporary World 1*, 1–10.

59. M. Fethullah Gülen, *Love and the Essence of Being Human* (Istanbul: Journalists and Writers Foundation Publication, 2004); M. Fethullah Gülen, *Toward a Global Civilization of Love and Tolerance* (Somerset, N.J.: The Light, 2004).

60. Pim Valkenberg, *Sharing Lights on the Way to God: Muslim-Christian Dialogue and Theology in the Context of Abrahamic Partnership* (New York: Editions Rodopi, 2006), 312–29; Gürkan Çelik and Pim Valkenberg, "Gülen's Approach to Dialogue

will instead mention my colleagues who have studied Gülen's texts about intercultural and interreligious dialogue. First, in a special issue of *The Muslim World* devoted to Fethullah Gülen, Zeki Saritoprak and Sidney Griffith have given an overview of his ideas about the so-called People of the Book.[61] Quite a few of the contributions to the conferences on the so-called Gülen Movement focus on Gülen's ideas about intercultural and interreligious dialogue and related notions such as tolerance, love, and peace.[62] Some of these contributions refer to comparative or interfaith dimensions in dialogues between Christians and Muslims.[63] The best summary of these

---

and Peace: Its Theoretical Background and Some Practical Perspectives," *International Journal of Diversity in Organisations, Communities and Nations* 7, no.1 (2007): 29–37.

61. Zeki Saritoprak and Sidney Griffith, "Fethullah Gülen and the 'People of the Book': A Voice from Turkey for Interfaith Dialogue," *The Muslim World* 95 (2005), 329–40.

62. Paul Weller, "Fethullah Gülen, Religions, Globalization, and Dialogue," in *Muslim Citizens of the Globalized World. Contributions of the Gülen Movement*, ed. Robert A. Hunt and Yüksel A. Aslandoğan (Somerset, N.J.: The Light, 2007), 85–100; John Borelli, "Interreligious Dialogue as a Spiritual Practice," in *Islam in the Age of Global Challenges*, 144–63; Heon Kim, "Gülen's Dialogic Sufism: A Constructional and Constructive Factor of Dialogue," in *Islam in the Age of Global Challenges.*, 374–406; Adnan Aslan, "Interfaith Dialogue in the Context of New Theological Language and Fethullah Gülen," in *Islam in the Contemporary World 1*, 312–23; Yetkin Yildirim and Madeline Maxwell, "Tolerance and Dialogue in Fethullah Gülen's Writings," in *Islam in the Contemporary World 1*, 35–46; Irinia Vainovski-Mihai, "The Limits of the Otherness in Fethullah Gülen's Dialogic Methodology for Interfaith Encounters," in *Islam and Peacebuilding: Gülen Movement Initiatives*, ed. John L. Esposito and İhsan Yilmaz (New York: Blue Dome Press, 2010), 85–101; Karina V. Korostelina, "Dialogue as a Source of Peaceful Co-existence," in *Islam and Peacebuilding: Gülen Movement Initiatives*, ed. John L. Esposito and İhsan Yilmaz (New York: Blue Dome Press, 2010), 103–21; Zeki Saritoprak, "Fethullah Gülen's Theory of Peacebuilding," in *Islam and Peacebuilding: Gülen Movement Initiatives*, ed. John L. Esposito and İhsan Yilmaz (New York: Blue Dome Press, 2010), 169–87; Paul Weller, "Dialogical and Transformative Resources: Perspectives from Fethullah Gülen on Religion and Public Life," in *European Muslims, Civility and Public Life: Perspectives On and From the Gülen Movement*, ed. Paul Weller and Ihsan Yilmaz (New York: Continuum, 2012), 3–19.

63. Yetkin Yildirim and Virginia Burnett, "Interfaith Dialogue for Muslims and Catholic Christians," in *Islam and the Contemporary World 4: The Fethullah Gülen Movement in Thought and Practice* (Somerset, N.J.: Tughra Books, 2009), 109–15;

theoretical perspectives might have been provided by M. Hakan Yavuz in the chapter on the "Theology of Interfaith Dialogue" in his recent book on the Hizmet Movement.[64] Finally, a very interesting book about dialogue in Islam in which Gülen's name is not mentioned but which is entirely based on his approach to dialogue, is the booklet published by London's Dialogue Society.[65]

Others have studied particular initiatives of the movement in specific contexts – often interlocking with initiatives in education – such as the following countries in Europe: (Northern) Ireland,[66] the United Kingdom,[67] and the Netherlands.[68] Other regions studied

---

Richard Penaskovic, "Gülen on Healing the Rift between Islam and the West," in *Islam and Peacebuilding: Gülen Movement Initiatives*, ed. John L. Esposito and İhsan Yilmaz (New York: Blue Dome Press, 2010), 123–43; Turan Kayaoglu, "Preachers of Dialogue: International Relations and Interfaith Theology," in *Islam and Peacebuilding: Gülen Movement Initiatives,* 147–68; Douglas Pratt, "Islamic Prospects for Interreligious Dialogue: The Voice of Fethullah Gülen," in *Islam and Peacebuilding: Gülen Movement Initiatives*, 189–206; Pim Valkenberg, "The Hizmet Movement in the Dialogue between Muslim and Christian Religious Traditions," in *The Gülen Hizmet Movement and Its Transnational Activities*, ed. Pandya and Gallagher, 35–54;

64. M. Hakan Yavuz, "The Theology of Interfaith Dialogue," in *Toward an Islamic Enlightenment: the Gülen Movement* (New York: Oxford University Press, 2013), 173–97.

65. Ahmet Kurucan and Mustafa Kasım Erol, *Dialogue in Islam. Qur'ān – Sunnah – History* (London: Dialogue Society, 2011).

66. Jonathan Lacey, "Investigating the Contribution of Fethullah Gülen through the Activities of a Gülen-Inspired Religio-Cultural Society Based in Ireland," in *Islam and Peacebuilding: Gülen Movement Initiatives*, ed. John L. Esposito and İhsan Yilmaz (New York: Blue Dome Press, 2010), 249–72; Jonathan Lacey, "An Exploration of the strategic dimensions of dialogue in a Gülen movement organization in Northern Ireland," in *European Muslims, Civility and Public Life: Perspectives On and From the Gülen Movement*, ed. Paul Weller and Ihsan Yilmaz (New York: Continuum, 2012), 127–39.

67. Paul Weller, "Robustness and Civility: Themes from Fethullah Gülen as Resource and Challenge for Government, Muslims and Civil Society in the United Kingdom," in *European Muslims, Civility and Public Life: Perspectives on and from the Gülen Movement*, ed. Paul Weller and Ihsan Yilmaz (New York: Continuum, 2012), 143–59.

68. Kate Kirk and Gürkan Çelik, "Opening the Road to Dialogue: An Amalgamation of Gülen's and Spinoza's Ideas on Tolerance and Dialogue Applied to the Situation of Muslims in the Netherlands," in *Peaceful Coexistence: Fethullah Gülen's Initiatives in the Contemporary World* (London: Leeds Metropolitan University Press, 2007), 169–82.

are in Asia,[69] Australia,[70] and the United States.[71] The two studies on Australia together give a very good idea of how interfaith initiatives gradually grow from first initiatives to well-established institutions. The three studies on dialogue initiatives in the United States are in fact case studies of three separate institutions, namely Rumi Forum (Washington, D.C.), Institute of Interfaith Dialog (Houston, Tx.), and Pacifica Institute (Los Angeles, Calif.). I will come back to these institutions later in this chapter. As I said before, the Hizmet organizations that concentrate on dialogue activities are not centrally organized. Yet the Istanbul based Journalists and Writers Foundation (Gazeteciler ve Yazarlar Vakfı) can certainly be seen as the "mother" of many similar organizations that came into existence later.

My first contact with the Journalists and Writers Foundation was with its vice-president, Cemal Uşşak who was present at the first symposium on Abraham as the forefather of three faiths that the "Islam en Dialoog" Foundation organized near Nijmegen in the Netherlands in 2003. A year later, I was invited, together with Alper Alasağ and Tamarah Benima, a Jewish friend and colleague, to participate in the second Harran Meeting on "Religion and Peace in the Vision of Prophet Abraham," organized by the Jour-

69. Mohamed Nawab bin Mohamed Osman, "Towards a Middle Way: Islam in Southeast Asia and the Contributions of the Gülen Movement," in *Islam and Peacebuilding: Gülen Movement Initiatives*, ed. John L. Esposito and İhsan Yilmaz (New York: Blue Dome Press, 2010), 291–309; Heon C. Kim, "Humanism in Islam and in East Asia: Gülen's Vision in Dialogue with East Asian Religious Cultures," in *The Gülen Hizmet Movement and Its Transnational Activities*, ed. Pandya and Gallagher, 55–72.

70. Barton, "How the Hizmet Works: Islam, Dialogue and the Gülen Movement in Australia," in *Islam in the Age of Global Challenges*, 114–43; Emre Çelik, "The Influence of Fethullah Gülen in the Australian Experience of Interfaith Dialogue," in *Islam in the Contemporary World 3: The Fethullah Gülen Movement in Thought and Practice* (Somerset, N.J.: Tughra Books, 2009), 134–43.

71. Zeynep Sahin, "Interfaith Dialogue Organizations as Actors of Peace Building: Case of Rumi Forum," in *Islam in the Age of Global Challenges*, 694–710; JoAnn Long, "Fethullah Gülen and Interfaith/cultural Dialogue: The Lubbock Christian University Experience," in *Islam in the Contemporary World 4: The Fethullah Gülen Movement in Thought and Practice* (Somerset, N.J.: Tughra Books, 2009), 58–62; Nancy Gallagher, "Hizmet Intercultural Dialogue Trips to Turkey," in *The Gülen Hizmet Movement and Its Transnational Activities*, ed. Pandya and Gallagher, 73–93.

nalists and Writers Foundation in Mardin and Istanbul in 2004. During this conference, I gathered a number of brochures about the work of the Journalists and Writers Foundation and its different programs (Intercultural Dialogue Platform, Dialog Eurasia, Abant Platform) in English and Turkish. This information was updated during a visit with others from Rumi Forum Maryland on August 17, 2009.[72]

We were welcomed by Arzu Çingay and Faruk Tuncer, together with project coordinators Elfide Süt and Mustafa Kasım Erol. They told us that the Journalists and Writers foundation was established in 1994 at Gülen's explicit request. He wanted a group of writers and journalists to act as facilitators and mediators in processes of intercultural and interfaith dialogue with a view to achieving peaceful coexistence in the Turkish society. Hocaefendi was actively involved in the first conferences and *iftar* (fast-breaking during Ramadan) interreligious dialogue meetings. He was also present at a benefit soccer game for peace in Bosnia in 1995 and he still is the honorary president of the Journalists and Writers Foundation. Every year, the foundation organizes a number of award ceremonies for persons from different professional fields in society, such as politics, arts, diplomacy, scholarship, family, and environment, both in Turkey and abroad.

Since 1998, the Journalists and Writers Foundation has functioned as an umbrella organization for five platforms that promote different forms of dialogue. The first is the Abant platform that brings together intellectuals from different walks of life in Turkey in order to discuss basic issues in Turkish culture and society.[73] Among the issues discussed in its conferences have been: Islam and

72. The information in 2004 consisted of a number of brochures on the Journalists and Writers Foundation, the Abant platform, the Intercultural Dialogue Platform, and Dialog Eurasia. The information in 2009 consisted of one brochure on the Journalists and Writers Foundation, together with a DVD. The most recent information can be found on the Internet: http://www.gyv.org.tr (accessed June 23, 2014). The different platforms have their own websites as well.

73. http://www.abantplatform.org and http://www.abantplatform.org/Etkin likler/Index (accessed June 23, 2014) for past events.

Secularism (1998); Religion, State and Society (1999); Globalization (2002); Alevism (2007); Diverse Perspectives on Turkey (2013); and Freedom of Speech and Respect to the Sacred (2014). While most of the Abant meetings took place in Turkey, some of them were organized abroad in connection with the themes discussed: Islam, Secularism, and Democracy (2004, Washington, D.C.); Culture, Identity, and Religion in the Process of Turkey's EU membership (2004, Brussels); Republic, Multiculturalism, and Europe (2005, Paris); and Islam, the West, and Modernization (2007, Cairo). Among the most recent of the thirty-three Abant meetings were meetings on the Kurdish problem (2008 in Turkey; 2009 in Arbil, Iraq); on Democratization for Social Consensus (2009); and on Egypt, Stability in the Middle East, and Turkey (2010 in Cairo). In their contributions to conferences on the Hizmet Movement in London and Rotterdam in 2007, Etga Ugur and Niyazi Öktem gave an analysis of these Abant conferences, the participants, and the results.[74]

The Intercultural Dialogue Platform (in Turkish KADİP; Kültürler Arası Diyalog Platformu) mainly focuses on dialogue with non-Muslims.[75] It also extends its invitations to a number of neighboring countries with Christian majorities, such as Armenia, Greece, Rumania, and Russia. This platform has organized a number of interreligious conferences, among which the two Harran Meetings – named after the presumed place of the birth of Abraham – in Urfa (2000) and Mardin (2004) stand out because of their intensity and overwhelming number of participants. Both conferences were organized partly as public events with a sizeable participation of religious leaders, in southeast Anatolia, and partly as

74. Etga Ugur, "Religion as a Source of Social Capital? The Gülen Movement in the Public Sphere," in *Muslim World in Transition: Contributions of the Gülen Movement* (London: Leeds Metropolitan University Press, 2007), 152–62; Niyazi Öktem, "Necessity and Importance of Intercultural – Interreligious Dialogue," in *Peaceful Coexistence: Fethullah Gülen's Initiatives in the Contemporary World* (London: Leeds Metropolitan University Press, 2007), 483–88.

75. See http://www.kadip.org.tr and for events: http://www.kadip.org.tr/Etkinlikler (accessed on June 23, 2014).

scholarly conferences, in Istanbul. Other conferences are organized on a smaller scale, as is the case with a number of Muslim-Christian symposia held jointly by the IDP and Catholic communities in Turkey. Among the themes are "Being a Foreigner and Dialogue with the Other" (September 2012), "An Experience of Coexistence" (April 2013 in Sanliurfa and Rome), "The Virgin Mary in the Holy Book and the Qur'ān" (November 2013, Istanbul), followed by "The Blessed Mary's Patience" (May 2014 in Izmir). Other activities focus on intercultural rather than interreligious dialogue, for instance a recent panel on hospitality in Anatolian and Asian cultures (April 2014 in Bangkok). Another activity is "Prayers of Peace," which brings together religious leaders in order to pray for peace. Finally, the Intercultural Dialogue Platform each year organizes a number of *iftar* dinners at the breaking of the fast during the month Ramadan to which non-Muslims are explicitly invited.

The Eurasian Dialogue Platform focuses on the contacts between Turkey and its neighbors in the "Eurasian region" that formed after the disintegration of the Soviet Union. This platform has as its second language not English but Russian, and it publishes a journal, *DA*, which stands for *Yes* in Russian, but also for *Diyalog Avrasya* in Turkish.[76] I attended the conference on "From Terror to Universal Ethics: Religions and Peace" in Moscow in June 2005. It contained much of the same symbolism as the Harran Meetings, but included non-Abrahamic religions as well. Other conferences organized by the Eurasian Dialogue Platform took place in Kyrgyzstan, Kazakhstan, Georgia, Ukraine, and Tadjikistan.

The fourth platform is the Medialog Platform which promotes dialogue through the media and invites foreign correspondents to Turkey in order to discuss common issues, especially how to create more positive language in the media.[77] During the meeting in August 2009, our hosts introduced the fifth and final platform as a platform on culture and art that seeks contact with young people and artists, and tries to get them involved as well. In fact, the infor-

76. http://www.daplatform.org (accessed June 23, 2014).

77. http://www.medialogplatform.org (accessed June 23, 2014).

mation on GYV's website suggests that this platform has now been transformed into a Women's Platform that organized conferences on "Family Policies" (November 2014, Istanbul) and a panel on the "Education of Girls in Afghanistan" (March 2014, New York).[78] Finally, the sixth "pillar" on the website of the Journalists and Writers Foundation is a research center that organizes conferences as well, for instance a conference (with a banner in French) on "Diversity and Cohesion in a Globalized World" (February 2013 in Dakar, Senegal), and on "Philanthropy and Peacebuilding" (April 2014).[79]

During the conversation that followed the presentation about the several platforms of the Journalists and Writers Foundation, we talked about the influence of Fethullah Gülen on the organization. Our hosts were of the opinion that Gülen does influence individual persons but that the institutions are independent, and therefore they all have their own policies. Mustafa Erol told us that he wanted to study theology at Fatih University, and at first the university seemed to make such plans possible; but after the 1997 "soft coup" they became more cautious and they cancelled the plans so that Erol had to go to Birmingham in the United Kingdom in order to study theology. Mustafa stressed that nonreligious people or people with other religions are working in the organization as well, because they can be inspired by Gülen on an individual basis to engage in service for humankind.[80]

An activity that is loosely connected to the Journalists and Writers Foundation, but that may certainly be placed under its umbrella, is organizing travel in Turkey for persons from abroad who have been invited by the many sister organizations of the Journalists and Writers Foundation. Since this activity is more vital to the image of these sister organizations than to the Journalists and Writers Foundation itself, it does not occupy an important

78. http://www.gyvkadinplatformu.org (accessed June 23, 2014).

79. http://www.arastirmamerkezi.org (accessed June 23, 2014).

80. Conversation with Arzu Çingay, Faruk Tuncer, Elfide Süt, and Mustafa Kasım Erol, Journalists and Writers Foundation, Istanbul, August 17, 2010.

position in the foundation's activities, although the brochure we received as prospective visitors showed pictures of a number of foreign guests (including a picture of a sizeable delegation of students from my own department of religious studies at the university in Nijmegen in 2005).[81] The Journalists and Writers Foundation publishes magazines and books, among others books by Fethullah Gülen, some of which have been mentioned in the third chapter of this book. It is not clear how the publication activities of the Journalists and Writers Foundation relate to the activities of Kaynak publishers and their imprints. Sometimes, one gets the impression that there might be some rivalry between the two publishing houses as they do not refer to each other in their catalogues of works by Gülen. The research center contains an online library that has a few books on Gülen in English, and some 240 articles in English taken from the proceedings of the conferences in Washington, D.C. (2008); Dallas (2006); Oklahoma (2006); Melbourne (2009); Los Angeles (2009); London (2007); Houston (2005); Rotterdam (2007); Jakarta (2010); and Berlin and Potsdam, (2009).[82]

One of the things that we discussed with our hosts from the Journalists and Writers Foundation is that they have many sister organizations throughout the world, but every local organization creates its own initiatives. While the Journalists and Writers Foundation, with all of its platforms, has an extensive range of activities, most sister organizations concentrate on only a few of these activities, although most of them share a number of important activities, such as *iftar* dinners, cultural exchanges, award ceremonies, and interreligious activities. Islam en Dialoog in the Netherlands,

81. As will become clear later in this chapter, these intercultural trips to Turkey form a substantial part of the agenda of the local organizations in the Hizmet Movement in the United States. On these trips, see among others Gallagher, "Hizmet Intercultural Dialogue Trips to Turkey."

82. The books are at http://www.arastirmamerkezi.org/Kutuphane/Kitaplar; the articles in English (German and Turkish articles are available as well) are at http://www.arastirmamerkezi.org/Kutuphane/Makaleler/2 (accessed June 23, 2014). I found some papers that have not been published elsewhere to my knowledge, for instance the papers from the conference in Berlin and Potsdam that I attended in 2009.

for instance, is mainly active in organizing courses about Islam, getting together interreligious groups of younger people, organizing local events in Rotterdam, and a special Ramadan excursion to Istanbul. They also organize a "Ramadan tent" where people can come together to eat. Placing such a Ramadan tent was also one of the activities mentioned at the *sohbet* that I witnessed in Izmir last year, and recently Rumi Forum organized a similar event in Virginia. The basic idea behind the Ramadan tent is that it makes it possible to share food with the poor as well.[83] The Dialoog Academie, which has its base in Rotterdam as well, organizes lectures and debates and conferences, and therefore aims at a more intellectual public.[84]

When I moved to the United States from the Netherlands in the summer of 2006, I had to change my dialogue partners as well. In this case, the transition went rather smoothly, since my friend Alper Alasağ, who was one of the pioneers of the Islam en Dialoog Foundation, was a good friend of Ali Yurtsever, the president of Rumi Forum at that time. So one of the first trips that I made from my present residence in Baltimore was to Rumi Forum where I was received very warmly. Rumi Forum is one of the many dialogue organizations inspired by Gülen in the United States. Thomas Michel thinks that there might be more than fifty of them.[85] Most of these organizations operate regionally, and they all have their—sometimes very sophisticated—websites that contain information about their multiple activities. Although I do not know all of them, I can mention at least those whose representatives I encountered in

83. The website www.islamendialoog.nl is no longer active; the Islam and Dialogue foundation has become part of a new foundation, Platform INS. See www.platformins.nl. As I mentioned in the first chapter, the Dutch Hizmet Movement, in response to unfavorable political reaction—a new debate in the Dutch Parliament in May 2014 about the "Gülen Movement" is one of the symptoms—wants to become more transparent. Two new websites have been created (both in Dutch): www.fethullahgulen.nl and http://www.gulenbeweging.nl (both accessed June 23, 2014).

84. The website of the Dialogue Academy has been discontinued as well; information has been transferred to the websites mentioned in the previous footnote.

85. Michel, "Fighting Poverty with Kimse Yok Mu," in *Islam in the Age of Global Challenges*, 526.

the last couple of years, such as the Turkish Cultural Center in New York.[86] It has a number of local offices in the state of New York. Covering a somewhat broader region is the Peace Islands Institute with branches in the states of New York, including upstate New York; New Jersey; Connecticut; Pennsylvania; and Massachusetts.[87] The Niagara Foundation, based in Chicago, has branches in Illinois, Indiana, Iowa, Michigan, Minnesota, Missouri, Nebraska, Ohio, and Wisconsin.[88] It was one of the co-organizers of a major conference in 2010 on "The Gülen Movement: Paradigms, Projects, and Aspirations."[89] Going from the Midwest to the Northwest of the United States, we encounter the Acacia Foundation in the state of Washington.[90] Further to the south, the Pacifica Institute (Los Angeles) has several branches in California, but it has offices in Oregon, Utah, and Idaho as well.[91] The Pacifica Institute was a partner in organizing one of the major conferences on the Hizmet Movement in 2009, but it also organizes other activities such as intercultural dialogue trips to Turkey and intercultural food festivals.

One of the oldest (founded in 2002) and maybe the most active of the centers is the Institute of Interfaith Dialog, recently renamed the Dialogue Institute of the Southwest.[92] This institute was one of the organizing partners of some of the first conferences on the Gülen Movement in Texas (Houston and Dallas), Oklahoma,

86. http://www.turkishculturalcenter.org/ (last accessed on June 23, 2014).

87. See http://www.peaceislands.org (accessed on June 23, 2014).

88. http://www.niagarafoundation.org/ (accessed on June 23, 2014).

89. Information about this conference can be found on the following websites: http://gulenmovement.ca/gulen-conferences/2010-gulen-conference-chicago-gulen-movement-paradigms-projects-aspirations and http://gulenconferences.com (both accessed on June 23, 2014).

90. http://www.acaciafoundation.org/kt/about-us (new web address, accessed on June 23, 2014).

91. http://www.pacificainstitute.org/

92. The internet address, however, is still http://www.interfaithdialog.org. (accessed on June 23, 2014). When I attended the first conference on "Islam in the Contemporary World: The Fethullah Gülen Movement in Thought and Practice" at Rice University in Houston in December 2005, I received a full-color brochure that gives a very detailed impression of the activities of the Institute of Interfaith Dialog between 2002 and 2005.

and Louisiana. This institute has chapters in Texas, New Mexico, Mississippi, Kansas, Arkansas, and Oklahoma as well. Recently, it was one of the founding partners of the Gülen Institute, which has built one of the most informative websites on Gülen and his spiritual heritage.[93] It seems that the Gülen Institute is more oriented toward academic research, and in that sense it is an American sister of the research center at the Journalists and Writers Foundation.[94]

My overview of institutes on intercultural and interreligious collaboration related to the Hizmet Movement in the United States is certainly not complete.[95] Nevertheless, the institutes that I mentioned and their websites give a fairly good idea of what the supporters of the Hizmet Movement in the United States are doing. With some variations, they all follow more or less the same programs with *iftar* dinners, art exhibitions, cultural trips to Turkey, lectures, and some more specifically local or regional activities, for instance a very popular Anatolian cultures and food festival in California.

Since Rumi Forum is to my knowledge the oldest of all the Gülen-inspired organizations in the United States (it was founded in 1999) and since it is the organization with which I have the longest working relationship, it makes sense to write in more detail about its history and its activities.[96] The name of the organization in full is: Rumi Forum for Interfaith Dialogue and Intercultural Understanding, and it is based in Washington, D.C. with chapters in Virginia, Maryland, Delaware, Kentucky, and North Carolina.[97]

93. http://www.guleninstitute.org (last accessed on June 23, 2014). The Gülen Institute has published a number of informative brochures and booklets on Gülen, for instance *Fethullah Gülen: Biographical Album*.

94. The website http://gulenconferences.com (with the motto "Academic Gatherings on Gulen Movement") carries the logo of the Gülen Institute as well.

95. For instance, I am not familiar with the Atlantic Institute in Georgia with branches in Florida, Alabama, South Carolina, and Tennessee, even though a few years ago I visited the Peace Valley Foundation in Alabama which is now a branch of the Atlantic Institute. See http://theatlanticinstitute.org (accessed June 24, 2014).

96. See also Sahin, "Interfaith Dialogue Organizations as Actors of Peace Building: Case of Rumi Forum."

97. The best source of information for Rumi Forum is, of course, its website:

In 1999, from a small office near Georgetown University, Zeki Saritoprak founded Rumi Forum as an institute to foster interfaith and intercultural dialogue, and to promote education and the exchange of information. He was the first president of Rumi Forum, between 1999 and 2004, when he accepted a position as professor of Islamic studies at John Carroll University in Cleveland, Ohio. Between 2004 and 2009 Ali Yurtsever was Rumi Forum's president; in 2009 Emre Çelik from Australia took over this position. The fact that Rumi Forum is situated in the political center of the country determines the nature of some of its activities, such as congressional dinners, a congressional speaker series, and an ambassadorial speaker series. These activities are coordinated by the Center for Policy Studies of Rumi Forum.

A second center coordinates activities in the area of interfaith and intercultural dialogue. The fact that this center has a female director, Jena Luedtke, is important to counter one of the usual critiques of Gülen-inspired organizations, namely, that women are always veiled, do not have public functions, and stay in the background.[98] Even though many women in the Hizmet tend to work in the background rather than in the forefront, I like the fact that they can be either veiled or unveiled, shy or outspoken, withdrawn or prominent, and that they can be each other's best friends, as I have seen not only at Rumi Forum but in Turkey and the Netherlands as well. The most important activities of this center are the intercultural trips to Turkey, interfaith dialogue events, Rumi Peace and Dialogue Awards, and academic conferences – often in collaboration with Georgetown University or other local universities, as was the case at the most recent international symposium on the Hizmet Movement and peacebuilding in October 2013.[99] Rumi

---

http://www.rumiforum.org/ (accessed June 24, 2013). I also used a number of brochures that I received during several activities organized by Rumi Forum, and drew on my memory of some of the speeches on the occasion of Ali Yurtsever's farewell dinner as president of Rumi Forum on July 2, 2009.

98. See Ebaugh, *The Gülen Movement*, 120.

99. See the conference website http://www.peacebuilding2013.org (accessed June 23, 2014).

Forum participates in assistance programs as well, for instance in soup kitchens and international relief.[100] The forum pays attention to Fethullah Gülen in its public relations materials since he is its honorary president, but Jalaluddin Rūmī is also mentioned prominently. The Peace and Dialogue Awards programs on Capitol Hill bring together eminent personalities from the worlds of politics, religion, academics, and community relations. To me as a Catholic theologian, the list of recipients reads like an homage to some of the best models in Jewish-Christian-Muslim dialogue and peacemaking: John J. DeGioia, John Esposito, Seyyed Hossein Nasr, Marc Gopin, David Smock, and Krista Tippett in 2007; Akbar Ahmed, Suleyman Nyang, and Thomas Michel in 2008; John Borelli, Sidney Griffith, and Maureen Fiedler in 2009. In recent years, however, the tendency of the award ceremony has tended to shift more to the worlds of politics, international service, and the media. It seems that the interfaith aspect of promoting peaceful coexistence, which is the core of Rumi Forum's mission statement, has become less important than its policy aspect. At the same time, an opposite movement may sometimes be discerned as well. In Baltimore, where I live, Turkish Americans living in Maryland are building a new Turkish Community Center, but unlike what I have seen thus far in the Hizmet Movement, this center is to include a mosque.[101] When I visited the center for an *iftar* dinner during Ramadan in 2013, my hosts showed me around and were clearly very pleased that they will soon have a place of prayer annexed to their community center. On the occasion of Ali Yurtsever's departure as president, one of Rumi Forum's most interesting publications was

100. Some details in Sahin, "Interfaith Dialogue Organizations as Actors of Peace Building: Case of Rumi Forum," 706–7.

101. MARTI (Maryland Turkish American Inhabitants, with headquarters in Baltimore and Rockville, Maryland) and ATFA (American Turkish Friendship Association, with headquarters in Fairfax, Virginia) are organizations of Turkish entrepreneurs that are associated with the Hizmet Movement and with Rumi Forum Maryland branch, but not identical with it. For more information, see their websites: http://www.themarti.org/About/About-Us.html and http://www.atfa.us/about-us (both accessed June 23, 2014).

distributed, a booklet with reflections on cultural trips to Turkey, entitled *When I was in Turkey*.[102] All in all, Rumi Forum is able to organize an extremely interesting range of activities that testify to the mind of the man who inspired it, Fethullah Gülen.

Before I finish this section, I need to mention that the different organizations related to the Hizmet Movement and its dialogue activities have recently founded an umbrella organization named The Alliance for Shared Values. It describes itself as "a non-profit umbrella organization that serves as a voice for civic and service organizations associated with the Hizmet social initiative in the U.S"[103] The idea behind this organization is that it would be good to be able to speak with one voice if necessary, and I know that representatives of different organizations in the Hizmet Movement, both in and outside the United States, regularly come together to discuss publications, policy questions, and common interests. At the same time, this also implies that the decentralized character of the organizations working in the context of the Hizmet Movement tends to be watered down. Those who say that there is now an intellectual center in Saylorsburg, Pa. (where Gülen lives) and a business center in Manhattan (where the Alliance for Shared Values has its offices) may have some justification after all, even though I think that they do not understand the central idea of faith-based service behind the Hizmet Movement. The Hizmet may become more businesslike but that does not necessarily stop it from being *hizmet*.

CHARITY AS FAITH-BASED SERVICE

The third field in which the Hizmet Movement became active is the field of charity. The history of this involvement is somewhat different from the history of the Hizmet's involvement in education and dialogue. In the first place, the movement's engagement

102. These reflections can be read as well on Rumi Forum's website dedicated to Fethullah Gülen: http://www.fethullah-gulen.org/turkey-impressions/.

103. Quote taken from its website, http://www.afsv.org (accessed June 24, 2014).

with charity is fairly recent and thus has not been studied in depth. In the second place, this engagement has a somewhat different structure since one overarching organization is active in this field: Kimse Yok Mu, which can be translated as "Isn't there anybody who cares?" In fact, this cry for help was the name of a reality program on Samanyolu TV in the aftermath of an earthquake in the Marmara region in 1999 in which a relatively well-to-do family set out to help another family whose life was severely disrupted by the earthquake.[104] The broadcast was a great success and gifts were donated for a long time, so that in 2002 some people from the Hizmet Movement decided to found the Kimse Yok Mu Solidarity and Aid Association.

Again, the circumstances under which this organization came into existence are somewhat coincidental, but at the same time the ideas of "service" and "doing good for humankind" have always been central in Gülen's discourse and the movement has always developed this dimension of religious life. As was the case with "education" and "dialogue," "charity" is a value that has been important for Muslims from the very beginning. As several authors, including Ebaugh and Koç (2007) and Kalyoncu (2009), have noticed,[105] there is a strong relationship between the two terms that we analyzed in chapter five, *hizmet* (service) and *sohbet* (religious conversation) on the one hand, and commitment to and passion for giving on the other. Apart from the *zakāt*, a mandatory form of giving that is often mentioned in the Qur'ān, the *sadaqa* is a voluntary form of giving that is widespread in Islamic cultures such as Turkey.[106] Another traditional notion that is important in Gülen's thinking is

104. Ebaugh, *The Gülen Movement*, 87. Here, Ebaugh refers to an earthquake near Istanbul in 2004, but on page 101 she refers to the earthquake as taking place in 1999, which is probably more accurate because of the year in which the organization was founded.

105. Helen Rose Ebaugh and Dogan Koç, "Funding Gülen-Inspired Good Works: Demonstrating and Generating Commitment to the Movement," in *Muslim World in Transition: Contributions of the Gülen Movement* (London: Leeds Metropolitan University Press, 2007), 539–51; Mehmet Kalyoncu, "Understanding the Hizmet Discourse of the Gülen Movement," in *Islam in the Contemporary World*, 4, 25–27.

106. Muhammed Çetin, "Voluntary Altruistic Action: Its Symbolic Challenge

that of *himmah* or *himmet* (aspiration or resolve) that is studied in its relation to the Christian notion of "charity" by Özgüç Orhan in an excellent comparative theological study that shows how the two concepts converge in the basic notion of the love of God.[107] Already in 2003, Yavuz pointed to the narrow connection between *hizmet* (rendering service to religion and state), *himmet* (giving donations and protecting good work) and *ihlas* (seeking God's appreciation for every action) in the Gülen Movement.[108] Apart from these conceptual studies, there are a few studies about the Kimse Yok Mu organization and its activities.[109] While Koç and Ebaugh give the best idea of how exactly the charity is channeled from the givers to the receivers, Kirk gives a very insightful perspective on how Kimse Yok Mu works in practice in Southeastern Turkey.[110] The concept of "sister families" that she discusses, and that was already visible

---

Against Sinecures of Vested Interests," in *Islam in the Contemporary World* 3, 46; Zachary Baskal and Helen Rose Ebaugh, "The Turkish-Islamic Culture of Giving," in Helen Rose Ebaugh, *The Gülen Movement: A Sociological Analysis of a Civic Movement Rooted in Moderate Islam* (Dordrecht: Springer, 2010), 70.

107. Özgüç Orhan, "Islamic *Himmah* and Christian *Charity*: An Attempt at Inter-Faith Dialogue," in *Islam in the Age of Global Challenges*,561–82.

108. M. Hakan Yavuz, *Islamic Political Identity in Turkey* (New York: Oxford University Press, 2003), 186.

109. Greg Barton, "Preaching by Example and Learning for Life: Understanding the Gülen *Hizmet* in the Global Context of Religious Philanthropy and Civil Religion," in *Muslim World in Transition: Contributions of the Gülen Movement* (London: Leeds Metropolitan University Press), 650–62; Helen Rose Ebaugh and Dogan Koç, "Funding Gülen-Inspired Good Works: Demonstrating and Generating Commitment to the Movement," in *Muslim World in Transition: Contributions of the Gülen Movement* (London: Leeds Metropolitan University Press, 2007), 539–51; Ozcan Keles, "Promoting Human Rights Values in the Muslim World: Towards an Inclusive Civilization in Gülen's Thought and Practice," in *Peaceful Coexistence: Fethullah Gülen's Initiatives in the Contemporary World* (London: Leeds Metropolitan University Press), 447–70; Michel, "Fighting Poverty with Kimse Yok Mu," in *Islam in the Age of Global Challenges*, 523–33; Dogan Koç, "Generating an Understanding of Financial Resources in the Gülen Movement: 'Kimse Yok Mu' Solidarity and Aid Association," in *Islam in the Age of Global Challenges*, 435–54; Martha Ann Kirk, "'Second Rabi'a's': Women's Gratitude, Compassion, and Altruism," in *Islam in the Contemporary World* 4, 46–57.

110. Dogan Koç, "Generating an Understanding of Financial Resources in the Gülen Movement"; Ebaugh, *The Gülen Movement*, 101–3; Martha Ann Kirk, "Seeds of Peace: Solidarity, Aid, and Education Shared by the Gülen Movement in Southeastern Turkey," in *Islam in the Age of Global Challenges*, 407–34.

in the Samanyolu TV series, makes clear how "charity" can be used to build long-standing relationships instead of just short-term aid.

The tour that the guests from the Rumi Forum Maryland Chapter made in Turkey in August 2009 did not include a visit to the Kimse Yok Mu organization, so I cannot compare these studies with my own observations, but I can show the engagement of institutions and persons from the Hizmet Movement in a different manner. First, the institutional dimension will be exemplified in a report on our meeting with some of the staff members of Şifa Hospital in Izmir. After that, the personal dimension will be exemplified by telling about some of the persons that I encountered in Izmir a week before that.

In the evening of August 12, 2009 we – the guests from Rumi Forum Maryland – were received at a very nice dinner given by staff members of Şifa Hastanesi (Health Recovery Hospital) in Izmir. This hospital was established in 1984 as one of two Şifa hospitals in Izmir (the third Şifa hospital is in Erzurum). Bülent Taş, the general director of the hospital, told us that the initiators of the plan went to see Hocaefendi Fethullah Gülen and asked him what he would expect the hospital to be. He answered: "I want there to be very good facilities that can measure up to the best hospitals, and secondly I want you to take care for the patients as if they were your family." During the discussion that followed the presentation of the hospital in a short film, we noticed that the public relations materials of the hospital paid much attention to the first aspect, but did not really mention the second aspect.[111] When we asked how the hospital would treat patients differently from other hospitals, the director answered: "You should come and become a patient here, and you would notice the difference. At least, we do not only care for our patients, but we pray for them as well." The staff

111. The short video was given to us as a DVD as well. Furthermore, I consulted the hospital's website: http://www.sifatip.com.tr/index.php (accessed on August 27, 2010) and the brochures in English, German, Flemish, and Dutch are available through the website as well.

had heard that one person in our group, Jean-Pierre Lebouder, had been an important figure in the Central African Republic – he was prime minister in 1980–81 and minister of economy and finances in 2003–4 – and the hospital happened to have a relationship with a hospital in Bangui, the capital of that country. So after some searching they found some of the doctors who had volunteered to help in that hospital. Currently, people from the Şifa Hospital are establishing other hospitals in northern Iraq and in Dubai and they are sending out volunteer doctors in Nigeria, Senegal, and Congo, as well as training doctors from Niger. During our tour, they found a film about another form of collaboration between the Hizmet Movement and the Central African Republic, the École Internationale Centralafriquaine – Turque on the occasion of its fifth anniversary in 2009 showing another aspect of their work.

I must confess that this short visit to the Şifa hospital in Izmir not only gave our group from Maryland one of our first impressions of proverbial Turkish hospitality, but it also gave us a good idea about several aspects of *hizmet.* The importance of volunteer work abroad and of developmental cooperation show why the "Gülen Movement" should be characterized by the names of Hizmet Movement and volunteers movement.

At the level of individual forms of charity, Helen Rose Ebaugh gives a very detailed and therefore convincing overview of the local structure of the Hizmet Movement.[112] She shows how local businessmen become engaged in the movement, how they are motivated, and even how much they give to projects of the movement. As I discussed at the beginning of chapter two, the movement is a typical example of the rise of the "Anatolian tigers," entrepreneurs from the eastern part of Turkey who have made a lot of money since Turkey began to embrace the liberal market economy in the 1980s. Some of them have become very rich, and an amazing percentage of this affluence is directed to charity projects initiated by the Hizmet Movement (generally between 5 percent and 20 per-

112. Ebaugh, *The Gülen Movement*, 47–64.

cent but often 33 percent and sometimes 50 percent or more).[113] This explains, indeed, "where the water for the mill comes from," as the Turkish saying goes. It also gives a clear answer to the question that has occupied Tamarah Benima and me since we were pleasantly surprised but also slightly embarrassed by the free trips and the many gifts we received during the second Harran Conference in Mardin and Istanbul in 2004 (see the previous section). It is a combination of Turkish hospitality and the financial resources of the Hizmet Movement made possible by the generosity of its sponsors. Benima, a journalist and a rabbi in training, and myself, a scholar with some suspicious colleagues, were a bit concerned about the source of this largesse, but now I know that Ebaugh is right: because of the amount of donations from wealthy businessmen who sponsor the movement, the argument that the money must come from foreign governments – whether Saudi Arabia or the United States – does not make much sense.[114] One of my suspicious colleagues, a scholar of Islam, had a point when he said: "Of course they treat you right, because they have a mission and they hope that you will write nicely about them."[115] He is right, of course, and that explains why Rumi Forum – and other organizations as well – select people with some influence and standing for the trip to Turkey: their favorable opinion of Turkey and the Hizmet Movement is likely to have more impact than the opinion of random guests. I can see that some people might find this a form of elitism – the same objection that has frequently been made about the Jesuits, as I will discuss in the next chapter – but in itself I think it is for them just a matter of spending their money wisely.

113. Ibid., 54–59.

114. Ibid., 118.

115. As I explained in the introduction, another aspect of this invitation, or *da'wa,* to join them in their work, is that they hope they will convince you of the truth of their religion, according to the qur'ānic injunction to invite the People of the Book with friendliness and to discuss with them in the best possible way. I have no problem with that at all; in fact, I think that the best compliment my Muslim friends can give me is that they wonder why on earth I have not yet become a Muslim. For the role of da'wa in the Gülen Movement and a comparison with Christian missionary strategies, see David Tittensor, *The House of Service: The Gülen Movement and Islam's Third Way* (New York: Oxford University Press, 2014), 134–55.

After discussing the institutional dimension of activities sponsored by the Hizmet Movement, I want to give an impression of the personal dimension by reproducing small parts of three interviews with members of the Hizmet Movement in Izmir that clarify how the engagement works in practice, and how the ideas of *hizmet*, *sohbet,* and *himmet* are connected.

I met Mustafa Duğral in the showroom of his furniture store, together with Bişar Esen, who owns another furniture company, and Akif Topal, who has a staff function in the Izmir Employer's Organization İZİAD. Mustafa seems to be a very active member not only of the employer's organization but of the Hizmet Movement as well. The three businessmen told me that they are engaged in a number of *sohbetler* every week, where they discuss religious texts but also make plans for new charity projects. "At this moment," Mustafa told me,

> we are gathering money for a cultural center and a school. We now have one and a quarter of a million dollars, and we have vowed to support a project in Cameroon. A delegation went to Cameroon and we are now working on the floor plan of the buildings for a school. We wanted to help and we promised to do so, and God gave us the opportunity to work hard in order to reach our goals. We offered our gifts to Hocaefendi, but he refused to accept them. He said: you have to work hard in order to reach your goals. It is like a water well: the more you take out of it, the more water flows back to the well.[116]

I would like to add two notes to this interview. In the first place, I find Gülen's attitude toward money very remarkable. On the one hand, he is personally very austere and poor, and he does not want to possess anything since this would divert him from his main goal in life: to lead a life pleasing God.[117] Yet he encourages the businessmen in the Hizmet Movement to become wealthy so that they will be able to give a sizeable part of their wealth to the projects initiat-

116. Interview with Mustafa Duğral and some other members of IZIAD, Izmir, August 7 and August 10, 2009.

117. See Muhammed Çetin, *The Gülen Movement. Civic Service without Borders* (New York: Blue Dome Press, 2009), 156.

ed by the movement.[118] This combination of personal poverty and institutional capitalism is often compared to Calvinism by sociologists, and therefore some of them write about the "Turkish Calvinists."[119] In the second place, there are many organizations of Turkish businessmen with more or less clear connections to the Hizmet Movement. In Turkey, the Gülen-inspired business association was the Association for Solidarity in Business Life (İSHAD) and more recently the Confederation of Businessmen and Industrialists of Turkey (TUSKON).[120] TUSKON is now an internationally operating organization with offices in Istanbul, Brussels, Moscow, and Washington, D.C.[121] In the United States, Turkish businessmen often have their own business associations as well, and some of them visit events organized by the Hizmet Movement. During events organized by Rumi Forum, for instance, I have met representatives of TACTIC (Turkish American Chamber of Trade Industry and Commerce), MAFTAA (Mid-Atlantic Federation of Turkic American Associations), ATFA (American Turkish Friendship Association), and MARTI (Maryland Turkish American Inhabitants). In the Ramadan month of 2010, Rumi Forum organized an Iftar tent together with ATFA in Virginia, and Iftar dinners together with MARTI in Maryland. These structures of business associations can be seen as the "fourth leg" of the Hizmet Movement, running parallel to the educational, dialogue, and charity organizations.[122]

When I was in Izmir in August 2009, I asked a few businessmen about their daily activities in order to get a detailed picture

118. Çetin, *The Gülen Movement*, 155.

119. Yavuz, *Islamic Political Identity in Turkey*, 187; Rainer Hermann, *Wohin geht die türkische Gesellschaft? Kulturkampf in der Türkei* (Munich: Deutscher Taschenbuch Verlag, 2009), 102. As far as I can see, this term became famous through a report by the European Stability Initiative on "Islamic Calvinists: Change and Conservatism in Central Anatolia," published in September 2005. Hakan Yavuz is mentioned as one of the sources in this report. See http://www.esiweb.org/index.php?lang=en&id=156 (accessed August 27, 2010).

120. See Yavuz, *Islamic Political Identity in Turkey*, 192; Angel Rabasa and F. Stephen Larrabee, *The Rise of Political Islam in Turkey* (Santa Monica, Calif.: RAND Corporation, National Defense Research Institute, 2008), 53.

121. http://www.tuskon.org/index.php (accessed on August 27, 2010).

122. Rabasa and Larrabee, *The Rise of Political Islam in Turkey*, 53.

of what their involvement in the Hizmet Movement looks like. When I shared breakfast with Cemal Yavuzer and İhsan Taşpinar in Cemal's restaurant, they told me that they are involved in an educational organization as members of the board of directors. Cemal is also involved in Kimse Yok Mu, where they discuss applications for financial aid, both locally and internationally. The two friends also come together in different groups for *sohbetler*, four or five times every week. They discuss projects in Izmir, but they also try to give financial assistance to projects in Africa. Finally, they are involved in a local dialogue group where they try to bring together people with different backgrounds, such as Alevis and secularists. They also show the city to tourists in hopes of breaking down misunderstanding. They go to Christian communities and churches and invite them to join their activities, and finally they have personal contacts with Jews and Armenians.[123]

This chapter, like most chapters in this book, discusses mainly the stories of men, much less the stories of women. This is largely due to the segregation of the sexes, which is one of the main characteristics of most traditional cultures. In this respect, the Hizmet Movement certainly is traditional, but that does not imply that women have only passive roles. Female researchers such as Elizabeth Özdalga and Berna Turam have been able to sketch a different picture, based on participant observation and interviews with women.[124] Women researchers have also devoted a fair number of papers to the role of women in the Gülen Movement and the conference in Los Angeles in December 2009 even devoted an entire session to this topic.[125] Being a male non-Turkish researcher, I did not have many

123. Interview with Cemal Yavuzer and İhsan Taşpinar, Izmir, August 7, 2009.

124. Elizabeth Özdalga, "Following in the Footsteps of Fethullah Gülen," in *Turkish Islam and the Secular State*, ed.Yavuz and Esposito, 85–114; Berna Turam, *Between Islam and the State: The Politics of Engagement* (Stanford, Calif.: Stanford University Press, 2007).

125. See Margaret Rausch, "Progress Through Piety: *Sohbetler* (Spiritual Gatherings) of the Women Participants in the Gülen Movement," in *Islam in the Age of Global Challenges*, 610–34; Rausch, "Gender and Leadership in the Gülen Movement: Women Affiliates' Contributions to East-West Encounters," in *The Gülen Hizmet Movement and Its Transnational Activities*, ed. Pandya and Gallagher, 133–59.

occasions to hear the stories of women, but on one occasion I was invited to have dinner in the house of one of the volunteers on the board of the dormitory where I was lodged during my stay in Izmir in August 2009. The host, Ahmet Gürkan, allowed his wife and their daughter to be present at the dinner as well, and they told me that they were active in collecting money for the dormitory where I stayed. This dormitory, Özel Burç Yüksek Öğretim Erkek Öğrenci Yurdu, is located in the neighborhood of Buca in Izmir, and, as often in the Hizmet network, local people try to collect money for the students. Ahmet's wife said that she was excited about some of the things she heard while trying to collect this money. One woman told her that an anonymous person had told her in her dreams that she really should give some money for a good purpose. She was surprised when Ahmet's wife rang the doorbell the same day, so she was convinced that God had said in her dream that the dormitory was this good purpose. Another person had promised to give 2,000 lira, but he could only collect 500 lira from his own money since his business did not go well. But the night before he had to fulfill his promise an anonymous donor gave him the remaining 1,500 lira.[126]

I would like to finish with a story that one of the interviewees told me anonymously. It gives some insight into the mentality of the members of the Hizmet Movement and how they interpret what happens to them in religious terms. This person, who does not live in Turkey anymore, told me that he once left Turkey in order to go back to his country of residence. It is customary for those who live in countries with more affluence than Turkey to empty their pockets before they leave the country. Giving *sadaqa*, he said, is giving back from what you have received, and usually you will get a rich reward in return. This particular time, he did not give *sadaqa* before he passed the border, since the smallest amount of money in his purse was fifty lira, and he found that too much for *sadaqa*. Immediately beyond the border, an accident happened that cost him 250 lira, so he learnt his lesson and he now knows that it is always better to give. To this story he added a *hadith* that says you can "bring down" what

126. Interview with Ahmet Gürkan and family, Izmir, August 6. 2009.

is predetermined for you by giving *sadaqa*, as Hocaefendi says in his book on *Kader*. This story reminded me of what Mustafa Duğral told me about the water well that fills up with more water when you draw water from it. Some people may think this is a religious or perhaps magical form of *do ut des* (I give to you [God] so that you will give back to me) but that would be a misunderstanding of the form of religion involved. It sounds more like one of the contradictory pieces of advice from Jesus in the Gospel, where he discusses the parable of the talents – a big sum of money at that time – and compares the situation of someone who received five talents and made another five with that of someone who received one talent and buried it in the ground: "For to everyone who has, more will be given and he will grow rich; but from the one who has not, even what he has will be taken away" (Matthew 25:29). And this is from the same chapter in which Jesus says at the Last Judgment: "Amen, I say to you, whatever you did for one of these least brothers of mine, you did for me" (Matthew 25: 40). Just like Fethullah Gülen and the Hizmet Movement, Jesus seems to stress personal poverty ("Blessed are you who are poor, for the Kingdom of God is yours," Luke 6: 20) and an austere way of life ("Foxes have dens and birds of the sky have nests, but the Son of Man has nowhere to rest his head," Luke 9: 58) but at the same time he seems to endorse using your talents because they are gifts from God. In that sense, it is not strange that some sociologists have noticed that Max Weber's famous observation about "the Protestant ethic and the Spirit of Capitalism" holds true for recent developments in central Anatolia as well. Apparently, Gülen's inspiration may lead to a form of "this-worldly asceticism" that is very similar to the Christian "this-worldly asceticism" that contributed to economic development in northwestern Europe and certain parts of the United States. Although this is an interesting comparative perspective, it will not be the perspective pursued in the next and final chapter. That will concentrate more on the nexus between religious life and service as phenomena that can be found not only in the Hizmet Movement, but in certain forms of Christian religious life as well.

7

RELIGIOUS LIFE AND SERVICE IN CHRISTIANITY AND ISLAM

In this final chapter I want to draw a comparison between some of the most important elements from my analysis of the Hizmet Movement and similar phenomena in Christian forms of religious life. I want to be explicit in this comparison since, as I wrote in the introduction, this makes clear why I stressed certain elements in the life and works of Fethullah Gülen and the Hizmet Movement that he inspired. I did so because I saw parallels to some forms of religious life in my own religious tradition and that helped me to understand Fethullah Gülen and those he inspired in a certain particular way. I will leave to others the judgment as to whether this way of understanding is helpful or not, but I want to be as clear as possible about what I recognized and why I recognized it. Some of these parallels are quite obvious and have been noticed by others as well, such as certain parallels between the Hizmet Movement and the Jesuits in emphasizing the importance of excellent education. Yet some parallels are not so obvious and they require some explanation of the background.

In this chapter I will begin with one aspect that is not so obvious but that helps us to discover what John Haughey has named "the driver in the mind of Fethullah Gülen"[1] This can also be described, in somewhat less intellectual words, as Gülen's "spirituality." In chapter five, I have identified the notion of *rıza-i İlahi* (God's pleasure) as the driving force of Gülen's *hizmet* activity, and at the end of chapter four I have mentioned feelings of love and yearning and practices of austerity as common traits of Rūmī, Nursi, and Gülen. In the first section of this chapter, I will show how Gülen expresses this religious characteristic by discussing the frequent observation that Gülen often cries while preaching. I will analyze this crying as an expression of sincere sadness about the distance between our human situation here and now and the ideal situation of being with God that is the future for which Christians and Muslims hope in their God-centered religious life, and I will connect this intense religious feeling with what is called in the Christian tradition "the gift of tears," which is a manifestation of what the Latin patristic and medieval monastic tradition calls *compunctio cordis* (transfixion or piercing of the heart).

While by this first comparison I hope to elucidate an aspect of Gülen's preaching for the persons inspired by him, I also hope to clarify the function of the religious conversation (*sohbet*) by comparing it to the function of sacred reading (*lectio divina*) in the second section of this chapter. For these first two sections, I will use the monastic tradition of Christianity as an example, since I think it has a function in Christianity analogous to the Sufi tradition for Gülen: while many people do not share the strictly regulated religious life of the monks or the Sufis, they can draw inspiration from sermons and religious conversations originating from these traditions.

While the first and second section will compare elements of the spiritual life of Fethullah Gülen and the service community that he inspired with what is known as monasticism or "contemplative life" in Christianity, the third section will compare two ele-

1. John Haughey, SJ, "The Driver in the Mind of Fethullah Gülen," in *Islam in the Age of Global Challenges: Alternative Perspectives of the Gülen Movement* (Washington, D.C.: Rumi Forum, 2008), 333–49.

ments of the practice of the Hizmet community inspired by Gülen with what is known as "active religious life" in Christianity. I will focus on a comparison between the Hizmet Movement and the Society of Jesus, better known as the Jesuits, on the issues of education and service. Since these comparisons are more obvious than the first two, and already noted by other scholars before me, I can discuss these two issues in one shorter section.

PRELIMINARY REMARKS

In order to understand correctly what I try to establish in this chapter, it may be useful to give some preliminary remarks. The first remark is that I do not try to establish a form of dependence, as if Gülen would have borrowed some of his spiritual techniques from Christian sources. I do not think that Gülen has borrowed anything except from his own tradition, the Qur'ān, and the Sunna of Prophet Muhammad and his Companions (see chapter four for this point), but I do think that the spiritual life of some Muslims and some Christians centers around the same God albeit with different approaches in these two traditions. Therefore, there are both similarities and differences from which we can learn, as the Qur'ān (49:13) incites us to do: "We created you from a single pair of a male and a female, and made you into nations and tribes, that ye may know each other."

In the second place, I use the phrase "religious life" in the title of this chapter in a somewhat ambiguous sense. I refer not only to forms of religiosity in general, but also specifically to the life of religious persons who decide to follow a specific lifestyle in service and devotion to God. In the Muslim tradition, this is known as the *tarīqa* (way) of the Sufi brotherhoods, in the Christian tradition it is known as a specific "order" or "congregation" or "society" that follows a specific rule established by the founder of that specific form of religious life, such as the Order of Saint Benedict (OSB, the Benedictines, a contemplative or monastic religious order) or the Society of Jesus (SJ, the Jesuits, an active religious order). My point here is that Muslims and Christians can recognize some forms of spirituality that find their authoritative expression in a specific form of (Christian or Muslim) religious life because these forms of spirituality can be lived and practiced by others (Muslims and Christians) who do not belong to this specific form of religious life, but have nevertheless a certain connatural understanding of the God-centered life expressed in these specific forms of spirituality, or "religious life." This is the basis on which I have tried to approach Al-Ghazālī as a theologian whose basic spiritual insights are in harmony with those of Thomas Aquinas.[2] I have approached Said Nursi and Fethullah Gülen as modern Muslim thinkers whose spirituality is connatural with Teresa of Avila.[3] Most scholars would agree that Fethullah Gülen could be seen as "a Sufi in his own way."[4] He does not belong to the *tarīqa* of the (Mevleviyya or Nakşibendi) Sufi brotherhoods, nor to the *cemaat* of the followers of Said Nursi, but,at the same time, he has so much in common with both forms of religious life in Turkish Islam that those inspired by him share certain characteristics of this religious life. Similarly, some Christians can share some of the basic characteristics of the specific form of religious life of the Order of Saint Benedict or the Society of Jesus, without entering the Benedictine or Jesuit communities.[5]

2. Pim Valkenberg, *Sharing Lights on the Way to God: Muslim-Christian Dialogue and Theology in the Context of Abrahamic Partnership* (New York: Editions Rodopi, 2006), 213–54; Pim Valkenberg, "Being Found While Seeking: In Search of a Basic Structure of Root Metaphors in Muslim Spirituality," *Studies in Spirituality* 16 (2006): 39–58.

3. Valkenberg, *Sharing Lights*, 271–321.

4. Zeki Saritoprak, "Fethullah Gülen: A Sufi in His Own Way," in *Turkish Islam and the Secular State: The Gülen Movement*, ed. M. Hakan Yavuz and John L. Esposito (Syracuse, N.Y.: Syracuse University Press, 2003), 156–69.

5. See, for instance, Christopher Jamison, OSB, *Finding Sanctuary: Monastic Steps for Everyday Life*, (Collegeville, Minn.: Liturgical Press, 2006). When I was asked to write about "Jesuit Spirituality" as part of my application to Loyola University Maryland in Baltimore, I became aware of the fact that I had lived with Benedictines, Dominicans (OP, the Order of Preacher friars founded by St. Dominic), Franciscans (OFM, the Order of Friars Minor founded by St. Francis), and Augustinians (OSA, the Order of Saint Augustine) for quite some time in the Netherlands and that I was influenced by their specific "spiritualities" or forms of religious life. I was privileged

In the second section of the fifth chapter, I have identified the notion of *rıza-i İlahi*, "seeking God's pleasure," and the rite of *sohbet*, "religious conversation," as the internal and the external sides of the specific form of religious life in the Hizmet Movement, and in the first two sections of this chapter I seek to elucidate these notions by juxtaposing them to the Christian notions of *compunctio cordis* (piercing of the heart) and *lectio divina* (sacred reading), which can be seen as internal and external sides of the contemplative life as exemplified in the Christian religious orders of the Benedictines and the Cistercians.[6] In the same way, I seek to elucidate the notion of *hizmet* that we have discussed in the remainder of chapter five, and the notion of "educating a new golden generation" by juxtaposing them to notions of service and education in the mission of the Jesuits.

A third preliminary remark: I have decided to select two "classical" examples of Christian religious life although I could have chosen more contemporary examples as well. This would have had the advantage that I could have included interreligious dialogue and charity as two important fields of *hizmet*, and in that way I could also have given parallels for all the activities described in the last chapter. It would have had the added advantage of examining a suggestion made by Gülen in his book *Towards the Lost Paradise*, where he writes: "New movements of religious revival are being observed in Christendom. These movements will one day find their true course and play a significant part in world-wide revival of mankind."[7] This sounds a bit like Nursi's suggestion that Islam and a reformed Christianity can together work to the benefit of human-

---

to read most of the literature used in this chapter while preparing classes for the Department of Theology at Loyola University Maryland.

6. These two sections were published before as the second part of the article "The Hizmet Movement in the Dialogue between Muslim and Christian Religious Traditions," in *The Gülen Hizmet Movement and Its Transnational Activities: Case Studies of Altruistic Activism in Contemporary Islam*, ed. Sophia Pandya and Nancy Gallagher (Boca Raton, Fla..: BrownWalker Press, 2012), 35–54. I thank the publisher and the editors for their permission to use most of the article here.

7. M. Fethullah Gülen, *Towards the Lost Paradise* (Izmir: Kaynak, 1998), 68.

kind.[8] Yet I decided against that, mainly because the description of these contemporary forms of religious life would have required a chapter of its own. Fortunately, John Borelli refers to two of these "new movements of religious revival" in the Catholic tradition when he describes interreligious dialogue as a spiritual practice in his contribution to a conference organized by Rumi Forum in Washington, D.C., in 2008: the Community of Sant'Egidio and the Focolare Movement.[9] The members of these two new religious movements are not religious in the specific sense described above, but they are lay people who, while living a life "in the world," come together to pray and to discuss service activities, just like the people in the Hizmet Movement. The *Focolare* (hearth or family in Italian) Movement was founded by Chiara Lubich in Trent during the Second World War.[10] The movement tries to embody a new spirituality in the Catholic Church that fosters the unity of the human family enriched by diversity. Since the end of the 1970s the movement has embraced interreligious dialogue as part of its mission. As Borelli writes, it has engaged in a special partnership with the African American Muslim community under the spiritual leadership of Warith Deen Mohammed, who brought the Nation of Islam back to mainstream Sunni Islam. Together with Cardinal Keeler of Baltimore, Warith Deen Mohammed visited Rome in 1996 and met with Pope John Paul II, the Focolare Movement, and the Sant' Egidio Community, and in 1997 he hosted Chiara Lubich in the famous Malcolm Shabazz Mosque in the Harlem neighborhood of New York.[11] The American section of the Focolare Movement

8. Said Nursi, *Letters 1928–1932*, trans. from the Turkish *Mektûbat* by Şükran Vahide in a new edition (Istanbul: Sözler Neşriyat, 2001), 515: "A zealous and self-sacrificing community known as a Christian community but worthy of being called 'Muslim Christians,' will work to unite the true religion of Jesus (Upon whom be peace) with the reality of Islam, and will kill and rout that society of the Dajjal, thus saving humanity from atheism."

9. John Borelli, "Interreligious Dialogue as a Spiritual Practice," in *Islam in the Age of Global Challenges*, 44–63.

10. See the self-presentation (*chi siamo* = who we are) on the English version of the international official website of the *Movimento dei Focolari*: http://www.focolare.org/en/chi-siamo (accessed June 24, 2014).

11. Borelli, "Interreligious Dialogue as a Spiritual Practice," 155–56.

is still engaged in dialogue between Christians and Muslims, as a recent item on their website attests.[12]

The Community of Sant'Egidio was founded by Andrea Riccardi and some other high school students in Rome in 1968. It encourages leading a life of prayer and social service to the poor. Apart from its activities in the field of interreligious dialogue, Sant' Egidio has made a name as peace brokers, since they have been instrumental in a number of peace negotiations around the world. On its website, the community shares photos of Pope Francis's recent visit and their shared concern for the fate of immigrants in Italy and worldwide.[13] This short description may suffice to give at least some impression of the parallels between these two new religious lay movements within the Catholic Church and the Hizmet Movement inspired by Fethullah Gülen. In all cases, interreligious dialogue is an important field of their missions, but the activities in this field are nourished by a life of prayer and reading Scripture, and are implemented in activities to promote peace and the unity of humankind. John Borelli concludes: "The Gülen Movement, if we can use that expression for a diversity of projects promoted mostly by Muslims of Turkish descent, is a true Muslim counterpart to the Community of Sant'Egidio and the Focolare Movement."[14]

Finally, I am aware of the fact that a comparative approach that looks for parallels in religious life, and more specifically in monastic life, will be frowned upon by some Muslims who may argue that there is no place for "monkery" in Islam, since at one place the Qur'ān seems to speak negatively about some of the ascetic and monastic traditions in Christianity: "We sent after them Jesus the son of Mary, and bestowed on him the Gospel; and We ordained in the hearts of those who followed him compassion and mercy; but the Monasticism which they invented for themselves, We did

12. http://www.focolare.org/usa/en/news/2014/06/20/christians-and-muslims-on-a-journey-together (accessed June 24, 2014) mentions a meeting between young Muslims from the Harlem: WD Mohammed community and members of the Focolare community at Fordham University in New York.

13. http://www.santegidio.org/index.php?&idLng=1064 (accessed June 24, 2014).

14. Borelli, "Interreligious Dialogue as a Spiritual Practice," 157.

not prescribe for them: (We commanded) only the seeking of the Good Pleasure of Allah."[15] Apparently, monasticism (*rahbānīya*) is seen as an intensive but erratic form of seeking the good pleasure of God (*ibtighā'a ridwān Illāhi*). I conclude from this that the Qur'ān is not opposed to an intense form of religious life as such, but it rejects forms of spirituality that have not been revealed. So with some reservation the Qur'ān recognizes the connection between what is central in Gülen's spiritual life, namely *rıza-i İlahi*, "seeking God's pleasure," and monasticism as an intensive yet deviating form of that pursuit. This is confirmed by two places where the Qur'ān speaks positively about religious characteristics of some Christians, namely those who stand upright reciting the Signs of God during the night and prostrate themselves, and those who are devoted to learning, who have renounced the world (*ruhbanan*) and are not arrogant.[16] For a Christian who reads these words, it is quite clear that the Qur'ān here seems to praise the monks in their liturgy of the hours, where they recite the psalms standing, bow down for the doxology, and prostrate themselves in prayer. The devotion to learning can easily be associated to the *lectio divina* – itself a practice against arrogance – in which the Scriptures are read, ruminated on, and contemplated. Gülen clearly has an affinity with the Sufi tradition that forms a parallel with what the Qur'ān praises in Christians who adore God at night, recite their Scriptures, and are humble and upright. I am convinced that the notion of "seeking God's pleasure" and of "piercing of the heart" that I will discuss below comes very close to this "adoring God at night, being humble and upright" that is seen as the best possible approach between Muslims and Christians in the Qur'ān.

15. Qur'ān 57: 27 in the interpretation of 'Abdullah Yusuf 'Ali.

16. These two places in the Qur'ān are *Āl-'Imrān* 3:113, and *al-mā'ida* 5:82. In both cases, disputes with Christians about the right worship of God and the place of Christ in this worship form the context.

THE CRYING PREACHER AND THE PIERCING OF THE HEART

While preparing for this book I often visited Fethullah Gülen's official English website. When I was writing about his biography, I obviously consulted the documents gathered under "biography" under the heading "about Fethullah Gülen."[17] The first two documents in the section "about Fetullah Gülen," before its restructuring, did not immediately give the kind of biographical information that one would expect. The first entry was "Relation with Literature and Music," and contained some of Gülen's answers to questions about his literary and musical preferences. The second entry bore the title "Why Does He Cry?" This is a question posed to Gülen by Nuriye Akman during an interview in the Turkish daily *Sabah* back in 1995: "In your sermons I watched on video cassettes to get to know you, I saw that you frequently cry. What makes you so soft-hearted?" Gülen answered: "I guess the biggest factor is God's creating me like that. On the other hand, I grew up in a place that resembled 'ruined towns, ruined homes.' In Akif's words, 'homeless deserts, headless communities, days without work, evenings with no thought for tomorrow, domination, oppression' .... Seeing those, I can't help but feeling sad when wistfully remembering the past. It's made me soft-hearted like a child."

This is an interesting observation that certainly matches with the biographical details of Gülen's early life discussed in chapter three, and with the analysis of his discourse on yearning and love in chapter four. But it is remarkable that this item was so prominently displayed on Gülen's website, and therefore I think that there is more to say about this crying than just the biographical reference.[18] The fact that Gülen can be seen as one of the emerging

17. www.fethullahgulen.org/about-fethullah-gulen/biography.html (accessed July 23, 2009). This website has been restructured since and this item can now no longer be found on this website. However, it can be found under http://fgulen.com/en/fethullah-gulens-life/about-fethullah-gulen/biography/24660-why-does-he-cry (accessed June 24, 2014).

18. Of course the fact that it now has been reallocated to a less prominent place

"emotional preachers"[19] and that his weeping is sometimes considered his trademark,[20] tells something about his spiritual drive.[21] My analysis is that it displays a profound religious attitude that may be compared to a not so well-known but important phenomenon in Christian spirituality: the gift of tears.

In his magnificent study of monastic culture, *The Love of Learning and the Desire for God*, Benedictine monk Jean Leclercq devotes a paragraph to what he calls "the gift of tears."[22] He explains the monastic culture of the early Middle Ages as a confluence of love for the humane letters and a desire for the heavenly kingdom. The tears shed by the monks are indicative of their religious mood that is sad and hopeful at the same time. It is sad because the monks realize how far they are from being worthy of attaining the heavenly kingdom, and it is hopeful at the same time because they hope that God will not withhold his divine grace from those who sincerely seek him. Leclercq describes these tears as being born from the piercing of love, and as a gift from God. In his famous *Rule*, Saint Benedict says that the prayer of the monks should not

---

is significant as well. It may show a side of Gülen that is difficult to grasp immediately for the average reader brought up in an English culture with the saying "real men don't cry."

19. Olivier Roy, *Globalized Islam: The Search for a New Ummah* (New York: Columbia University Press, 2004), 191.

20. See Daniel Steinvorth, "The Fethullah Gülen Movement: Pillar of Society or Threat to Democracy?" on the German website Qantara: http://en.qantara.de/content/the-fethullah-gulen-movement-pillar-of-society-or-threat-to-democracy (accessed June 24, 2014). The article was published in May 2009, and Steinvorth is a correspondent in Turkey for the German news magazine *Der Spiegel*.

21. In a strange article in the *Wall Street Journal* of January 20, 2014 (written by Joe Parkinson and Ayla Albayrak) with the headline "Gulen Blasts Turkey Leader," we read the following about Gülen: "Known to cry during sermons, the preacher has built a world-wide movement that operates charter schools in 160 countries, including the U.S., where Cemaat has forged ties with local and national political leaders, paying for congressional trips to Turkish cities. But the movement's opaque structure and Calvinist work ethnic has spurred comparisons to Opus Dei, the Masons and the Mormon Church." Retrieved from http://online.wsj.com/news/articles/SB40001424052702304027204579332670740491570 on June 24, 2014.

22. Jean Leclercq, OSB, *The Love of Learning and the Desire for God: A Study of Monastic Culture* (New York: Fordham University Press, 1961), 158.

be long or ostentatious, since "God regards our purity of heart and tears of compunction, not our many words."[23] It is important to see that the Latin notion of *compunctio cordis* refers to being touched by God's grace and love, and therefore the translation of this word by the English word "compunction" implying feelings of remorse, guilt, regret, and scruples, "will not do at all."[24] The Latin word and the English homonym seem to imply two totally different forms of spirituality. The "piercing of heart" is perhaps represented most famously by Gian Lorenzo Bernini's famous sculpture of the Ecstasy of Saint Teresa of Avila (also called the Transverberation of Saint Teresa) in which she seems to swoon when an angel transfixes her heart with a lance. The description that Saint Teresa gives of this mystical event in her autobiography has such clear erotic overtones that many modern interpreters think that she is in fact describing an orgasm.[25] One need not be scandalized by such an interpretation if one realizes that yearning for the divine is in fact an important part of religious life. It explains, for instance, why one of the most famous spiritual works in the Middle Ages is Saint Bernard's series of sermons on the Song of Songs in which the Cistercian monk interprets the secular love songs from this biblical source as a longing for the arrival of God's incarnated Word.[26] In this context, the compunction can be "begotten of sadness over sin," but it can also be "begotten of joy over having benefited from the divine benignity."[27] As Denys Turner explains, according to Bernard, "the longing of the patriarchs and prophets for the coming of Christ . . . can outstrip in intensity the Christian's complacency in his possession of Christ."[28] Bernard begins

23. Benedict of Nursia, "The Rule of Saint Benedict," in *The Benedictine Handbook* (Collegeville, Minn.: Liturgical Press, 2003), chapter 20.

24. Denys Turner, *Eros and Allegory: Medieval Exegesis of the Song of Songs* (Collegeville, Minn.: Cistercian Publications, 1995), 251.

25. Teresa of Avila, *The Life of Teresa of Jesus, The Autobiography of Teresa of Avila* (New York: Doubleday, 2004), 244–45.

26. Bernard of Clairvaux, *The Works of Bernard of Clairvaux, 2: Song of Songs I*, trans. Kilian Walsh OCSO (Collegeville, Minn.: Cistercian Publications, 2008).

27. Walsh, in *The Works of Bernard of Clairvaux,* 2, xv.

28. Turner, *Eros and Allegory*, 85.

his second sermon on the Song of Songs, discussing its first line, "let him kiss me with the kiss of his mouth," as follows:

> During my frequent ponderings on the burning desire with which the patriarchs longed for the incarnation of Christ, I am stung with sorrow and shame. Even now I can scarcely restrain my tears, so filled with shame am I by the lukewarmness, the frigid unconcern of these miserable times. For which of us does the consummation of that event fill with as much joy as the mere promise of it inflamed the desires of the holy men of pre-Christian times? Very soon now there will be great rejoicing as we celebrate the feast of Christ's birth! But how I wish it were inspired by his birth! All the more, therefore, do I pray that the intense longing of those men of old, their heartfelt expectation, may be enkindled in me by these words: "Let him kiss me with the kiss of his mouth."[29]

As we will see in a moment, the emotions described by these words strikingly parallel the emotions evoked in Gülen and the listeners to his sermons when he describes the difference between the heartfelt faith of the Prophet and his Companions, and the lukewarm faith of present-day Muslims. So, *compunctio cordis* is literally a pinching through the heart by God's grace and love which results in a heightened awareness of the insufficiency of one's present situation, and thus in repentance; but it results in a more fiery devotion and a longing for the future as well. For Christians, this future has nowhere better been described than in the final words of the New Testament in the book of Revelation, "Behold, God's dwelling is with the human race. He will dwell with them and they will be his people and God himself will always be with them [as their God]. He will wipe every tear from their eyes, and there shall be no more death or mourning, wailing or pain, [for] the old order has passed away."[30] So, tears are a sign of "the old order" of the monastic or the Sufi who has not yet traversed the mystical path to its final destination. The same image can be found in the book of Isaiah, "The Lord God will wipe away the tears from all faces. The

29. Bernard of Clairvaux, *Song of Songs I*, 8.

30. Revelation 21: 3–4, according to the New American Bible (NAB) translation.

reproach of his people he will remove from the whole earth; for the Lord has spoken."[31]

Saint Ignatius Loyola, the founder of the Jesuits, mentions the combination of great devotion and many tears so often in his spiritual diary, written in 1544, that it becomes a refrain that may deter the modern observer not accustomed to such baroque emotions.[32] A short, random example will suffice: Ignatius's entry for Friday, February 22, Mass of the Trinity:

> Throughout the customary prayer I was helped by great grace – it was warm and shone in some way – and felt much devotion. For my part I sometimes felt I should have no difficulty in discontinuing; yet I continued to be helped by great grace. Later, when I prepared the altar, some impulses to weep: I kept repeating, "I am not worthy to invoke the name of the Blessed Trinity." This thought, and the repetition of the phrase, caused greater interior devotion. When I vested, turning over these and other considerations, my soul opened more to tears and sobs. I began mass and reached the Gospel which I said with considerable devotion: I was being helped by a warm grace which later battled like fire with water against some thoughts.[33]

Although it seems that Ignatius may be somewhat obsessed with his spiritual emotions – he repeatedly writes about weeping and sobbing, so much so that he threatens to become blind – he writes these pages at a time when he is very busy establishing the Society of Jesus in Rome, being engaged in very exacting apostolic and administrative tasks. Precisely because of the combination of an intense spiritual life and an active engagement in establishing a brighter future by educating a new generation, Ignatius may remind us of Fethullah Gülen.

If this is true, Bernard and Teresa and Ignatius – all three of them saints in the Catholic tradition – and Jalaluddin Rūmī, Said

31. Isaiah 25:8, NAB.

32. Text of the "Spiritual Diary" in Ignatius of Loyola, *Personal Writings: Reminiscences, Spiritual Diary, Select Letters including the text of The Spiritual Exercises* (London: Penguin Books, 1996), 73–109.

33. Ignatius of Loyola, "Spiritual Diary" in *Personal Writings*, 84.

Nursi, and Fethullah Gülen – all three of them great models in the Muslim tradition – must be gifted with an exceptional religious yearning that made them receive the "gift of tears." This is not the kind of gift that will be recognized by many as a gift that could go together with a "normal" or even "healthy" spiritual or religious life. William James, in his famous Gifford Lectures on *The Varieties of Religious Experience,* would not include them in his description of "the Religion of Healthy-Mindedness," but would tend to deal with them when he describes "the Sick Soul."[34] Yet in fact James discusses saints Ignatius and Teresa when he talks about mysticism as a special state of consciousness that cannot be measured with medical or psychological criteria, underlining that their mystical experiences energized them to become very active in the world.[35] They were, indeed, very actively involved in the political and ecclesial situation of their times and they can be named as great renewers in their age.[36] The same can be said about saints Benedict and Bernard as well.

This combination of the "gift of tears" and a very energetic active life is precisely how Fethullah Gülen was described by some of his closest friends in Izmir during the years in which the Hizmet Movement originated, as I described in the third chapter. Mehmet Yıldız, who met Hocaefendi a decade later when he preached at Izmir's Bornova Mosque, told me that Gülen was very popular during these years (1977–80), and that people crowded the mosque hours before he was to give his *vaaz* (a catechetical sermon that precedes the Friday afternoon prayer). People were used to being moved to tears by some preachers, but Gülen was the first

34. William James, *The Varieties of Religious Experience* (New York: Triumph Books, 1991), 76–108 and 112–39 respectively (1st ed. 1902).

35. James, *The Varieties of Religious Experience*, 312–18.

36. Patrick Howell, "Dialogue between Jesuit and Gülen Educational and Spiritual Foundations," in *East and West Encounters: The Gülen Movement* (Conference Proceedings December 5–6, 2009, University of Southern California, Los Angeles), 59–69. This text can be found in the online library on the website of the Journalists and Writers Foundation: http://www.arastirmamerkezi.org/Kutuphane/Makaleler/2/16 (accessed June 24, 2014).

preacher who cried himself because of his deep piety and his love for humankind.[37]

I heard and saw two examples of this in the collected sermons of Gülen. For instance, in a *khutba* (*hutpe* in Turkish) on faith in the hereafter, preached in Bornova Mosque, Izmir, on January 21, 1978, Gülen mentioned the example of Ammar ibn Yasir who gave himself totally in a defensive battle for the love of God, knowing that he would probably die. He contrasted this fervor of the first generation of followers of the Prophet with the lukewarm faith of contemporary Muslims. "If my faith would have been as strong as the faith of the Companions of the Prophets, I would not sleep in a soft bed; I would not long for material gains. But still I do need food; I do need sleep, while human beings suffer." After this example of "the gift of tears" with a crying voice, Gülen ends his sermon in a strong voice by saying "let us promise to God and the Prophet that we will not sleep again till humanity has been saved!"[38]

Another example in which one can actually see Gülen crying is a videotaped sermon on the "knowledge of the heart" from Şadırvan Mosque in Izmir (January 28, 1990) in which Gülen has just heard about children dying in Azerbaijan, and he refers to this with these words: "We want to talk only about love, but people make problems even about that; we cannot change the situation with weapons, we can only change it by praying and weeping, moistening our prayer rugs."[39]

It is important to note that Gülen describes Prophet Muhammad as someone who was compassionate and tender-hearted as well.[40] "Despite being sinless, he spent more than half the night praying and crying, and sometimes fasted two or three consecu-

37. Interview with Mehmet Yıldız, teacher, Izmir, August 7, 2009.

38. *Minberden Yükselen Ses* [The rising voice from the pulpit], CD 10 from the *Vaaz Külliyatı* collection, first part, *hutbe 21 Ocak 1978, Bornova Camii / İzmir.*

39. *Vuslat Arzusu* [Good news about meeting with the Beloved], first part of DVD 6 from the *Vaaz Külliyatı* collection, *vaaz 28 Ocak 1990, Şadırvan Camii / Izmir*. Some of these videotaped *vaazlar* can also be watched on YouTube.

40. M. Fethullah Gülen, *Emerald Hills of the Heart: Key Concepts in the Practice of Sufism,* 2. (Somerset, N.J.: The Light, 2004), 262.

tive days."[41] Prophet Muhammed is described as crying over the death of his son Ibrahim and as caring for women and children.[42] Gülen considers Muhammad and his Companions, as special models for this soft-heartedness that leads to "the gift of tears," yet he may also have derived a sensitivity to this spiritual mood of sadness about our situation as human beings from the two main sources of his writings: Rūmī and Nursi.[43] At the end of chapter four of this book I have mentioned the wailing of the *ney* (reed flute) during the *sema* liturgy of the Whirling Dervishes in connection with Rūmī's "Song of the Reed" and in connection with Nursi's experience of *gurbet* (*ghurba* in Arabic) as living in exile and being estranged from one's true nature.[44] It is possible to connect this with the idea of *huzn* as the proper emotion evoked by the beautiful recitation of the Qur'ān. Just like *compunctio cordis* in Latin, the Arabic word *huzn* has the notion of sadness, sorrow, or grief, but beyond that it indicates our awareness as human beings of our state in relation to our Creator. As Kristina Nelson summarizes in her book on *The Art of Reciting the Qur'ān*: "*Huzn* is the awareness of the human state vis-à-vis the creator. With *huzn* one knows true humility, awe of the divine, human frailty and mortality. This awareness, and the emotion it stirs on the part of the reciter, is communicated through the reciter's voice and artistry, heightening the listeners' sensitivity and awareness and moving them to tears."[45] What connects Gülen with Rūmī and Nursi is a deep awareness of our relationship with our Creator, and of our

41. M. Fethullah Gülen, *Muhammad, the Messenger of God: Aspects of His Life* (Somerset, N.J.: The Light, 2005), 292.

42. Gülen, *Muhammad, the Messenger of God*, 166.

43. I gave a lecture on "The Role of *Ghurba* (Exile) as Physical and Spiritual Category in Jalalluddin Rūmī and Said Nursi" at a conference on Rūmī and Nursi in Konya, in May 2013. The conference was organized by the Risale Akademi: see http://www.risaleakademi.org/?page=9&YaziID=76 (accessed June 24, 2014; page in Turkish).

44. Yvonne Yazbeck Haddad, "*Ghurba* as Paradigm for Muslim Life: A *Risale-i Nur* Worldview," *The Muslim World* 89 (1999): 297–313.

45. Kristina Nelson, *The Art of Reciting the Qur'ān* (Cairo: The American University in Cairo Press, 2001), 53.

being exiled in this life; it is the living sound of the Word of God that reminds us of our true nature and of our future encounter with the Beloved.[46]

In my discussion of the Christian concept of the "gift of tears," I wrote that it is a sign of being on the way to God, a way that has not yet been traversed completely. Sufi spirituality has a tradition of attentiveness to these specific states and stages that human beings must cross on their way to God.[47] Gülen reflects on this situation of being wayfarers to God when he discusses the "self-accusing self" in his exposition of the Sufi notion of *Sayr u suluk* (journeying and initiation) as follows:

> Those who have reached the stage of self-accusation intend to set out toward Him. However, they falter, making errors that stain their good deeds, and beautiful things follow ugly ones in their life. But whenever they stumble and fall, they pull themselves upright in remorse for the evils committed, cleanse themselves of sin by sincerely asking God for forgiveness and by trying to uproot their inclinations toward evil through prayer. Not content with these, they continuously accuse themselves, and suffer pangs of conscience. A time comes when they express these pangs with sighs from the depth of the heart, and when they put these feelings into invocations and tears in seclusion."[48]

In his book *The Statue of Our Souls* Gülen describes a new generation of devout people who will be true Muslims and will bring a new religious consciousness. Gülen often uses this notion of a new generation or a "golden generation" (*altın nesil*) in his books, and it is also the name of the retreat center where Gülen now stays in Pennsylvania. One of these descriptions contains the following:

> Humanity is terribly in need of people with inner depths and sincerity now, more than anything else, for people who suffer and cry for the sins

46. *Vuslat Arzusu* [Good news about meeting with the Beloved] was the title of the series of sermons just quoted. And *Gurbet solukları* [Breathings from a faraway country] is the title of a long series of *sohbetler* given by Gülen during his exile in the United States.

47. Valkenberg, "Being Found While Seeking."

48. M. Fethullah Gülen, *Emerald Hills of the Heart,* 2, 252.

and errors of others; who look forward to forgiveness and pardon of others before their own; who, instead of entering Paradise, and taking their pleasures individually there, prefer to stay in the *A'raf* [the plain separating Paradise and Hell] and from there try to take all the people to Paradise along with them; and who, even if they enter Paradise, will not be able [to] find time to enjoy the pleasures of Paradise because of their thoughts for others and their concern to save them from the hell-fire.[49]

I discussed in detail this first parallel between Gülen on the one hand and the founders of the Benedictine and Jesuit religious orders in Christianity on the other because, to my knowledge, the idea of the "gift of tears" is not well-known but it may shed some light on the driving force for Gülen's active engagement and therefore on the origins of the Hizmet Movement. The other parallels that I will discuss are more well-known and therefore have been discussed in the literature about Gülen and Christianity so that I can describe them much more succinctly.

RELIGIOUS CONVERSATIONS AND SACRED READING

When Saint Benedict of Nursia, the "father of Western monasticism," wrote his Rule in sixth century Italy, one of the most important things he did was to divide the time of the monks, who would live together under the guidance of an abbott, into three basic activities: praying, reading, and working.[50] Benedictine religious life is often characterized as *ora et labora* (pray and work), and this is correct insofar as the Liturgy of the Hours, or the *opus Dei* (divine office) as Benedict calls it, is a form of praying and reading at the same time. On the other hand, the reading that is called *lectio divina* (sacred or divine reading) has more in common with prayer than with modern forms of reading. In fact, the Benedictine daily activi-

49. M. Fethullah Gülen, *The Statue of Our Souls. Revival in Islamic Thought and Activism.* (Somerset, N.J.: The Light, 2005), 97. This text contains quite remarkable parallels to the Mahayana Buddhist notion of the *bodhisattvas*.

50. Benedict of Nursia, "The Rule of Saint Benedict."

ties contain three different forms of reading. The first is the liturgical reading of the divine office, where texts from the Old and New Testaments are read aloud, but mostly chanted. In his rule, Benedict takes great care to divide the 150 Psalms over the week in such a way that the entire Psalter is chanted in the course of one week. While I will not focus on this form of reading here, it is important to note that the original function of the Christian Scriptures was a liturgical one, which implied that they were chanted and thus heard instead of read or studied (as the very word Qur'ān – recitation – implies, the same holds true for Islamic Scripture).

The second form of reading takes place during the meals, and Benedict specifies in his rule that one monk will read aloud from the Scriptures or the Lives of the Saints or another edifying work during an entire week, while all the others listen silently while eating.[51] After some of these meals, there is another reading period in which the monks sit quietly and listen to some devotional lecture, such as the *Collationes* ("Conferences," but the word refers to shared meals as well) by John Cassian or the Lives of the Fathers by St. Gregory.[52] Yet the third form of reading comes closest to the silent reading that we practice today; it is an individual reading by monks in their cells during specified hours. Benedict specifies that they should be given a book from the abbatial library – books, or rather manuscripts, were extremely scarce and expensive at that time – and the monks were to read these books in their entirety. Moreover, they should read during fixed hours of the day, on Sundays and during Lent more often than on other days.[53] The Cistercian monk Michael Casey uses these indications in the Rule of Saint Benedict to show some of the characteristics of *lectio divina* in its contemporary form.[54] This form of reading is not aimed at obtaining information, but it is a "sacred reading," in which the text – often from the Bible or from the tradition of the church –

51. Ibid., chap. 38.

52. Ibid., chap. 42.

53. Ibid., chaps. 48–49.

54. Michael Casey, *Sacred Reading. The Ancient Art of* Lectio Divina (Liguori, Mo.: Liguori/Triumph, 1996).

forms the occasion for meditation. The book is received as a given, as a source of God's message for me that I need to uncover by continuous reflection on its contents. It is a patient reading and a reading that waits for unexpected developments to take place. Casey shares Benedict's presumption that you do not choose the book but that the book chooses you – which of course implies that only a certain kind of books is suitable for *lectio divina* – and this idea differentiates sacred reading from any form of modern reading in which we choose to read a text or not, and stop reading as soon as we have found what we were looking for. The four characteristics of such sacred reading mentioned by Casey are fidelity (staying with it even though it does not seem to bring anything), assiduity (concentration and density of intent), reverence (respect for the text, and a willingness to be challenged by the text), and compunction (a willingness to be touched by the text).[55] Here we meet the idea of *compunctio cordis* again as a willingness to be touched by what God wants to tell me through this text, and an awakening of our desire to lead a different kind of life because of what we have read in the text.[56]

In his autobiographical *Reminiscences*, Ignatius of Loyola tells about a similar *lectio divina* in which he had to engage while lying in his bed for a long time because of a severe injury – during a battle, a cannonball had smashed his leg. He describes his conversion to a religious life while reading the lives of Christ and the saints, and he tells us that his mind was torn between the world that he served before, and the models of Christ and the saints that seemed less attractive to him but in the end gave him more happiness while thoughts about the world gave him more immediate satisfaction but a lasting sadness.[57] This process of reading has the four characteristics of the *lectio divina* as analyzed by Casey, even though or maybe just because it was not a voluntary reading. But one can see how in this process some of the most important char-

55. Casey, *Sacred Reading*, 16–32.

56. Ibid., 29.

57. Ignatius of Loyola, "Reminiscences" in *Personal Writings*, 15.

acteristics of Ignatius's *Spiritual Exercises* and of the Society of Jesus were formed. Reading the life of Christ and the Lives of the Saints helped Saint Ignatius to make the right choices in his life, just as Fethullah Gülen was formed in his spiritual outlook by reading the lives of the Prophet and his Companions, and later books such as Said Nursi's *Risale-i Nur*.

Ignatius makes texts from the Bible the point of departure for the imagination in the *Spiritual Exercises*, the core of which is summarized in the "Principle and Foundation" as follows: "The human person is created to praise, reverence and serve God Our Lord, and by so doing to save his or her soul. The other things on the face of the earth are created for human beings in order to help them pursue the end for which they are created."[58] Immediately after this "Principle and Foundation," Ignatius talks about the importance of the daily *Examen*, which is an exercise in five points: first, giving thanks to God for the benefits received; second, asking for grace to know one's sins and reject them; third, asking for an account of one's soul about one's thoughts, words, and deeds; fourth, asking God for pardon for sins; and fifth, determining to do better with God's grace.[59] This daily examination of one's conscience is still widely used in Jesuit education. In his *Key Concepts in the Practice of Sufism,* Fethullah Gülen tells about a similar practice: *muhasaba* (self-criticism or self-interrogation). Quoting Ibn al-'Arabi, he tells that righteous people during the first centuries of Islam used to do very much the same: "write down or memorize their daily actions, thoughts, and words, and then analyze and criticize themselves for any evil or sin they had committed."[60] While this comes quite close to the "self-accusing self" that we discussed in the previous section, the important function of *lectio divina* and the *Examen* is not only to create a daily space for meditative reading and guided reflection,

58. Ignatius of Loyola, "Spiritual Exercises: Principle and Foundation," in *Personal Writings*, 289.

59. Ignatius of Loyola, "Spiritual Exercises: Daily Examen," in *Personal Writings*, 293.

60. Gülen, *Emerald Hills of the Heart, 1*, 6.

but also to lead one to specific actions. While there are many "book clubs" and reading circles in which people may read together and have conversations about spiritual subjects, the *sohbet* functions, as I wrote in chapter five, as a bridge between the spiritual discourse and the action-oriented discourse in the Hizmet Movement. The Benedictine and Cistercian *lectio divina* might be more akin to the *dershane* in the Nursi reading circles in that they are evidently based on the sacred Scripture in the respective traditions, and they seek to shape the lives of the faithful who participate in them, but they are not directly action-oriented. The Jesuit *Examen* and the *Spiritual Exercises,* of which it forms a part, are directly action-oriented because they are meant to help human beings in making well-reasoned choices. "Making an election," therefore, is one of the most important parts of the *Spiritual Exercises*; it is placed by Ignatius of Loyola at the end of the second week, precisely in the middle of the Exercises.[61] In his personal writings, such as the "Spiritual Diary" and the "Reminiscences," Ignatius tells about the importance of the process of election or discernment for the development of the Society of Jesus. The texts that function as the basis of the *Spiritual Exercises* are not read because of their informative value, but they are read because of their life-shaping potential. In a similar way, those who come together in reading circles like *sohbetler* in the Hizmet's Houses of Light base the choices in their lives on what they heard and discussed in these texts, as the followers of Saint Benedict do in their *lectio divina* and the followers of Ignatius in their "Spiritual Exercises." They choose a particular course of action and they discuss how they can shape their lives in such a way that they are faithful to the model that is embodied in the basic texts that are read in a "sacred reading."

61. Ignatius of Loyola, "Spiritual Exercises: Making an Election," in *Personal Writings*, 316–20.

EXCELLENT EDUCATION AND SERVICE TO OTHERS

Now that we have discussed the similarities between two manifestations of the spiritual core of particular forms of religious life in Islam and Christianity, namely the "crying preacher" and the "gift of tears," and also the similarities between two ritual enactments that form the bridge between this spiritual life and the specific forms in which this life is put into action, the last task is to describe similarities in these actions themselves. This is, as I said, the easiest task since the similarities are quite obvious and have been noticed by other researchers as well. Since both the Society of Jesus and the Hizmet Movement are action-oriented, it could be possible to describe just the similarity in their actions, namely excellent education and service to others. But in order to do justice to the religious character of these actions, it is necessary to start with their spiritual motivation once again. At the beginning of this chapter, we already observed the similarity between the idea of doing everything "to the greater glory of God" (*ad maiorem Dei gloriam*), the motto of the Society of Jesus, and the idea of "pleasing God by serving humankind" for the Hizmet Movement. More specifically, David Graskemper sees a similarity between "themes found in the Gülen educational movement, such as the Golden Generation and the concept of *hizmet*" and "Jesuit notions such as A.M.D.G., *cura personalis*, and 'Men and Women for Others.'"[62] Similarly, Patrick Howell sees similarities in the mystical and religious roots, in the emphasis on experience and pragmatic action, and finally in the devotion to building up community.[63]

The active engagement is visible first and foremost in excellent education in which excellence in the sciences and humanities—

62. Michael David Graskemper, "A Bridge to Inter-Religious Cooperation: The Gülen-Jesuit Educational Nexus," in *Muslim World in Transition: Contributions of the Gülen Movement* (London: Leeds Metropolitan University Press, 2007), 622–31.

63. Patrick Howell, "Dialogue between Jesuit and Gülen Educational and Spiritual Foundations," 59.

often in the form of a liberal arts core – is paired to a virtuous moral life. The Jesuit engagement in excellent education goes back to Ignatius of Loyola himself, who decided seven years after the conversion on his sickbed that he needed to go to Paris in order to receive the best possible education. Here, at the Sorbonne in Paris, the first group of Jesuit followers was formed.[64] Just over forty years after Ignatius's death, the Jesuits published a *ratio studiorum* (an official study plan) that became basis for their many educational institutions.[65] There are many similarities between the educational mission of the Gülen-inspired schools and of the Jesuit schools, for instance the fact that both types of education only included religious education when this was allowed, and refrained from doing so if that could be perceived as proselytizing.[66] Also, Gülen-inspired education and Jesuit education both tend to focus on the higher strata of society, trying to change the leaders in the presumption that the rest will follow. They are therefore sometimes seen as elitist and also accused of having a hidden agenda and of justifying the means because of the end.[67] The suspicions that both types of education awakened because of their apparent successes has led some governments to ban the Jesuits, which has happened to the Gülen schools in some countries as well.[68]

I have no room to discuss the different opinions about the characteristics of Jesuit education, since even the history of the Jesuits in America already gives a great number of viewpoints on Jesuit education.[69] I will limit myself here to a particular address in which

64. Ignatius of Loyola, "Reminiscences," in *Personal Writings*, 53.

65. Howell, "Dialogue between Jesuit and Gülen Educational and Spiritual Foundations," 60.

66. Ibid., 61.

67. Nancy Gallagher, "Hizmet Intercultural Dialogue Trips to Turkey," in *The Gülen Hizmet Movement and Its Transnational Activities: Case Studies of Altruistic Activism in Contemporary Islam*, ed. Sophia Pandya and Nancy Gallagher (Boca Raton, Fla.: BrownWalker Press, 2012), 76.

68. I owe these insights to a discussion with Jean-Pierre Lebouder while driving from our interview with Fatih University to our interview with the Journalists and Writers Foundation on August 17, 2009.

69. Raymond A. Schroth, SJ, *The American Jesuits: A History* (New York: New York University Press, 2007).

father Peter-Hans Kolvenbach, the superior general for the Society of Jesus in 2000, talked about "The Service of Faith and the Promotion of Justice" at a conference on "commitment to Justice in Jesuit Higher Education" organized by the twenty-eight Jesuit colleges and universities in the United States.[70] One of the core points in this address was that the most important thing in education is not "what our students do but who they become." This means that attention should be focused not so much on the career perspectives of students, but on the type of persons they become. This is the meaning of the Latin phrase *cura personalis* that describes personal care for the whole person. It is also summarized in the expression "forming men and women for others" — a term that dates back to the former Superior General Pedro Arrupe who used it in 1973. It is now sometimes emended to men and women with and for others and has become one of the trademarks of Jesuit education in the United States. As Graskemper observes, this term gives a very interesting parallel to the idea of a "golden generation" so often mentioned by Fethullah Gülen.[71] In both cases, it is not the knowledge or the skills of the students that is the central educational goal, but their personalities as men and women who are ready to serve. Thus, the term "service" is often used in the Jesuit educational setting to refer to "doing service to others," as a specific adaptation of the notion of "men and women for others." This leads to an explosion of service-initiatives implemented by students at Jesuit institutions such as service-learning, community service, and immersion programs. This activism forms a parallel to the countless initiatives of the Hizmet Movement. In this central notion of "doing good to humankind in order to please God," Muslims and Christians who went to Gülen-inspired schools or to Jesuit educational institutions can easily find one another, and this may indeed be one of the most promising avenues for future Christian-Muslim dialogue.[72]

70. See http://www.loyola.edu/Justice/commitment/kolvenbach.html (accessed August 29, 2010).

71. Graskemper, "A Bridge to Inter-Religious Cooperation," 628.

72. Ibid., 630.

Of course there are many forms of service that are not based on faith, but in institutions that are based on a faith identity, a danger arises if the term "service" is no longer recognized in its faith-based sense.[73] For believers, "doing good" is only possible in so far as we are enabled to give back something of what has been given to us. In much of the enthusiasm for "service" as a contemporary form of exerting one's faith, there lurks the danger of what in the Christian tradition has been labeled as Pelagianism, a tendency to rely mainly on our own power and to forget that we can only give to others after having received our gifts from God first. So, if some Jesuits interpret "to the greater glory of God" as meaning that God should be glorified by helping human beings, they tell the truth but not the whole truth. If one of the benefits of interfaith dialogue is that we can learn from one another, as the Qur'ān states (49:13), I may venture to give my personal opinion here on what students in Jesuit education could learn from the Gülen-inspired *hizmet*, and what the Hizmet Movement could learn from the Jesuits. I admire the activism of many students in Jesuit education who show their faith in doing service and thereby becoming "men and women with and for others," but I question the fact that some of them seem to identify their faith with performing service. They could learn from the Hizmet Movement about the fact that activism needs a spiritual foundation.

Something of this critique is also implied in Father Kolvenbach's address when he explains that "the service of faith" is in fact a form of proclamation of faith, because the word "service" goes back to the Greek word *diakonia* in the New Testament. In the title of Kolvenbach's lecture, "service of faith" is paired with and qualifies "promotion of justice." This prevents us from getting the impression that justice might be available apart from faith. This is a discussion within the Jesuit discourse on education, and as I said, the Hizmet Movement could help those who work at Jesuit institutions to realize how and why they are working at faith-based

73. One may be reminded here of Martin Luther, who was of the opinion that the danger of "sanctifying yourself through works," instead of being sanctified through God's grace, lurked in both Islam and Roman Catholicism.

institutions. On the other hand, the Jesuit stress on justice might influence the type of service that is organized by the Hizmet community in the sense of adding the commitment to justice as an important part of our Abrahamic faiths. In this sense, we can learn from one another and that is why God has created us in different nations and religions.

CONCLUSION

In this book, I have tried to show how Fethullah Gülen and the Hizmet Movement that he inspired by his life and works can be seen as contributing to the renewal of faith by service. The interreligious nature of my approach may serve to not only explain some of the characteristics of this faith-based service movement to non-Muslims, but also to show how the renewal of faith by service may extend beyond the world of Islam.

In the first chapter, I described the awakening of my interest in the movement and in Fethullah Gülen's writings through the friendships developed at a number of interreligious events in the Netherlands. The second chapter described the special place of Turkey as a country with a long and deep history of engagement both with the heartlands of Islam and with Western political and cultural realities. This sketch formed the background against which the life and writings of Fethullah Gülen could be discussed in chapter three, and the major influences on his theological thinking in chapter four. From the fifth chapter on, the main attention shifted from Gülen to the network of volunteers inspired by him that has become known as the Hizmet Movement. I have tried to describe some of the basic elements of the religious identity of this movement in chapter five, and the three main forms of its service in chapter six. This final chapter is most explicitly comparative in its outlook, since it tried to gain a deeper understanding of Fethullah Gülen and the volunteers inspired by him through the presentation of a couple of explicit parallels in Christian religious life.

Even though I am fully aware that the Hizmet Movement is

not very transparent in its structure, and that political considerations may sometimes prevent it from talking openly about its inspiration, I am convinced that the religious core of its faith-based service may offer important lessons for the future of interreligious relationships. Members of the Hizmet Movement may not only renew the religion of Islam by doing service to humankind in order to please God, but they may also help Christians to find new resources for the renewal of their own faith.

BIBLIOGRAPHY

Afsaruddin, Asma. *The First Muslims: History and Memory*. Oxford: Oneworld, 2008.

———. "Education: Classical Views and M. Fethullah Gülen's Perspectives." In *Islam in the Contemporary World 1: The Fethullah Gülen Movement in Thought and Practice.* Conference Proceedings, November 12–13, 2005, Rice University, Houston, Tex. Somerset, N.J.: Tughra books, 2009.

Agai, Bekim. "The Gülen Movement's Islamic Ethic of Education." In *Turkish Islam and the Secular State: The Gülen Movement,* edited by M. Hakan Yavuz and John L. Esposito, 48–68. Syracuse N.Y.: Syracuse University Press, 2003.

———. *Zwischen Netzwerk und Diskurs: Das Bildungsnetzwerk um Fethullah Gülen (geb. 1938): Die flexible Umsetzung modernen islamischen Gedankenguts*. Bonner Islamstudien 2. Schenefeld: EB-Verlag, 2004.

———. "Discursive and Organizational Strategies of the Gülen Movement." In *Islam in the Contemporary World 1: the Fethullah Gülen Movement in Thought and Practice.* Conference Proceedings, November 12–13, 2005, Rice University, Houston, Tex., 47–59. Somerset, N.J.: Tughra Books, 2009.

Akşin, Sina. *Turkey from Empire to Revolutionary Republic. The Emergence of the Turkish Nation from 1789 to the Present*. Translated from the Turkish by Dexter H. Mursaloğlu. New York: New York University Press, 2007.

Aktay, Yasin. "New Media Figures and Instruments of Religious Authority in Turkey: Understanding Gülen and his Religious Leadership." In *Islam in the Contemporary World 1: The Fethullah Gülen Movement in Thought and Practice.* Conference Proceedings, November 12–13, 2005, Rice University, Houston, Tex., 297–304. Somerset, N.J.: Tughra Books, 2009.

Akyol, Harun. "The Role of Turkish Schools in Building Trusting Cross-ethnic Relationships in Northern Iraq." In *Islam and Peacebuilding: Gül-*

en Movement Initiatives, edited by John L. Esposito and İhsan Yilmaz, 311–39. New York: Blue Dome Press, 2010.

Albayrak, İsmail, ed. *Mastering Knowledge in Modern Times: Fethullah Gülen as an Islamic Scholar*. New York: Blue Dome Press, 2011.

Alimuhamedov, Farhod. "Peaceful Muslim – non-Muslim Coexistence in a Secular Context." In *Peaceful Coexistence: Fethullah Gülen's Initiatives in the Contemporary World*, 373–81. London: Leeds Metropolitan University Press, 2007.

Aras, Bülent. "Turkish Islam's Moderate Face." *Middle East Quarterly* 5, no.3 (1998): 23–31.

Ashton, Loye, and Tamer Balci. "A Contextual Analysis of the Supporters and Critics of the Gülen/Hizmet Movement." In *Islam in the Age of Global Challenges: Alternative Perspectives of the Gülen Movement*. Conference Proceedings, Georgetown University, Washington, D.C., November 14–15, 2008, 73–113. Washington, D.C.: Rumi Forum, 2008.

Aslan, Adnan. "Interfaith Dialogue in the Context of New Theological Language and Fethullah Gülen." In *Islam in the Contemporary World 1: The Fethullah Gülen Movement in Thought and Practice*. Conference Proceedings, November 12–13, 2005, Rice University, Houston, Tex., 312–23. Somerset, N.J.: Tughra Books, 2009.

Aslandoğan, Y. Alp. "Pedagogical Model of Gülen and Modern Theories of Learning." In *Islam in the Contemporary World 2: the Fethullah Gülen Movement in Thought and Practice*. Conference Proceedings, March 4–5, 2006, Southern Methodist University, Dallas, Tex., 115–23. Somerset, N.J.: Tughra Books, 2009.

Aslandoğan, Yüksel A., and Muhammed Çetin, "Gülen's Educational Paradigm in Thought and Practice." In *Muslim Citizens of the Globalized World*, edited by Robert A. Hunt and Yüksel A. Aslandoğan, 34–61. Somerset, N.J.: The Light, 2007.

Aydin, Hasan, and Stephen K. Lafer. "Promoting Multicultural Harmony in Nigeria: the Gülen-Inspired Schools." In *The Gülen Hizmet Movement and its Transnational Activities. Case Studies of Altruistic Activism in Contemporary Islam*, edited by Sophia Pandya and Nancy Gallagher, 195–211. Boca Raton, Fla.: BrownWalker Press, 2012.

Barton, Greg. "Preaching by Example and Learning for Life: Understanding the Gülen *Hizmet* in the Global Context of Religious Philanthropy and Civil Religion." In *Muslim World in Transition: Contributions of the Gülen Movement*. Conference Proceedings, London, 25–27 October 2007, 650–62. London: Leeds Metropolitan University Press, 2007.

———. "How the Hizmet Works: Islam, Dialogue and the Gülen Movement in Australia." In *Islam in the Age of Global Challenges. Alternative Perspectives of the Gülen Movement.* Conference Proceedings, Georgetown University, Washington, D.C., November 14–15, 2008, 114–43. Washington, D.C.: Rumi Forum, 2008.

———. "Progressive Islamic Thought, Civil Society, and the Gülen Movement in the National Context: Parallels with Indonesia." In *Islam in the Contemporary World 1: The Fethullah Gülen Movement in Thought and Practice.* Conference Proceedings, November 12–13, 2005, Rice University, Houston, Tex., 224–70. Somerset, N.J.: Tughra Books, 2009.

Baskal, Zachary, and Helen Rose Ebaugh. "The Turkish-Islamic Culture of Giving." In Helen R. Ebaugh, *The Gülen Movement: A Sociological Analysis of a Civic Movement Rooted in Moderate Islam*, 65–81. Dordrecht: Springer, 2010.

Baum, Gregory. *The Theology of Tariq Ramadan: A Catholic Perspective.* Notre Dame, Ind.: University of Notre Dame Press, 2009.

Benedict of Nursia. "The Rule of Saint Benedict." In *The Benedictine Handbook.* Collegeville, Minn.: Liturgical Press, 2003.

Bernard of Clairvaux. *The Works of Bernard of Clairvaux, 2: Song of Songs I.* Translated by Kilian Walsh, OCSO. Collegeville, Minn.: Cistercian Publications, 2008.

Bommel, Abdulwahid van. *Het Lied van het Riet: Djalâluddîn Rûmî Masnawî.* Vertaald door Abdulwahid van Bommel. Amsterdam: Türkevi Productions, 2008.

Borelli, John. "Interreligious Dialogue as a Spiritual Practice." In *Islam in the Age of Global Challenges. Alternative Perspectives of the Gülen Movement.* Conference Proceedings, Georgetown University, Washington, D.C., November 14–15, 2008, 144–63. Washington, D.C.: Rumi Forum, 2008.

Brodeur, Patrice. "The Ethics of Bediüzzaman Said Nursi's Dialogue with the West in Light of his Concept of 'Europe.'" In *Globalization, Ethics and Islam. The Case of Bediuzzaman Said Nursi*, edited by Ian Markham and Ibrahim Ozdemir, 89–98. Burlington, Vt.: Ashgate.

Bruinessen, Martin van. *De Fethullah Gülenbeweging in Nederland. Een rapport opgesteld op verzoek van de Minister voor Wonen, Wijken en Integratie.* [The Fethullah Gülen Movement in the Netherlands. A report on behalf of the Minister of Living, Neigborhoods, and Integration]. Utrecht: Universiteit Utrecht, 2010.

Bruckmayr, Philipp. "Pnom Penh's Fethullah Gülen School as an Alternative to Prevalent Forms of Education for Cambodia's Muslim Minority." In *Islam and Peacebuilding: Gülen Movement Initiatives*, edited by John L. Esposito and İhsan Yilmaz, 225–48. New York: Blue Dome Press. 2010.

Bulaç, Ali. *Din-Kent ve Cemaat: Fethullah Gülen Örneği*. Istanbul: Ufuk Kitap, 2007.

Burrell, David B., CSC. *Faith and Freedom. An Interfaith Perspective*. Malden, Mass.: Blackwell Publishing, 2004.

Can, Şefik. *Fundamentals of Rumi's Thought: A Mevlevi Perspective*. Foreword by M. Fethullah Gülen. Translated by Zeki Saritoprak and Cüneyt Eroğlu. Somerset, N.J.: The Light, 2004.

Çapan, Ergün. "Gülen's Teaching Methodology in his Private Circle." In *Mastering Knowledge in Modern Times: Fethullah Gülen as an Islamic Scholar*, edited by İsmail Albayrak, 127–56. New York: Blue Dome Press, 2011.

Çarkoğlu, Ali, and Barry Rubin. *Turkey and the European Union: Domestic Politics, Economic Integration and International Dynamics*. Portland Ore.: Frank Cass, 2003.

Carroll, B. Jill. *A Dialogue of Civilizations. Gülen's Islamic Ideals and Humanistic Discourse*. Somerset, N.J.: The Light, Inc., 2007.

Casey, Michael. *Sacred Reading. The Ancient Art of* Lectio Divina. Liguori, Mo: Liguori/Triumph, 1996.

Çelik, Emre. "The Influence of Fethullah Gülen in the Australian Experience of Interfaith Dialogue." In *Islam in the Contemporary World 3: The Fethullah Gülen Movement in Thought and Practice*. Conference Proceedings, University of Oklahoma, November 4–5, 2006, 134–43. Somerset, N.J.: Tughra Books, 2009.

Çelik, Gürkan. *The Gülen Movement. Building Social Cohesion through Dialogue and Education*. Delft: Eburon, 2010.

Çelik, Gürkan, and Pim Valkenberg. "Gülen's Approach to Dialogue and Peace: Its Theoretical Background and Some Practical Perspectives." *The International Journal of Diversity in Organisations, Communities and Nations* 7, no.1 (2007): 29–37.

——, eds. *Fethullah Gülen & de Vrijwilligersbeweging*. Budel: Damon, 2010.

Çelik, Gürkan, et al. *Voorlopers in de vrede*. Budel: Damon, 2005.

Çetin, Muhammed. *The Gülen Movement: Civic Service without Borders*. New York: Blue Dome Press, 2009.

——. "Voluntary Altruistic Action: Its Symbolic Challenge against Sinecures of Vested Interests." In *Islam in the Contemporary World 3: The Fethullah Gülen Movement in Thought and Practice*. Conference Proceedings, University of Oklahoma, November 4–5, 2006, 42–55. Somerset, N.J.: Tughra Books, 2009.

Chittick, William. *The Sufi Path of Love: The Spiritual Teachings of Rumi*. Albany, N.Y.: State University of New York Press, 1983.

Çitlak, M. Fatih, and Hüseyin Bingül, eds. *Rumi and His Sufi Path of Love*. Somerset, N.J.: The Light, 2007.

Clooney, Francis X., SJ. *Comparative Theology: Deep Learning across Religious Borders*. Chichester: WileyBlackwell, 2010.

Creemers, Iris, et al., eds., *Erasmus en Gülen. Inspiratoren voor vrede en dialoog* [Erasmus and Gülen: Inspiring peace and dialogue]. Budel: Damon, 2009.

Demir, Emre. "The Emergence of a neo-communitarian discourse in the Turkish diaspora in Europe: the implantation stategies and competition logics of the Gülen Movement in France and in Germany." In *European Muslims, Civility and Public Life: Perspectives on and from the Gülen Movement*, edited by Paul Weller and Ihsan Yilmaz, 101–12. New York: Continuum, 2012.

Ebaugh, Helen Rose. *The Gülen Movement: A Sociological Analysis of a Civic Movement Rooted in Moderate Islam*. Dordrecht: Springer, 2010.

Ebaugh, Helen Rose, and Dogan Koç, "Funding Gülen-Inspired Good Works: Demonstrating and Generating Commitment to the Movement." In *Muslim World in Transition: Contributions of the Gülen Movement*. Conference Proceedings, London, 25–27 October 2007, 539–51. London: Leeds Metropolitan University Press, 2007.

Erdem, Emrullah, ed. *Mewlana Djalaladdin Rumi en zijn "mystieke pad van de liefde."* Rotterdam: Stichting Islam en Dialoog, 2007.

Ergene, Mehmet Enes. *Tradition Witnessing the Modern Age: An Analysis of the Gülen Movement*. Somerset, N. J.: Tughra Books, 2008.

Esposito, John L., and İhsan Yilmaz, eds. *Islam and Peacebuilding: Gülen Movement Initiatives*. New York: Blue Dome Press, 2010.

Fitzgerald, Michael L., and John Borelli. *Interfaith Dialogue: A Catholic View*. Maryknoll, N.Y.: Orbis, 2006.

Fortuyn, Pim. *De islamisering van onze cultuur. Nederlandse identiteit als fundament*. [The Islamization of our culture: Dutch identity as foundation.] Rotterdam: Speakers Academy, 2001.

Gaffney, Patrick D. *The Prophet's Pulpit: Islamic Preaching in Contemporary Egypt*. Berkeley: University of California Press, 1994.

Gallagher, Nancy. "Hizmet Intercultural Dialogue Trips to Turkey." In *The Gülen Hizmet Movement and its Transnational Activities. Case Studies of Altruistic Activism in Contemporary Islam*, edited by Sophia Pandya and Nancy Gallagher, 73–93. Boca Raton, Fla.: BrownWalker Press, 2012.

Ghazālī, Abu Hamid Muhammad al-. *Love, Longing, Intimacy and Contentment. Kitāb al-mahabba wa'l shawq wa'l uns wa'l ridā*. Book 36 of The Revival of the Religious Sciences, *Ihyā' 'ulūm al-dīn*. Translated with an introduction and notes by Eric Ormsby. Cambridge: Islamic Texts Society, 2011.

Gioia, Francesco, ed. *Interreligious Dialogue: The Official Teaching of the Catholic Church from the Second Vatican Council to John Paul II (1963–2005)*. Boston: Pauline Books and Media, 2006.

Gokcek, Mustafa. "Gülen and Sufism." In *Islam in the Contemporary World 1: The Fethullah Gülen Movement in Thought and Practice*. Conference Proceedings, November 12–13, 2005, Rice University, Houston, Tex., 305–11. Somerset, N.J.: Tughra Books, 2009.

Gramlich, Richard. *Muhammad al-Gazzālī's Lehre von den Stufen zur Gottesliebe*. Wiesbaden: Franz Steiner Verlag, 1984.

Graskemper, Michael David. "A Bridge to Inter-Religious Cooperation: The Gülen-Jesuit Educational Nexus." In *Muslim World in Transition: Contributions of the Gülen Movement*. Conference Proceedings, London, 25–27 October 2007, 622–31. London: Leeds Metropolitan University Press, 2007.

Gülen, M. Fethullah. *Towards the Lost Paradise*. İzmir: Kaynak, 1998.

———. *Essentials of the Islamic Faith*. Translated by Ali Ünal. Fairfax, Va.: The Fountain, 2000.

———. *Fethullah Gülen: Advocate of Dialogue*. Compiled by Ali Ünal and Alphonse Williams. Translated by Ali Ünal. Fairfax, Va.: Fountain Publications, 2000.

———. *Pearls of Wisdom*. Translated by Ali Ünal. Fairfax, Va.: The Fountain, 2000.

———. *Essays, Perspectives, Opinions*. Compiled by the Fountain. Rutherford, N.J: The Light, 2002.

———. *Emerald Hills of the Heart: Key Concepts in the Practice of Sufism, 1*. Translated by Ali Ünal. Rutherford, N.J.: The Light, 2004.

———. *Emerald Hills of the Heart: Key Concepts in the Practice of Sufism, 2*. Translated by Ali Ünal. Somerset, N.J.: The Light, 2004.

———. *Love and the Essence of Being Human*. Prepared for publication by Faruk Tuncer. Translated by Mehmet Ünal and Nilüfer Korkmaz. Istanbul: Journalists and Writers Foundation Publication, 2004.

——. *The Necessity of Interfaith Dialog: A Muslim Perspective*. Somerset, N.J.: The Light, 2004.

——. *Toward a Global Civilization of Love and Tolerance*. Foreword by Thomas Michel. Somerset N.J.: The Light, 2004.

——. *Muhammad, the Messenger of God: Aspects of His Life*. Translated by Ali Ünal. Somerset, N.J: The Light, 2005.

——. *Questions and Answers about Islam, 2*. Somerset, N.J.: The Light, 2005.

——. *The Statue of Our Souls: Revival in Islamic Thought and Activism*. Translated from the Turkish by Muhammed Çetin. Somerset, N.J.: The Light, 2005.

——. *Questions and Answers about Islam, 1*. Somerset, N.J.: The Light, 2006.

——. *Fatiha Üzerine Mülâhazalar*. Istanbul: Nil Yayınları, 2007.

——. *Emerald Hills of the Heart: Key Concepts in the Practice of Sufism, 3*. Somerset, N.J.: Tughra Books, 2008.

——. *Vuslat muştusu*. Kirik Testi, 8. Istanbul: Gazeteciler ve Yazarlar Vakfı Yayınları, 2008.

——. *Enginliğiyle Bizim Dünyamiz*. Istanbul: Nil Yayınları, 2009.

——. *Hitap Çiçekleri*. Istanbul: Nesil Yayınları, 2009.

——. *Kader. Kitap ve sünnet perspektifinde*. Istanbul: Nil Yayınları, 2009.

——. *Kur'ân'dan İdrake Yansıyanlar*, Istanbul: Nil Yayınları, 2009.

——. *Reflections on the Qur'ān: Commentaries on Selected Verses*. Translated by Ayşenur Kaplan and Harun Gültekin. Clifton, N.J.: Tughra Books, 2012.

Haddad, Yvonne Yazbeck. "*Ghurba* as Paradigm for Muslim Life: A *Risale-i Nur* Worldview." *The Muslim World* 89 (1999): 297–313.

Harrington, James C. *Wrestling with Free Speech, Religious Freedom, and Democracy in Turkey: The Political Trials and Times of Fethullah Gülen*. Lanham, Md.: University Press of America, 2011.

Haughey, John, SJ. "The Driver in the Mind of Fethullah Gülen." In *Islam in the Age of Global Challenges: Alternative Perspectives of the Gülen Movement*. Conference Proceedings, Georgetown University, Washington, D.C., November 14–15, 2008, 333–49. Washington, D.C.: Rumi Forum, 2008.

Hendrick, Joshua. *Gülen: The Ambiguous Politics of Market Islam in Turkey and the World*. New York: New York University Press, 2013.

Hermann, Rainer. *Wohin geht die türkische Gesellschaft? Kulturkampf in der Türkei*. Munich: Deutscher Taschenbuch Verlag, 2009.

Hermansen, Marcia. "The Cultivation of Memory in the Gülen Community." In *Muslim World in Transition: Contributions of the Gülen Movement.* Conference Proceedings, London, 25–27 October, 2007, 60–76. London: Leeds Metropolitan University Press, 2007.

———. "Understandings of 'Community' within the Gülen Movement." In *Islam in the Contemporary World 1: The Fethullah Gülen Movement in Thought and Practice.* Conference Proceedings, November 12–13, Rice University, Houston, Tex., 2005, 280–96. Somerset, N.J.: Tughra Book, 2009.

Hick, John. *An Interpretation of Religion: Human Responses to the Transcendent.* London: MacMillan, 1989.

Homolka, Walter, Johann Hafner, Admiel Kosman, Ercan Karakoyun, eds. *Muslime zwischen Tradition und Moderne. Die Gülen-Bewegung als Brücke zwischen den Kulturen.* Freiburg: Herder, 2010.

Howard, Douglas A. *The History of Turkey.* Westport, Ct.: Greenwood Press, 2001.

Howell, Patrick. "Dialogue between Jesuit and Gülen Educational and Spiritual Foundations." In *East and West Encounters: the Gülen Movement.* Conference Proceedings, December 5–6, 2009, University of Southern California at Los Angeles, 59–69.

Hunt, Robert A., and Yüksel A. Aslandoğan, eds. *Muslim Citizens of the Globalized World: Contributions of the Gülen Movement.* Somerset, N.J.: The Light, 2007.

Ignatius of Loyola. *Personal Writings: Reminiscences, Spiritual Diary, Select Letters including the text of The Spiritual Exercises.* Translated with Introductions and Notes by Joseph A. Munitiz and Philip Endean. London: Penguin Books, 1996.

Irvine, Jill. "The Gülen Movement and Turkish Integration in Germany." In *Muslim Citizens of the Globalized World: Contributions of the Gülen Movement*, edited by Robert A. Hunt and Yüksel A. Aslandoğan, 62–84. Somerset, N.J.: The Light, 2007.

James, William. *The Varieties of Religious Experience.* New York: Triumph Books, 1991. First published 1902.

Jamison, Christopher, OSB. *Finding Sanctuary: Monastic Steps for Everyday Life.* Collegeville, Minn.: Liturgical Press, 2006.

Kalyoncu, Mehmet. "Gülen Inspired Schools in East Africa: Secular Alternative in Kenya and Pragmatist Approach to Development in Uganda." In *Islam in the Age of Global Challenges. Alternative Perspectives of the Gülen Movement.* Conference Proceedings, Georgetown University,

Washington, D.C., November 14–15, 2008, 350–73. Washington, D.C.: Rumi Forum, 2008.

Kalyoncu, Mehmet. "Understanding the Hizmet Discourse of the Gülen Movement." In *Islam in the Contemporary World, 4: The Fethullah Gülen Movement in Thought and Practice*. Conference Proceedings, San Antonio, November 3, 2007, 25–27. Somerset, N.J.: Tughra Books, 2009.

———. "Building Civil Society in Ethno-Religiously Fractured Communities: The Gülen Movement in Turkey and Abroad." In *Islam and Peacebuilding: Gülen Movement Initiatives*, edited by John L. Esposito and İhsan Yilmaz, 273–90. New York: Blue Dome Press, 2010.

Kayaoglu, Turan. "Preachers of Dialogue: International Relations and Interfaith Theology." In *Islam and Peacebuilding: Gülen Movement Initiatives*, edited by John L. Esposito and İhsan Yilmaz, 147–68. New York: Blue Dome Press, 2010.

Keles, Ozcan. "Promoting Human Rights Values in the Muslim World: Towards an Inclusive Civilization in Gülen's Thought and Practice." In *Peaceful Coexistence: Fethullah Gülen's Initiatives in the Contemporary World*, 447–70. London: Leeds Metropolitan University Press, 2007.

Kim, Heon. "Gülen's Dialogic Sufism: A Constructional and Constructive Factor of Dialogue." In *Islam in the Age of Global Challenges. Alternative Perspectives of the Gülen Movement*. Conference Proceedings, Georgetown University, Washington, D.C., November 14–15, 2008, 374–406. Washington, D.C.: Rumi Forum, 2008.

Kim, Heon C., "Humanism in Islam and in East Asia: Gülen's Vision in Dialogue with East Asian Religious Cultures." In *The Gülen Hizmet Movement and its Transnational Activities: Case Studies of Altruistic Activism in Contemporary Islam*, edited by Sophia Pandya and Nancy Gallagher, 55–72. Boca Raton, Fla.: BrownWalker Press, 2012.

Kirk, Kate, and Gürkan Çelik. "Opening the Road to Dialogue: An Amalgamation of Gülen's and Spinoza's Ideas on Tolerance and Dialogue Applied to the Situation of Muslims in the Netherlands." In *Peaceful Coexistence: Fethullah Gülen's Initiatives in the Contemporary World*, 169–82. London: Leeds Metropolitan University Press., 2007.

Kirk, Martha Ann. "Seeds of Peace: Solidarity, Aid, and Education Shared by the Gülen Movement in Southeastern Turkey." In *Islam in the Age of Global Challenges: Alternative Perspectives of the Gülen Movement.* Conference Proceedings, Georgetown University, Washington, D.C., November 14–15, 2008, 407–34. Washington, D.C.: Rumi Forum, 2008.

——. "'Second Rabi'a's': Women's Gratitude, Compassion, and Altruism." In *Islam in the Contemporary World 4: The Fethullah Gülen Movement in Thought and Practice*. Conference Proceedings, San Antonio, November 3, 2007, 46–57. Somerset, N.J.: Tughra Books, 2009.

Knitter, Paul. *Introducing Theologies of Religions*. Maryknoll, N.Y.: Orbis Books, 2002.

Koç, Dogan. "Generating an Understanding of Financial Resources in the Gülen Movement: 'Kimse Yok Mu' Solidarity and Aid Association." In *Islam in the Age of Global Challenges: Alternative Perspectives of the Gülen Movement.* Conference Proceedings, Georgetown University, Washington, D.C., November 14–15, 2008, 435–54. Washington, D.C.: Rumi Forum, 2008.

——. *Strategic Defamation of Fethullah Gülen. English vs. Turkish.* Lanham, Md.: University Press of America, 2012.

Korostelina, Karina V. "Dialogue as a Source of Peaceful Co-existence." In *Islam and Peacebuilding: Gülen Movement Initiatives*, edited by John L. Esposito and İhsan Yilmaz, 103–21. New York: Blue Dome Press, 2010.

Kramer, Heinz. *A Changing Turkey. The Challenge to Europe and the United States*. Washington, D.C.: Brookings Institution Press, 2000.

Kuru, Ahmet T. "Changing Perspectives on Islamism and Secularism in Turkey: The Gülen Movement and the AK Party." In *Muslim World in Transition: Contributions of the Gülen Movement*, 140–51. London: Leeds Metropolitan University Press, 2007.

Kurucan, Ahmet, and Mustafa Kasım Erol. *Dialogue in Islam. Qur'an – Sunnah – History*. London: Dialogue Society, 2011.

Kuschel, Karl-Josef. *Streit um Abraham: was Juden, Christen und Muslime trennt – und was sie eint*. Munich: Piper, 1994.

Lacey, Jonathan. "Investigating the Contribution of Fethullah Gülen through the Activities of a Gülen-inspired Religio-cultural Society Based in Ireland." In *Islam and Peacebuilding: Gülen Movement Initiatives*, edited by John L. Esposito and İhsan Yilmaz, 249–72. New York: Blue Dome Press, 2010.

——. "An Exploration of the strategic dimensions of dialogue in a Gülen movement organization in Northern Ireland." In *European Muslims, Civility and Public Life: Perpectives On and From the Gülen Movement*, edited by Paul Weller and Ihsan Yilmaz, 127–39. New York: Continuum, 2012.

Leaman, Oliver. "Nursi's Place in the *Ihya'* Tradition." *The Muslim World* 89 (1999): 314–24.

Leclercq, Jean, OSB. *The Love of Learning and the Desire for God: A Study of Monastic Culture*. Translated by Catherine Misrahi. New York: Fordham University Press, 1961. (First published as *L'Amour des lettres et le désir de Dieu. Initiation aux auteurs monastiques du moyen âge*, Paris 1957.)

Levinskaya, Victoria. "Resemblance of Fethullah Gülen's Ideas and Current Political Developments in Uzbekistan." In *Peaceful Coexistence: Fethullah Gülen's Initiatives in the Contemporary World*, 331–43. London: Leeds Metropolitan University Press, 2007.

Lewis, Bernard. *The Emergence of Modern Turkey*. 3rd ed. New York: Oxford University Press, 2002.

Lewis, Franklin D. *Rumi: Past and Present, East and West. The Life, Teachings and Poetry of Jalāl al-Din Rumi*. Oxford: Oneworld, 2003.

Long, JoAnn. "Fethullah Gülen and Interfaith/cultural Dialogue: The Lubbock Christian University Experience." In *Islam in the Contemporary World 4: The Fethullah Gülen Movement in Thought and Practice*. Conference Proceedings, University of Texas, San Antonio, Tex., November 3, 2007, 58–62. Somerset, N.J.: Tughra Books, 2009.

Lumbard, Joseph E. B. "The Decline of Knowledge and the Rise of Ideology in the Modern Islamic World." In *Islam, Fundamentalism, and the Betrayal of Tradition*. Revised and expanded. Edited by Joseph E. B. Lumbard, 39–77. Bloomington, Ind.: World Wisdom, 2009.

Markham, Ian. *Engaging with Bediuzzaman Said Nursi: A Model of Interfaith Dialogue*. Burlington, Vt.: Ashgate, 2009.

Mattson, Ingrid. *The Story of the Qur'an: Its History and Place in Muslim Life*. Malden, Mass.: Blackwell Publishing, 2008.

McAuliffe, Jane Dammen. "The Tasks and Traditions of Interpretation." In *The Cambridge Companion to the Qur'ān*, edited by Jane Dammen McAuliffe, 181–209. Cambridge: Cambridge University Press, 2006.

Mehmeti, Jeton. "The Role of Education in Kosovo and the Contribution of the Gülen Movement." In *The Gülen Hizmet Movement and Its Transnational Activities. Case Studies of Altruistic Activism in Contemporary Islam*, edited by Sophia Pandya and Nancy Gallagher, 213–21. Boca Raton, Fla.: BrownWalker Press, 2012.

Michel, Thomas, SJ. "Turkish Experience for Muslim-Christian Dialogue. A Thinker: B. S. Nursi; An Activist: M. F. Gülen." In *Travelling Together beyond Dialogue: Peace and Dialogue in a Plural Society: Common Values and Responsibilities*, 33–40. Melbourne: Australian Intercultural Society, 2002.

——. "Fethullah Gülen as Educator." In *Turkish Islam and the Secular State: The Gülen Movement*, edited by M. Hakan Yavuz and John L. Esposito, 69–84. Syracuse, N.Y.: Syracuse University Press, 2003.

——. *Reflections on Said Nursi's Views on Muslim-Christian Understanding.* Istanbul: Söz Basım Yayın, 2003.

——. "Fighting Poverty with Kimse Yok Mu." In *Islam in the Age of Global Challenges. Alternative Perspectives of the Gülen Movement.* Conference Proceedings, Georgetown University, Washington, D.C., November 14–15, 2008, 523–33. Washington, D.C.: Rumi Forum, 2008.

——. *Insights from the Risale-i Nur: Said Nursi's Advice for Modern Believers.* Clifton, N.J.: Tughra Books, 2013.

Mitchell, Lynn E. "M. Fethullah Gülen: A Preacher of Piety and Integrity of Action: A Study in Analogy between the Gülen Movement and the Clapham Circle." In *Islam in the Age of Global Challenges: Alternative Perspectives of the Gülen Movement.* Conference Proceedings, Georgetown University, Washington, D.C., November 14–15, 2008, 534–60. Washington, D.C.: Rumi Forum, 2008.

Mohamed, Yasien. "The Educational Theory of Fethullah Gülen and Its Practice in South Africa." In *Muslim World in Transition: Contributions of the Gülen Movement.* Conference Proceedings, London, 25–27 October 2007, 552–71. London: Leeds Metropolitan University Press, 2007.

Nelson, Kristina. *The Art of Reciting the Qur'an.* Cairo: The American University in Cairo Press, 2001.

Nursi, Said. *The Words: From the Risale-i Nur Collection.* Translated from the Turkish by Şükran Vahide. Istanbul: Sözler Neşriyat, 1992.

——. *The Damascus Sermon.* Translated by Şükran Vahide. 2nd. ed. Istanbul: Sözler Neşriyat, 1996.

——. *Letters 1928–1932.* Translated from the Turkish *Mektûbat* by Şükran Vahide, new edition. Istanbul: Sözler Neşriyat, 2001.

——. *Signs of Miraculousness: The Inimitability of the Qur'an's Conciseness.* Translated by Şükran Vahide. Istanbul: Sözler Neşriyat, 2004. (First published as *Ishārāt al-I'jāz fi mazann al-Ijāz*, 1918.)

Orhan, Özgüç. "Islamic *Himmah* and Christian *Charity*: An Attempt at Inter-Faith Dialogue." In *Islam in the Age of Global Challenges. Alternative Perspectives of the Gülen Movement.* Conference Proceedings, Georgetown University, Washington, D.C, November 14–15, 2008, 561–82. Washington, D.C.: Rumi Forum, 2008.

Osman, Mohamed Nawab bin Mohamed. "Towards a Middle Way:

Islam in Southeast Asia and the Contributions of the Gülen Movement." In *Islam and Peacebuilding: Gülen Movement Initiatives*, edited by John L. Esposito and İhsan Yilmaz, 291–309. New York: Blue Dome Press, 2010.

Öktem, Niyazi. "Necessity and Importance of Intercultural – Interreligious Dialogue." In *Peaceful Coexistence: Fethullah Gülen's Initiatives in the Contemporary World*, 483–88. London: Leeds Metropolitan University Press, 2007.

Özdalga, Elizabeth. "Following in the Footsteps of Fethullah Gülen." In *Turkish Islam and the Secular State: The Gülen Movement*, edited by M. Hakan Yavuz and John L. Esposito, 85–114. Syracuse, N.Y.: Syracuse University Press, 2003.

Pandya, Sophia, and Nancy Gallagher, eds. *The Gülen Hizmet Movement and Its Transnational Activities: Case Studies of Altruistic Activism in Contemporary Islam*. Boca Raton, Fla.: BrownWalker Press, 2012.

Penaskovic, Richard. "Gülen on Healing the Rift between Islam and the West." In *Islam and Peacebuilding: Gülen Movement Initiatives*, edited by John L. Esposito and İhsan Yilmaz, 123–43. New York: Blue Dome Press, 2010.

Peppinck, Tineke. "From 'New Man' to 'World Citizen': The Replication of Fethullah Gülen's Renovation Vision in the Dutch Context." In *European Muslims, Civility and Public Life: Perspectives On and From the Gülen Movement*, edited by Paul Weller and Ihsan Yilmaz, 91–100. New York: Continuum, 2012.

Polat, Çemen. "Gülen-Inspired Schools in Australia and Their Funding." In *The Gülen Hizmet Movement and Its Transnational Activities: Case Studies of Altruistic Activism in Contemporary Islam*, edited by Sophia Pandya and Nancy Gallagher, 171–93. Boca Raton, Fla.: BrownWalker Press, 2012.

Pratt, Douglas. "Islamic Prospects for Interreligious Dialogue: The Voice of Fethullah Gülen." In *Islam and Peacebuilding: Gülen Movement Initiatives*, edited by John L. Esposito and İhsan Yilmaz, 189–206. New York: Blue Dome Press, 2010.

Rabasa, Angel, and F. Stephen Larrabee. *The Rise of Political Islam in Turkey*. Santa Monica, Calif.: RAND Corporation, National Defense Research Institute, 2008.

Rausch, Margaret. "Progress Through Piety: *Sohbetler* (Spiritual Gatherings) of the Women Participants in the Gülen Movement." In *Islam in the Age of Global Challenges. Alternative Perspectives of the Gülen Movement.* Conference Proceedings, Georgetown University, Washington, D.C., November 14–15, 2008, 610–34. Washington, D.C.: Rumi Forum, 2008.

———. "Gender and Leadership in the Gülen Movement: Women Affiliates' Contributions to East-West Encounters." In *The Gülen Hizmet Movement and Its Transnational Activities. Case Studies of Altruistic Activism in Contemporary Islam*, edited by Sophia Pandya and Nancy Gallagher, 133–59. Boca Raton, Fla.: BrownWalker Press, 2012.

Reed, Fred. *Anatolia Junction*. Burnaby: Talon, 1999.

Roy, Olivier. *Globalized Islam: the Search for a New Ummah*. New York: Columbia University Press, 2004.

Sahin, Zeynep. "Interfaith Dialogue Organizations as Actors of Peace Building: Case of Rumi Forum." In *Islam in the Age of Global Challenges: Alternative Perspectives of the Gülen Movement.* Conference Proceedings, Georgetown University, Washington, D.C., November 14–15, 2008, 694–710. Washington, D.C.: Rumi Forum, 2008.

Saritoprak, Zeki. "Fethullah Gülen: A Sufi in His Own Way." In *Turkish Islam and the Secular State: The Gülen Movement*, edited by M. Hakan Yavuz and John L. Esposito, 156–69. Syracuse, N.Y.: Syracuse University Press, 2003.

———. "Fethullah Gülen's Theory of Peacebuilding." In *Islam and Peacebuilding: Gülen Movement Initiatives*, edited by John L. Esposito and İhsan Yilmaz, 169–87. New York: Blue Dome Press, 2010.

Saritoprak, Zeki, and Sidney Griffith. "Fethullah Gülen and the 'People of the Book': A Voice from Turkey for Interfaith Dialogue." *The Muslim World* 95 (2005): 329–40.

Schroth, Raymond A., SJ. *The American Jesuits: A History*. New York: New York University Press, 2007.

Sevindi, Nevval. *Contemporary Islamic Conversations. M. Fethullah Gülen on Turkey, Islam, and the West.* Edited and with an Introduction by Ibrahim M. Abu-Rabiʿ. Translated by Abdullah T. Antepli. Albany, N.Y.: State University of New York Press, 2008.

Sirry, Mun'im. *Scriptural Polemics: The Qur'ān and Other Religions*. Oxford: Oxford University Press, 2014.

Soltes, Ori Z., and Margaret A. Johnson, eds. *Preventing Violence and Achieving World Peace: The Contributions of the Gülen Movement*. Washington College Studies in Religion, Politics, and Culture, 4. New York: Peter Lang, 2013.

Stoneman, Richard. *A Traveller's History of Turkey*. 5th ed. Northampton, Mass.: Interlink Books, 2009.

Teresa of Avila. *The Life of Teresa of Jesus. The Autobiography of Teresa of Avila*. New York: Doubleday, 2004.

Tittensor, David. *The House of Service: The Gülen Movement and Islam's Third Way*. New York: Oxford University Press, 2014.

Tuncer, Faruk. "Fethullah Gülen's Methodology of Interpreting Quran." In *Islam in the Contemporary World 2. The Fethullah Gülen Movement in Thought and Practice*. Conference Proceedings, Southern Methodist University, Dallas, Tex., March 4–5, 2006, 89–103. Somerset, N.J.: Tughra Books, 2009.

Turam, Berna. "National Loyalties and International Undertakings: The Case of the Gülen Community in Kazakhstan." In *Turkish Islam and the Secular State: The Gülen Movement*, edited by M. Hakan Yavuz and John L. Esposito, 184–207. Syracuse, N.Y.: Syracuse University Press, 2003.

———. *Between Islam and the State: The Politics of Engagement*. Stanford, Calif.: Stanford University Press, 2007.

Turner, Denys. *Eros and Allegory: Medieval Exegesis of the Song of Songs*. Collegeville, Minn.: Cistercian Publications, 1995.

Ugur, Etga. "Religion as a Source of Social Capital? The Gülen Movement in the Public Sphere." In *Muslim World in Transition: Contributions of the Gülen Movement*, 152–62. London: Leeds Metropolitan University Press, 2007.

Ünal, Ali. *M. Fethullah Gülen. Bir Portre Denemesi* [Essay of a portrait]. Izmir: Nil yayınları, 2002.

———. *Geçmişten Geleceğe Köprü Fethullah Gülen*. Istanbul: Işık yayınları, 2006.

———. *The Qur'ān: With Annotated Interpretation in Modern English*. Somerset, N.J.: Light, 2006.

Vahide, Sükran. "Bediüzzaman Said Nursi and the *Risale-i Nur*." In *Globalization, Ethics and Islam. The Case of Bediuzzaman Said Nursi*, ed. Ian Markham and Ibrahim Ozdemir, 3–35. Burlington, Vt.: Ashgate, 2005.

———. "An Outline of Bediüzzaman Said Nursi's Views on Christianity and the West." In *Globalization, Ethics and Islam. The Case of Bediuzzaman Said Nursi*, ed. Ian Markham and Ibrahim Ozdemir. 109–18. Burlington, Vt.: Ashgate, 2005.

Vainovski-Mihai, Irina. "The Limits of the Otherness in Fethullah Gülen's Dialogic Methodology for Interfaith Encounters." In *Islam and Peace-*

building: Gülen Movement Initiatives, edited by John L. Esposito and İhsan Yilmaz, 85–101. New York: Blue Dome Press, 2010.

Valkenberg, Wilhelmus GBM. *Words of the Living God: Place and Function of Holy Scripture in the Theology of St. Thomas Aquinas*. Publications of the Thomas Instituut te Utrecht 6. Leuven: Peeters, 2000.

Valkenberg, Pim. "Being Found While Seeking. In Search of a Basic Structure of Root Metaphors in Muslim Spirituality." *Studies in Spirituality* 16 (2006): 39–58.

———. *Sharing Lights on the Way to God: Muslim-Christian Dialogue and Theology in the Context of Abrahamic Partnership*. New York: Editions Rodopi, 2006.

———. "Fethullah Gülen's Contribution to Muslim-Christian Dialogue in the Context of Abrahamic Cooperation." In *Islam in the Contemporary World 1: The Fethullah Gülen Movement in Thought and Practice*. Conference Proceedings, November 12–13, 2005, Rice University, Houston, Tex., 1–10. Somerset, N.J.: Tughra Books, 2009.

———. "Towards 'Abrahamic Learning Communities': How to Learn from Violence and Prejudices in Interreligious Polemics on Abraham and his Family." In *Your Heritage and Mine: Teaching in a Multi-Religious Classroom*, Studies on Inter-Religious Relations 43, edited by Lena Roos and Jenny Berglund, 154–62. Uppsala: Swedish Science Press, 2009.

———. "Learned Ignorance and Faithful Interpretation of the Qur'an in Nicholas of Cusa (1401–1464)." In *Learned Ignorance. Intellectual Humility among Jews, Christians, and Muslims*, edited by James L. Heft, SM, et al., 34–52. New York: Oxford University Press, 2011.

———. "Sifting the Qur'an: Two Forms of Interreligious Hermeneutics in Nicholas of Cusa." In *Interreligious Hermeneutics in Pluralistic Europe*, edited by David Cheetham, et al., 27–48. New York: Editions Rodopi, 2011.

———. "The Hizmet Movement in the Dialogue between Muslim and Christian Religious Traditions." In *The Gülen Hizmet Movement and Its Transnational Activities: Case Studies of Altruistic Activism in Contemporary Islam*, edited by Sophia Pandya and Nancy Gallagher, 35–54. Boca Raton, Fla.: BrownWalker Press, 2012.

———. "Fethullah Gülen and Peace as Horizon of Tolerance and Dialogue." In *Preventing Violence and Achieving World Peace*. Washington College Studies in Religion, Politics, and Culture, 4, edited by Ori Z. Soltes and Margaret A. Johnson, 41–53. New York: Peter Lang, 2013.

Valkenberg, Pim, et al., eds. *In de voetsporen van Abraham*. Budel: Damon, 2004.

Volf, Miroslav, Ghazi bin Muhammad, and Melissa Yarrington, eds. *A Common Word: Muslims and Christians on Loving God and Neighbor*. Grand Rapids, Mich.: William B. Eerdmans, 2010.

Wagner, Walter. *Beginnings and Endings. Fethullah Gülen's Vision for Today's World.* New York: Blue Dome Press, 2013.

Weller, Paul. "Fethullah Gülen, Religions, Globalization, and Dialogue." In *Muslim Citizens of the Globalized World: Contributions of the Gülen Movement*, edited by Robert A. Hunt and Yüksel A. Aslandoğan, 85–100. Somerset, N.J.: The Light, 2007.

——. "Dialogical and transformative resources: perspectives from Fethullah Gülen on religion and public life." In *European Muslims, Civility and Public Life: Perspectives on and from the Gülen Movement*, edited by Paul Weller and Ihsan Yilmaz, 3–19. New York: Continuum, 2012.

——. "Robustness and Civility: Themes from Fethullah Gülen as Resource and Challenge for Government, Muslims and Civil Society in the United Kingdom." In *European Muslims, Civility and Public Life: Perspectives on and from the Gülen Movement*, edited by Paul Weller and Ihsan Yilmaz, 143–59. New York: Continuum, 2012.

Weller, Paul, and Ihsan Yilmaz. *European Muslims, Civility and Public Life: Perspectives on and from the Gülen Movement.* New York: Continuum, 2012.

White, Jenny. *Islamist Mobilization in Turkey: A Study in Vernacular Politics.* Seattle: University of Washington Press, 2002.

Williams, Ian. "'A Station Above That of Angels': The Vision of Islamic Education within Pluralistic Societies in the Thought of Fethullah Gülen – A Study of Contrasts between Turkey and the UK." In *Muslim World in Transition: Contributions of the Gülen Movement*. Conference Proceedings, London , 25–27 October 2007, 585–96. London: Leeds Metropolitan University Press, 2007.

——. "The Vision of Education within Pluralistic Societies in the Thought of Fethullah Gülen: the Contribution of Non-Denominational Education towards Inter-Religious and Communal Understanding, Peace and Identity: A Study of Contrasts in the UK, Turkey and the USA." In *Peaceful Coexistence: Fethullah Gülen's Initiatives in the Contemporary World*, 407–15. London: Leeds Metropolitan University Press, 2007.

Woodhall, Ruth. "An Examination of Fethullah Gülen's Philosophy of

Education and the Educational Activities of his Movement." In *Islam in the Contemporary World 1. The Fethullah Gülen Movement in Thought and Practice*. Conference Proceedings, November 12–13, 2005, Rice University, Houston, Tex., 60–77. Somerset, N.J.: Tughra Books, 2009.

Yavuz, M. Hakan. "The Gülen Movement: The Turkish Puritans." In *Turkish Islam and the Secular State: The Gülen Movement*, edited by M. Hakan Yavuz and John L. Esposito, 19–47. Syracuse, N.Y.: Syracuse University Press, 2003.

———. "Islam in the Public Sphere: the Case of the Nur Movement." In *Turkish Islam and the Secular State: The Gülen Movement*, edited by M. Hakan Yavuz and John L. Esposito, 1–18. Syracuse, N.Y.: Syracuse University Press, 2003.

———. *Islamic Political Identity in Turkey*. New York: Oxford University Press, 2003.

———. "*Nur* Study Circles (*Dershanes*) and the Formation of New Religious Consciousness in Turkey." In *Islam at the Crossroads: On the Life and Thought of Bediüzzaman Said Nursi*, edited by Ibrahim M. Abu-Rabi', 297–316. Albany: State University of New York Press, 2003.

———. *Towards an Islamic Enlightenment: The Gülen Movement*. New York: Oxford University Press, 2013.

Yildirim, Yetkin, and Virginia Burnett. "Interfaith Dialogue For Muslims and Catholic Christians." In *Islam and the Contemporary World 4: The Fethullah Gülen Movement in Thought and Practice*. Conference Proceedings, University of Texas, San Antonio, Tex., November 3, 2007, 109–15. Somerset, N.J.: Tughra Books, 2009.

Yildirim, Yetkin, and Madeline Maxwell. "Tolerance and Dialogue in Fethullah Gülen's Writings." In *Islam in the Contemporary World 1: The Fethullah Gülen Movement in Thought and Practice*. Conference Proceedings, November 12–13, 2005, Rice University, Houston, Tex., 35–46. Somerset, N.J.: Tughra Books, 2009.

Yilmaz, Ihsan. "*Ijtihad* and *Tajdid* by Conduct: The Gülen Movement." In *Turkish Islam and the Secular State: The Gülen Movement*, edited by M. Hakan Yavuz and John L. Esposito, 208–37. Syracuse, N.Y.: Syracuse University Press, 2003.

———. "State, Law, Civil Society and Islam in Contemporary Turkey." *The Muslim World* 95 (2005): 385–411.

INDEX

Renewing Islam by Service: A Christian View of Fethullah Gülen and the Hizmet Movement was designed in Agmena and typeset by Kachergis Book Design of Pittsboro, North Carolina. It was printed on 60-pound House Natural Smooth and bound by Sheridan Books of Ann Arbor, Michigan.